Books by Richard M. Nixon

Six Crises
RN: The Memoirs of Richard Nixon,
Volumes I and II
The Real War

Published by
WARNER BOOKS

The Real War

RICHARD NIXON

WARNER BOOKS

A Warner Communications Company

WARNER BOOKS EDITION

Copyright © 1980, 1981 by Richard Nixon
All rights reserved.

Maps by Paul J. Pugliese, G C I

Book design by Helen Roberts

Cover design by Gene Light

Type design by John Harrington

Warner Books, Inc., 75 Rockefeller Plaza, New York, N.Y. 10019

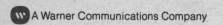 A Warner Communications Company

Printed in the United States of America

First Printing: May, 1981

10 9 8 7 6 5 4 3 2

To Our Grandchildren

Contents

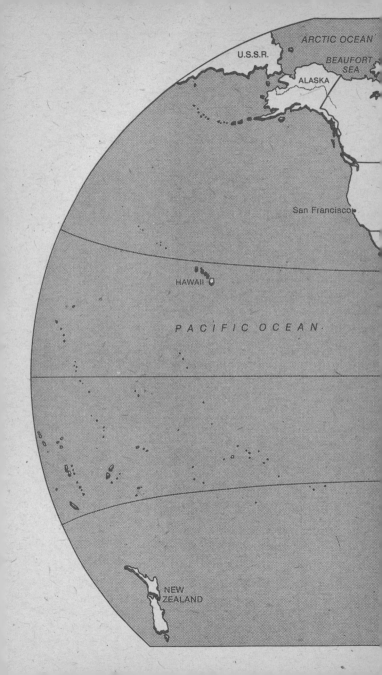

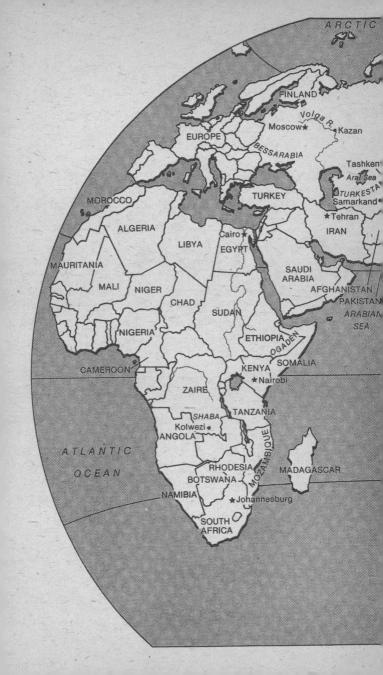

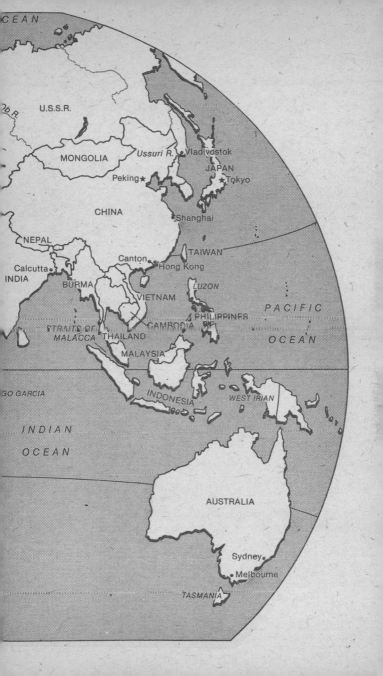

Introduction to the 1981 Edition

When I first wrote this book, I did so in a mood of short-term alarm but long-term optimism. I believed that unless the United States changed its policies, the West faced a catastrophe: either defeat in war or surrender without war. But I also had a basic, gut feeling that the "sleeping giant"—the United States—would be awakened in time, and that the catastrophe that otherwise faced the West could be averted.

In the period since the hardcover edition appeared in spring 1980, the most important world event has been the American election. The results of that election have substantially increased my optimism. The challenge continues— "The Real War" did not begin last year, and it will not end next year—but I am confident that President Reagan and the members of his administration will have the vision to see what needs to be done and the courage to do it. I also expect that the new Congress will be much more readily disposed to support the necessary actions.

The election not only brought in a new administration, and changed the complexion of Congress; it also signaled a crystalizing of American perceptions about where the danger lies and how to meet it. In the long run, this can be as important as the advent of an administration that takes the dangers seriously and addresses them realistically. For no administration acts in a vacuum. Public support is vital, especially for measures that require public sacrifice. And public understanding is vital to maintaining that support.

That is why I hope this book will be widely read, now and in the years ahead: to increase public understanding, and thereby to strengthen public support for the kinds of policies America must follow in order to survive.

This does not mean simply strengthening our military posture, however urgently necessary that strenthening is. To see the climactic struggle for the world in solely military terms is a fatal delusion. "The Real War" is being fought on many fronts. It takes place on the economic front, in the realms of ideas and ideals, in covert action and psychological warfare and propaganda—in all the various arenas of competing faiths and competing systems. We could be overwhelmingly superior militarily and still lose if we fail on the economic, ideological, or diplomatic front.

The most critical battle in 1980 will be on the economic front. If we lose the battle against inflation we will lose "The Real War."

We could also lose by ignoring the Soviet challenge around the periphery—those piecemeal advances into countries in Africa, Asia, Latin America, and the Middle East on which the West depends not only for oil, but for so many of the other vital resources without which a modern industrial economy cannot operate. We could lose by letting the Soviets get the upper hand psychologically, so that the West sinks into a gradual paralysis.

Eventual victory for the West will require advances on all the necessary fronts, recognizing that these advances will not be steady, that there will be setbacks along the way. We must press resolutely to overcome or compensate for these setbacks and continue the advance.

The 1980 election probably turned more on the state of the economy than on considerations of foreign policy. But even there, those who voted their pocketbooks voted, in effect, for a stronger America. The American economy was once the mainstay of the West; now it is in serious trouble. High inflation and low productivity take a heavy toll not only in terms of personal well-being, but also in terms of national morale, and they severely limit our capacity to put forth the effort required in the military and other areas. Taking measures to set the economy right, and particularly to bring the raging winds of inflation under control, must be a top priority. We must do what is necessary to accomplish this goal, even if in the short term what is necessary may be politically unpopular.

One of the central theses of this book is the importance of national willpower. We can marshal that willpower only if we see clearly the nature and extent of the challenge we face. I have sought in these pages to spell out the dimensions of that challenge. Some readers have reported themselves startled or even shocked by it. They were meant to be. The facts themselves are startling and shocking. If those facts shock us into a sufficiently strong and steady response, the West will prevail, and peace and freedom will survive.

Having dealt directly and at great length with the leaders of the Soviet Union, I know that they exploit weakness but respect strength. If they see a new strength in the American sinew, a new firmness in the American step, a new steel in the American eye, then two things will happen. They will be more cautious in their adventuring, and they will also be more realistic in their negotiating. If they think they can roll us, they will try to roll us. If they conclude that they have to deal with us, they will try to deal with us.

This book went to press (in its hardcover edition) in February 1980. Several major upheavals that have occurred since it was written have borne out its theses. The workers' rebellion in Poland underscored the problems the Soviet Union faces in Eastern Europe. By attacking Iran, Iraq has demonstrated its determination to be the predominant military power in the Persian Gulf area, while Iran's own further descent into chaos has highlighted the fragility of that entire vital area. Central America continues to be an imperiled target of revolutionary violence. China watches anxiously for signals about the extent of America's resolve.

This book should be read against the background of U.S. policies as they were in 1980; but this itself is the background of those new policies that will now begin to emerge as the new administration takes office. The conflicts it describes continue, and the principles remain unchanged. What is new is the promise of a new team that understands these principles.

The struggle described in this book will be a long one. The outlook is brighter now, because awareness of the needs is heightened now. But this is no time for euphoria. Our hope for a brighter future will be shattered unless we mobilize our military, economic, and spiritual forces to the hilt. Which side prevails in "The Real War" will determine the fate of Western civilization, and the struggle to determine which side prevails will dominate the remaining decades of the twentieth century.

—Richard Nixon

New York
December 2, 1980

The
Real War

1
No Time to Lose

> The history of failure in war can be summed up in two words: Too Late. Too late in comprehending the deadly purpose of a potential enemy; too late in realizing the mortal danger; too late in preparedness; too late in uniting all possible forces for resistance; too late in standing with one's friends.
>
> —*General Douglas MacArthur*

As I write this book, a third of a century has passed since I first entered Congress; five years have passed since I resigned the presidency.

When I resigned that office, I left unfinished the work that meant more to me than any I have ever been engaged in: the establishment of a new "structure of peace" that might prevent a major war, and at the same time maintain the security of the Western world during the balance of this century. Since that time, the position of the United States relative to that of the Soviet Union has seriously worsened, and the peril to the West has greatly increased. That "structure of peace" can still be completed, but it will be more difficult now, and there is less time in which to build it.

Since resigning, I have reflected at great length on the ways in which the world has changed during my third of a century in public life, and on the ways in which it has not.

I have also reflected at length on the challenges that my successors in the presidency have faced and will face. The President of the United States wields enormous power. The fate of the West depends on how well and how shrewdly he uses it. He can wield it to far greater effect if the American people understand what he confronts, and why the use of American power is necessary; if, in effect, they become partners with him in preserving the security of the West and the peace of the world. He cannot do it alone, and he cannot do it at all if the obstructionists block his way.

During most of my presidency America was fighting a bitter war in Vietnam. During all of my presidency we were engaged in a "war" with the Soviet Union. That struggle with the Soviets will continue to dominate world events for the rest of this century.

This book is about that struggle, and about the ways in which American power can be used to win it. We cannot win it unless we understand the nature and uses of power. Our adversaries understand these all too well.

I have dealt directly and sometimes bluntly with the leaders of the Soviet Union, of China, of Europe, and of the developed and developing nations of all continents. I have used both force and diplomacy in world affairs, and have seen how they are used by others. I have encountered the steel will of the Kremlin leaders, and have had to match their determination with my own. I have seen that they know what they want and will resort to any means to get it.

This book is a *cri de coeur,* addressed not only to our political leaders but to leaders in all walks of life—to take hold before it is too late, and to marshal America's strengths so as to ensure its survival.

The Soviet Union today is the most powerfully armed expansionist nation the world has ever known, and its arms buildup continues at a pace nearly twice that of the United States. There is no mystery about Soviet intentions. The Kremlin leaders do not want war, but they do want the world. And they are rapidly moving into position to get what they want.

In the 1980s America for the first time in modern history will confront two cold realities. The first of these is that if war were to come, we might lose. The second is that we might be defeated without war. The second prospect is more likely than the first, and almost as grim. The danger facing the West during the balance of this century is less that of a nuclear holocaust than it is of drifting into a situation in which we find ourselves confronted with a choice between surrender and suicide—red or dead. That danger can still be averted, but the time in which we can avert it is rapidly running out.

The next two decades represent a time of maximum crisis for America and for the West, during which the fate of the world for generations to come may well be determined.

Other nations have much longer experience than we have in the use of power to maintain the peace. But they no longer have the power. So, by default, the world looks to the United States. It looks today with nervous apprehension, as the bulwarks against Soviet expansion crumble in one nation after another, and as the United States appears so lost in uncertainty or paralyzed by propriety that it is either unable or unwilling to act.

Soviet ambitions present the United States with a strategic challenge of global proportion, which requires a renewed strategic consciousness and response. It requires a coherent national strategy based upon informed public support. Piecemeal temporizing will not do. Angola, Ethiopia, Afghanistan, South Yemen, Mozambique, Laos, Cambodia, and South Vietnam, all have been brought under communist domination since 1974; nearly 100 million people in the last five years. Iran has been plunged into bloody chaos and turned overnight from a bastion of Western strength to a cauldron of virulent anti-Westernism, its oil treasures lying provocatively exposed to lustful Russian eyes. Cuba acts increasingly as an agent of wide-ranging Soviet ambitions.

These are examples of how the pieces will continue to fall if we take a piecemeal approach. We have to recover the geopolitical momentum, marshaling and using our resources in the tradition of a great power.

The old colonial empires are gone. The new Soviet imperialism requires a new counterforce to keep it in check. The United States cannot provide this alone, but without strong and effective leadership from the United States, it cannot be provided at all. We cannot afford to waffle and waver. Either we act like a great power or we will be reduced to a minor power, and thus reduced we will not survive—nor will freedom or Western values survive.

To be effective, our response to the Soviet challenge must integrate long-term and short-term measures. It must also integrate the various levels on which it is mounted—military, economic, philosophical, political, diplomatic. We must recognize the relationships between what happens in Asia and what happens in the Middle East, between strategic resources and patterns of world trade, between economic productivity and military might, between philosophical commitment and national will, between national will and the effectiveness of a nation's military forces in preventing conflict.

We are at war. We are engaged in a titanic struggle in which the fates of nations are being decided. In war the fact that a surrounded garrison surrenders without any shots being fired makes its capture no less a military victory for one side and a defeat for the other. When the Soviet Union advances by using proxy troops, its conquests are still Soviet victories and Western defeats.

Since World War II the Soviet military buildup has been continuous and the Soviet expansionist pressure has been relentless. Moscow has fished assiduously in the troubled waters left in the wake of the dismantlement of the old colonial empires. It has blockaded Berlin, fomented revolutions in Latin America, Asia, and Africa, aided aggression by North Korea and North Vietnam. It has trained and subsidized guerrillas, disrupted elections, shot down unarmed planes, sponsored coups, shot refugees, imprisoned dissidents. It has threatened, blustered, connived, conspired, subverted, bribed, intimidated, terrorized, lied, cheated, stolen, tortured, spied, blackmailed, murdered—all as a matter of deliberate national policy.

The basic rule of Soviet behavior was laid down years ago by Lenin: Probe with bayonets. If you encounter steel, withdraw. If you encounter mush, continue. The question is which will the Soviets encounter: steel or mush?

The answer to that question lies with America's leadership. Not just its political leadership. What kind of world view the American President has, how well he understands the uses of power and the nuances of diplomacy, whether he has a strategic vision and the will and shrewdness to carry it out—all these are vital, even indispensable, elements. But more broadly, the answer lies with those segments of American leadership whose attitudes determine the limits of the possible for American policy.

Unfortunately, America is still suffering from the legacy of the 1960s. A rabid anti-intellectualism swept the nation's campuses then, and fantasy reigned supreme. Attacks on anything representing the established order were in fashion. The discords of that decade and of its aftermath critically weakened the nation's capacity to meet its responsibilities in the world, not only militarily but also in terms of its ability to lead.

Ironically, even as anti-intellectualism ravaged the campuses, the 1960s also saw an overly "intellectualized" new fashion take hold among many of those who thought professionally about arms and particularly about arms control: the notion that above a certain minimum, the less military strength you had, the better. The hope arose that if the United States limited its own arms, others—particularly the Soviets—would follow. But the Soviets did not perform according to theory. In fact, during the same period when this arms-control doctrine was winning favor among American theorists, and the theorists were winning influence, the Soviet five-year plans were charting ever greater increases in military spending, clearly guided by coherent strategic objectives. The Soviets were not bogged down in theory; they were driving toward supremacy.

There are many today who suggest that American civilization is suffering a terminal illness, that we are witnessing the beginning of the end of the West. Some American opinion leaders view this with despair. Some, especially in darkest academia, see it as the logical and overdue result of our being on the wrong side. Like the classic definition of fox hunting as "the unspeakable in pursuit of the uneatable," they see America as the aggressive in support of the oppressive. As playwright Eugene Ionesco reported after a recent visit to the United States, American intellectuals tend to be "masochists who want to be blamed for every thing wrong in the world." When he told American liberal friends that the United States was not as bad as other nations, "the liberals looked at me askance. For in order to be appreciated in America, one must, above all, never say that Americans are not the worst criminals of humanity."

What America does suffer from is not itself a terminal illness, but rather a sort of creeping paralysis that could become terminal unless treated. Together with our allies in the Western world, we have the capacity to survive, to prosper, to turn back the challenges to our security that are being mounted with increasing force. The question is whether we will use that capacity.

Nations live or die by the way they respond to the particular challenges they face. Those challenges may be internal or external; they may be faced by a nation alone or in concert with other nations; they may come gradually or suddenly. There is no immutable law of nature that says only the unjust will be afflicted, or that the just will prevail. While might certainly does not make right, neither does right by itself make might. The time when a nation most craves ease may be the moment when it can least afford to let down its guard. The moment when it most wishes it could address its domestic needs may be the moment when it most urgently has to confront an external threat. The nation that survives is the one that rises to meet that moment: that has the wisdom to recognize the threat and the will to turn it back, and that does so before it is too late.

The naïve notion that we can preserve freedom by exuding goodwill is not only silly, but dangerous. The more adherents it wins, the more it tempts the aggressor.

The central thesis of this book is that the West, today, has crossed the threshold of a period of acute crisis in which its survival into the twenty-first century is directly at stake. We have the material capacity, the economic and technological strength, to prevail—which means to maintain our freedom and to avert a major war. But the capacity alone is not enough. Sir Robert Thompson, the British expert on guerrilla warfare, has trenchantly defined national power as manpower plus applied resources, *times* will. We have the resources and the manpower. Have we the will to use them?

The situation today is ominously reminiscent of the period preceding World War II which Walter Lippmann described so perceptively:

> The American people were as unprepared in their minds as in their military establishment. Could the democracies be rallied, could they be collected and nerved for the ordeal . . . ? They had the superior assets. . . . But did they have the insight, the discipline to persevere, and the resolution to go through with it? Though they had the means, did they also have the will, and did they know how? . . . They were reacting to events and they were not governing them. . . . They had refused to take in what they saw, they had refused to believe what they heard, they had wished and they had waited, hoping against hope.

There are two aspects to national will. There is will as demonstrated by the nation itself, and there is will as perceived by the nation's adversaries. In averting the ultimate challenge, perceived will can be as important as actual will. Although an American President would launch a nuclear strike only with the most extreme reluctance, the Kremlin leaders must always assume that he might; and that if the truly vital interests of the nation or of the West required the use of nuclear weapons, that he would do so. If they are to be effectively deterred from the ultimate provocation, they must perceive that such a provocation carries with it the ultimate risk.

National will involves far more than readiness to use military power, whether nuclear or conventional. It includes a readiness to allocate the resources necessary to maintain that power. It includes a clear view of where the dangers lie, and of what kinds of responses are necessary to meet those dangers. It includes also a basic, crystalline faith that the United States is on the right side in the struggle, and that what we represent in the world is worth defending.

For will to be effective, it must necessarily include the readiness to sacrifice if necessary—to defer those goals that are merely desirable in order to advance those that are essential; to pay the costs of defense; to incur risks; to incur the displeasure of powerful constituencies at home and of raucous voices abroad.

America's failures of will in recent years have been partly the product of weariness after nearly forty years of bearing the burdens of world leadership. They clearly result in part from the traumas of Vietnam and Watergate. But more fundamentally, they reflect the failures of America's leadership class. Too many of those who profess to be the guardians of our ideals have instead become the architects of our retreat.

The answer cannot be to replace one leadership class with another. That is not going to happen. Individuals may change, one political party may lose ground to another, different factions may move into or out of intellectual fashion; but essentially, those groups to which the nation looks for leadership will remain pretty much the same throughout these critical two decades. What has to be done is to wake those who exercise leadership to the responsibilities of leadership.

In 1919 a starry-eyed Lincoln Steffens, after visiting the Soviet Union, exulted, "I have been over into the future, and it works." In our own time other starry-eyed reporters have glorified the "Brave New Worlds" of Maoist China, Vietnam, and Cuba. This romanticizing of revolution, this willful blindness to the human costs of tyranny as long as tyranny speaks the hypocritical language of the Left, permeates the ranks of those who report and those who teach, and it leaves a disastrous imprint on the minds of millions who read and listen.

Revolution itself is neither inherently good nor inherently evil. But what the United States confronts today is the advance of a tyranny marching under the banners of revolution: one that seeks to replace democracy with despotism in the name of "the people." But in these "people's democracies" the people have no meaningful vote; they have no voice; they have no freedom; they have no choice. The Soviet Union has built the most powerful war-making machine ever possessed by an aggressive power, not for the benefit—or by the choice—of the Russian people, but to extend the dominion of the Kremlin leadership.

Unfortunately for the West, a large segment of the American intellectual establishment, including many in the business establishment, falls for the sort of con-man spiel the Kremlin and its propagandists use. Just as the con man knows how to play on his victim's greed and self-importance, so does the Kremlin know precisely how to play on its target's romantic idealism and on his grandiose dreams of remaking whole societies in his own image.

With Africa now a crucible of great-power maneuver, we cannot afford to have our Africa policies hostage to the bitter memories still cherished by those who struggled for racial equality in America. We cannot let Africa become a stage on which Americans act out their psychic traumas. We must address it as the vitally important strategic battleground that Soviet adventuring has made it.

Nor can we ignore any part of the world as being too far from our concerns to care about. As the 1980s began, this was being vividly illustrated by events in Afghanistan—a fact that provided its own peculiar irony, because for many years American newsmen disparagingly referred to analyses of trends in distant lands as "Afghanistanism." Afghanistan—remote, land-locked, a harsh mountain region of primitive tribesmen as rugged as the land they lived on—was treated as a metaphor for all the dull and distant events that glazed the eyes of the American reader.

But in real life Afghanistan is much more than that. Despite its poverty and the harshness of its land, Texas-sized Afghanistan has long been a cockpit of great-power intrigue for the same reason that it used to be called "the turnstile of Asia's fate." With Iran on the west, Pakistan on the south, China to the east and a thousand-mile border with the Soviet Union on the north, Afghanistan has traditionally been one of those points where the great thrusts of empire met.

Throughout its history Afghanistan has been a cross-roads for conquerors; Alexander the Great, Genghis Khan, and Tamerlane have all ridden across Afghanistan's dusty hills in their quest for empire. The King of Afghanistan recalled for me when I visited him in 1953 that it was there that Alexander the Great said, "I have no further worlds to conquer." In the nineteenth century Great Britain and Imperial Russia played what Kipling called the "Great Game" in Afghanistan as they dueled all across Central Asia in a struggle for control of the continent. The British knew that Afghanistan's rugged Khyber Pass was the gateway to the Indian subcontinent, and they fought two brutal wars to deny the Russians control of it. Today Afghanistan is a testing ground for an ominous, brazen new phase in the Soviet expansionist drive.

A bloody Soviet-backed coup in April 1978 suddenly ousted President Mohammed Daoud, who was promptly murdered, and installed in his place a stridently anti-Western, Marxist regime under the leadership of Prime Minister Noor Mohammed Taraki. Taraki renamed his ruling party the "People's Democratic Party," and renamed his country the "Democratic Republic of Afghanistan," adopting as its new flag a bright red banner with the party symbol and a star in the corner—almost indistinguishable from the Soviet flag. Soon nearly every government ministry, as well as the 100,000-man Afghan Army, had Soviet "advisers," many of them Tadzhiks from Soviet Central Asia who speak a dialect most Afghans understand.

This abrupt renewal of centuries of Russian pressure against its repeatedly extended Asian borders sent shock waves through Afghanistan's already weakened immediate neighbors, Pakistan and Iran—vulnerable not only because of geography but also because of tribal ties. Baluchi tribesmen range through Afghanistan, Pakistan, and Iran; Pushtuns through Afghanistan and Pakistan's Northwest Frontier Province. Less than ten months later, in fact, the Shah's regime had fallen, and leftist guerrillas staged their first takeover of the U.S. Embassy in Tehran on the same day that the U.S. ambassador to Afghanistan was dragged from his car and murdered.

In the United States reaction to that initial Soviet seizure of power in Afghanistan was largely a yawn. The New York *Times* headlined an editorial "Keeping Cool about Kabul." The "so what" school—those whose reflexive response to Soviet subversion or Soviet militarism is to say, "So what?"—said "So what?" about Afghanistan, if they paid even that much attention.

After the communist regime came to power, however, fiercely independent Moslem tribesmen launched a *jihad,* or holy war, in a struggle to the death for control of their country and of their lives. Insurgents sold their cattle and their wives' jewelry to buy ammunition. The rebels fought Soviet-made tanks by starting landslides. They rushed directly into the machine-gun fire of the tanks and overwhelmed them, armed with nothing more than wooden sticks and iron bars.

The government's army suffered from purges, desertions, and defections to the rebels; by late 1979 it had reportedly dwindled from more than 100,000 to 50,000, with a hard core of no more than 10,000 to 15,000 effective troops.

It was doubtful that the communists could have survived another spring offensive by the rebels.

In a September 1979 coup, Taraki was ousted and executed by his number-two man, Hafizullah Amin, who installed himself as President. But Amin made little headway in putting down the rebellion. In a carefully prepared and brazenly executed move, the Soviets invaded Afghanistan on Christmas Eve. Hundreds of Russian transport planes airlifted thousands of Soviet troops into Kabul; tens of thousands of other prepositioned Soviet forces quickly moved across the border; Amin and his family were killed; a reliably pliant Soviet puppet, Babrak Karmal, whom the Russians had kept hidden away in reserve in Eastern Europe, was put in as Amin's replacement. He beamed his first message as President to the Afghan people from a radio station in the Soviet Union. Izvestia had the gall to denounce the deposed communist leader Amin as a tool of the CIA, while Brezhnev warmly congratulated Kamal on his "election." The proud people of Afghanistan were crushed in the iron fist of the Soviet Union, and Russia came one country closer to achieving its goals—now within tantalizingly short reach—of a warm-water port on the Arabian Sea and control over the oil of the Persian Gulf.

In neighboring Pakistan a high-ranking official who had been privately warning of Russia's expansionist ambitions told an American friend, "You see, this is what I have been telling you and now it's come true. You Americans don't seem to understand the world anymore. Next comes the Finlandization of Pakistan, and subversion of our country by the Russians. There is a very real possibility—likelihood even—of Soviet hegemony in this whole part of the world. Don't your people in Washington care?"

The Soviet seizure of Afghanistan is a continuation of the old tsarist imperialism—the relentless outward pressure that has continued since the Duchy of Muscovy threw off Mongol rule in 1480. It also is a stark reminder that America no longer has the luxury of considering any place on earth too remote to affect its own security.

What made the fall of Afghanistan so significant a loss

to the West was not just the fate of its 18 million people, 90 percent of whom are illiterate, and whose $160 per capita annual income makes Afghanistan one of the poorest countries of the world. Not even its strategic location would make its loss so significant, if that loss had occurred in isolation. But it did not occur in isolation. It was part of a pattern. And that pattern is what presents the challenge. It is a pattern of ceaseless building by the Soviets toward a position of overwhelming military force, while using subversion and proxy troops, and now even its own, to take over one country after another, until they are in a position to conquer or Finlandize the world.

Looking at the changes in the world since World War II, we can see grounds for pessimism and grounds for optimism.

Communist regimes have taken power not only in Eastern Europe, but also in China, North Korea, all of Vietnam, Cambodia, Laos, Afghanistan, Ethiopia, South Yemen, Angola, Mozambique, and Cuba. So far, no country that has come completely under communist control has escaped from that control. Twenty-one countries are now in the communist orbit. Territorially, the communist powers are advancing all over the world, and the West is retreating.

In terms of nuclear weapons, the United States had an absolute monopoly at the end of World War II. At the time of the Cuban missile crisis in 1962, the United States still had an overwhelming nuclear superiority, in the range of 15 to 1 or even more. In 1973, when we ordered a worldwide alert in order to keep Soviet forces out of the Middle East during the Yom Kippur War, the United States and the Soviet Union were approximately equal in both strategic nuclear capability and theater nuclear capability. But since 1973 the Soviet Union has been spending three times as much as the United States on strategic weapons alone.

With their rapid advances in nuclear missile technology and their vigorous development of new weapons systems—while new American weapons systems have been systematically canceled or postponed—the Soviets are quickly closing the gap in those areas in which we are ahead and increasing their superiority where they are ahead.

The Soviets have an enormous advantage in conventional ground forces. To some extent this should be expected, since the U.S.S.R. is primarily a land power, with two fronts to defend—against Europe and against China. But Russia's huge armies also pose a formidable threat to its neighbors, because while Russia has two fronts for defense it has three fronts for attack. Soviet military power threatens Europe in the west, China and Japan in the east, and the countries of Central Asia, the Persian Gulf, the Middle East, and Africa to the south.

Beyond this, the dramatic buildup of Soviet sea power has been particularly ominous. While the United States still has an advantage in aircraft carriers, the Soviets now have half again as many major surface combatant ships as the United States and three times as many submarines.

Unless the United States drastically increases its military budget, the Soviet Union by 1985 will have unquestioned nuclear superiority, overwhelming superiority on the ground, and at least equality at sea. In sum, unless we act fast, the period of the mid-1980s will be one of maximum peril for the United States and the West. In a nutshell: The Soviet Union will be number one; the United States will be number two.

Taken by themselves, these trends would be grounds for acute pessimism. If projected into the 1980s, they would give the Soviet Union the capacity to impose its will militarily on targets of its choosing around the globe.

But there is another side. Dwight D. Eisenhower was a shrewd strategist. I remember that during his presidency, when talk around the National Security Council table grew gloomy as its members surveyed the world, Eisenhower used to remind us that one of the first requirements for a successful military commander is the capability to assess realistically both the strengths and weaknesses of his own forces. But equally important, he added, is the ability to recognize not only the strengths but also the weaknesses and vulnerabilities of the opposing forces.

When we do that, we find major vulnerabilities on the Soviet side, and major strengths on the Western side.

The most dramatic of those vulnerabilities lies in the deep and perhaps irreconcilable differences between the Soviet Union and China. China's economy is still weak, and its nuclear capability is still relatively primitive. But with a billion of the world's potentially most able people on its longest frontier, under control of a government that looks toward Moscow with bitter hostility, the leaders of the Kremlin have reason to be apprehensive. In the long run China may pose an expansionist threat to the West. But for the present China fears the Soviet Union and needs the West.

A second vulnerability stems from the nature of the communist system. No people has ever freely chosen to live under communism. No nation remains under communist rule except through force. No system of government has been more successful at extending its domination over other nations and less successful at winning the approval of the people of those nations.

The tragic boat people of Vietnam, the dissidents attempting to leave the Soviet Union, the people who flee when they are able from Eastern Europe—all are dramatic proof that when people have a choice, they reject communist rule. Ironically, it was Lenin who said that refugees are people who vote with their feet. In that balloting, peoples in all parts of the world, frequently at risk of their lives, are overwhelmingly pro-freedom and anti-communist.

A third vulnerability, one that is potentially a decisive Western advantage, lies in the fact that economically, capitalism works and communism does not. As we survey the world's economies, we find that the United States, Western Europe, and Japan together have a gross national product four times as great as that of the entire Soviet bloc.

The communist nations have the advantage that being totalitarian, they can allocate their resources as their leaders choose, to serve the ambitions of the rulers rather than the needs of the people. Thus even relatively nonproductive economies can support enormous military establishments. But if there is to be an arms race, and if the West decides to compete, the West has the economic power to win it. The Soviets know this.

At the end of World War II the West, swept by waves of relief and exhaustion, let down its guard. We disarmed while Stalin used his armies to seize all the territory he could. Eventually, alarmed, the West mobilized to meet this new Soviet threat. Moscow then moderated its tone and became more cautious in its expansion. This was a change of the head, not a change of the heart. When China shifted its emphasis from external adventuring to internal development—and to shoring up its defense against what by then it perceived as a looming Soviet threat—that, too, was a change of the head.

This change of the head is what made our first steps toward détente possible. We must understand that détente is not a love feast. It is an understanding between nations that have opposite purposes, but which share certain common interests, including the avoidance of nuclear war. Such an understanding can work—that is, it can restrain aggression and deter war—only as long as the potential aggressor is made to recognize that neither aggression nor war will be profitable.

The capitalist system works on the basis of the profit motive economically. The Soviet system works on the basis of the profit motive militarily and territorially. When the Kremlin calculates that it has more to gain than to lose by an act of aggression, subversion, or intimidation, it will engage in such action.

As the power balance shifts in the Soviets' favor, the Kremlin's profit-and-loss calculations will shift with it. Each time the West appears weak or irresolute, the potential cost of aggression falls and the Kremlin's market "demand" increases. Each time the West shows itself ready to resist effectively, the cost rises and the market dries up.

• • • •

Woodrow Wilson once eloquently declared World War I a war to make the world "safe for democracy." However noble that intent, events soon made a mockery of it. Our aim must be a world within which democracy will be safe, but more fundamentally a world in which aggression is restrained and national independence secure. Just as the 1940s and 1950s saw the end of the old colonialism, the 1980s and 1990s must be the years in which we turn back the new Soviet imperialism. To chart our course for the future, we must know our enemies, understand our friends, and know ourselves—where we are, how we got here, and where we want to go.

To meet the challenge to our own survival and to the survival of freedom and peace, we must drastically increase our military power, shore up our economic power, reinvigorate our willpower, strengthen the power of our Presidents, and develop a strategy aimed not just at avoiding defeat but at attaining victory.

The decades ahead will not be easy. They will not be free of risk. But the risk we run if we fail will be infinitely greater. And the longer we wait, the harder it will be to catch up. Every day lost increases the danger.

In 1934, Winston Churchill told the House of Commons, "To urge the preparation of defense is not to assert the imminence of war. On the contrary, if war was imminent preparation for defense would be too late . . . but it is very difficult to resist the conclusion that if we do not begin forthwith to put ourselves in a position of security, it will soon be beyond our power to do so." In the 1930s Britain had what in effect was a "strategic reserve"—the vast industrial power of the United States, which, with the luxury of time, could be mobilized after war broke out in order to save the allied nations; and this "reserve" ultimately saved Britain from its own unpreparedness. The United States has no such reserve to fall back on.

It was shortly before the outbreak of World War II that General Douglas MacArthur observed, "The history of failure in war can be summed up in two words: Too Late."

MacArthur, then in the Philippines, had seen the war clouds on the horizon; he had been frustrated in his efforts to win support for a strengthening of forces in the Philippines. He warned of the danger, but too many said, "So what?"

When he made that statement the atomic bomb had not yet burst on Hiroshima, forever changing the potential nature of war and the consequences of a surprise attack. The United States had time to recover from a naval Pearl Harbor, and it had ample warning of impending war. We could have less than thirty minutes' warning of a nuclear Pearl Harbor, from which we would have no time to recover. The time to prevent that from happening is now. There is no time to lose.

2
World War III

The first characteristic of the Soviet Union is that it always adopts the attitude of bullying the soft and fearing the strong. The second characteristic of the Soviet Union is that it will go in and grab at every opportunity.

—*Deng Xiaoping*

For more than twenty-five years the countries of the Western Alliance have been preparing themselves against the dread possibility of a nuclear war with the Soviet Union. This war, which the strategists have called . . . the Third World War—has never come, and may never come. Meanwhile, the real Third World War has been fought and is being fought under our noses, and few people have noticed what was going on.

—*Brian Crozier*

World War III began before World War II ended. Even as Allied armies battled Nazi forces to the death in Europe, Stalin had his eye clearly fixed on his postwar objectives. In April 1945, as American and Russian soldiers were embracing at the Elbe River in Germany, Stalin was spelling out his blueprint for a divided postwar world. "This war is not as in the past," he said; "whoever occupies a territory also imposes on it his own social system. Everyone imposes his own system as far as his army can reach. It cannot be otherwise."

19

By then, the blacksmith who would later forge the Iron Curtain had already shown how cynically he would ensure that his "social system" prevailed. One of the most heroic chapters of World War II was written by the resistance movement in German-occupied Poland, and in particular by the Polish Home Army. Its members provided intelligence information, conducted sabotage, disrupted rail communications behind the German lines, carried out reprisals for acts of Nazi repression by executing German officials; they even staged pitched battles with German troops. They were Polish patriots, determined to restore and preserve Polish independence.

On August 1, 1944, Polish freedom fighters rose up against the Nazi occupiers in Warsaw as the Soviet army approached, just as French partisans had done when American and British forces neared Paris. But instead of aiding the liberation of the city, the Soviet forces sat outside for week after week and watched as the Nazis threw five divisions against the trapped Poles, finally crushing their heroic resistance after sixty-three days. The Soviet government even refused to allow the Western Allies the use of Soviet airfields to fly supplies to the beleaguered Poles until the uprising had been going on for seven full weeks. At the end of September the Soviet army marched west, bypassing Warsaw altogether. On October 3, cut off and abandoned, the resistance forces surrendered to the Germans. The cream of the Polish resistance movement had been eliminated; the city of Warsaw had been ravaged; the path for Soviet domination of Poland had been cleared. In March 1945 the Soviets followed this up by inviting the commander of the Polish Home Army and several other leaders of the underground resistance to Moscow for political talks. When they revealed themselves to the Soviet agents, however, they were arrested and imprisoned. All this while the war in Europe was still going on, while the Soviets and the Western Allies—and the Polish underground—were still supposedly fighting together to defeat the Nazis.

•   •   •

World War III has gone on now for a third of a century, since those closing days of World War II. At Tehran, Yalta, and Potsdam, as the postwar pattern of Europe was being set, Stalin maneuvered his way toward the advantages that he soon abruptly seized. The Soviet armies that followed the retreating Germans into Eastern Europe stayed, and the Iron Curtain clanged down across the continent. Locked under communist rule were the people of Poland, Hungary, Czechoslovakia, Yugoslavia, Romania, Bulgaria, Albania, East Germany, as well as those of the once-independent states of Latvia, Lithuania, and Estonia. It was a coldly calculated grab on Stalin's part; as he later commented, "The reason why there is now no Communist government in Paris is because in the circumstances of 1945 the Soviet Army was not able to reach French soil."

World War III has proceeded from the Soviet seizure of Eastern Europe, through the communist conquest of China, the wars in Korea and Indochina, and the establishment of a western hemisphere outpost of Soviet power in Cuba, to the present thrusts by the Soviet Union and its allies into Africa, the Islamic crescent, and Central America. The expansionism has been accompanied by a prodigious military buildup that has brought the Soviet Union to the verge of decisive supremacy over the West.

Korea and Vietnam were battles in that war, as were the coups that brought Soviet satellite regimes to power in places as remote as Afghanistan and South Yemen. So, too, have been the struggles to keep Communist parties from taking control in Italy and Portugal, and to contain Castro's export of revolution in Latin America.

World War III is the first truly global war. No corner of the earth is beyond its reach. The United States and the Soviet Union have both become global powers, and whatever affects the balance between us anywhere affects that balance everywhere. The Soviets understand this. We too must understand it, and must learn to think in global terms.

World War III is also the first truly total war: it is

waged on all levels of life and society. Military power, economic power, willpower, the strength of a nation's galvanizing ideas and the clarity of its sense of purpose—each of these is vital to the outcome. So, too, are other intangibles: whether the competitive spirit is honored or denigrated; whether the prevailing ethic is for the individual to do the least he can get away with or the best of which he is capable; whether the next generation are to be builders and creators or television zombies. It is also the first total war because of the nature of our adversaries: because theirs is a totalitarian system, advancing under the banner of an ideology in which even the minds of its people are the property of the state.

For the past third of a century, when we in the West have thought about World War III, the term has conjured up dreadful visions of a nuclear Armageddon. But while the West casually refers to the absence of nuclear war as peace, the Soviets have assiduously been fighting "a war called peace," trying to win World War III without risking a nuclear exchange. They know that the object of war is not to obliterate the opponent, but to make him surrender. As the Prussian military strategist Clausewitz observed long ago, the aggressor never wants war; he would prefer to enter your country unopposed.

If we study Soviet actions, they show a clear pattern: not necessarily a "master plan" or a predictable timetable for world conquest, but rather a constant strengthening of military forces and a consistent exploitation of every opportunity to expand their own power and to weaken that of the West. Just as water flows downhill, the Soviets press to extend their power wherever it can reach, by whatever means they calculate can be effective. They are totally amoral opportunists. They *will* carefully calculate cost-benefit ratios, but they will not fret over the sanctity of contracts, the value of human life, or "bourgeois" concepts of justice.

Apologists often argue that the Soviets are really trying to ensure their own security against what they perceive as real or potential threats from abroad, and that once they have sufficient strength to ensure that security, their appetites will be sated. There may be some truth to the first half of that argument, but the trouble with the second half is that the Russian appetite for "security" is insatiable. The more the Soviets acquire, the more they have to protect; and they define "security" only as domination, whether at home or abroad. They have no tradition of compromise, of accommodation, of consensus, or indeed of a rule of law. As long as there is one country or one person who might stand in opposition, they consider their security in jeopardy. To them, security, like power, can only be total. And so it can only be guaranteed by total elimination of all potential opposition. In the Soviet view, Russian gains in security must come from the losses of others; there is no increase in mutual security. For the Soviets to be secure, in their view, others must be rendered insecure.

The Soviet leadership has no concept of "peace" as we understand it, or of coexistence as we would define it. They do not believe in the concept of equals. An equal is, by their definition, a rival, to be eliminated before he eliminates you.

The Soviet goal is, reversing Woodrow Wilson, a world made unsafe for democracy: a world in which the Soviet state is secure and all others respect Soviet control and pay Soviet tribute. The Soviet ambition has been appropriately described as a desire for "the capability to control global economic, political, and strategic affairs directly from Moscow." The Chinese communists accuse the Soviets of seeking "hegemony," and the word aptly describes Soviet aims.

The meaning of World War III is written starkly and eloquently on the faces of the boat people of Vietnam, desperately risking death on the high seas, and rejection when they finally reach land, rather than continue to live in the prison that was once their country. Millions from other countries have risked all in their efforts to escape communism, or have abandoned homes, possessions, even families, in sad pilgrimages as their countries were partitioned. As villagers flee the advancing lava from a volcano, these new dispossessed flee the advance of a tyranny that calls itself "liberation."

Before the communist regime took power in mainland China, Hong Kong was a city of little more than a million people. Today it holds nearly 5 million. Most of that increase is accounted for by the flood of refugees from the mainland, which surged through despite the barbed wire and border guards put in place to halt it.

In my office is a lacquer painting given to Mrs. Nixon when she visited a refugee camp in South Vietnam in 1956. It serves as a constant reminder to me that when Vietnam was partitioned in 1954 nearly a million people fled from North to South.

I spent Christmas Day 1956 at a refugee camp in Austria, near the bridge at Andau. There I talked with some of those who had escaped from Hungary in the wake of that country's brief rebellion, as Soviet tanks were crushing resistance in the streets of Budapest. Their tales of escape were harrowing. Their courage was a tribute to the human spirit, and a measure of the cruelty that triumphed.

In divided Germany the Berlin Wall stands as what West German Foreign Minister Hans-Dietrich Genscher has called "a monument to slavery." Before the Wall, undivided Berlin was an accessible island of freedom in a sea of tyranny. It was an abomination to the communists because it represented choice. Before the Wall was built in 1961, over 3 million people took advantage of that choice, and fled communist rule: five hundred people a day for fifteen years.

Closed borders, barbed wire, walls, guards with orders to shoot on sight any attempting to flee—these are the mark of communist control and the symbols of Soviet advance.

The hundreds of thousands of Jews waiting to get out of the Soviet Union have engaged the world's sympathy. But they are not alone. It is not just anti-Semitism that causes the Soviet government to limit Jewish emigration. If free emigration were allowed, millions of Ukrainians, Lithuanians, and others would leave also.

It is a mark of our times that when one or two persons defect from the West to the East, that is big news. But when thousands flee communist rule, that is merely a statistic. Yet the human tragedy behind such statistics is one of the central dramas of the twentieth century, and the assault on human liberties these statistics represent is one of the defining characteristics of World War III.

Resources: The Weak Link

To the Soviets, anyone who stands in the way of their supremacy—of their hegemony—is an adversary. The Soviet Union's ultimate target in World War III is its chief rival, the United States. Its intermediate targets are Western Europe and Japan. Its immediate targets are those vulnerable and unstable areas of Africa, Asia, the Middle East, and Latin America, in which, at relatively little risk and cost, it can gain strategic advantages and place itself increasingly in position to control the world's resources and lifelines.

Stalin highlighted the vulnerability of the West to resource interdiction back in 1921. "If Europe and America may be called the front," he said, "the non-sovereign nations and colonies, with their raw materials, fuel, food, and vast stores of human material, should be regarded as the rear, the reserve of imperialism. In order to win a war one must not only triumph at the front but also revolutionize the enemy's rear, his reserves." More recently, Soviet President Leonid I. Brezhnev confided to Somalian President Siad Barre, then an ally of the U.S.S.R., that "Our aim is to gain control of the two great treasure houses on which the West depends—the energy treasure house of the Persian Gulf and the mineral treasure house of central and southern Africa."

While the United States is partially dependent on imported oil and strategic minerals, Europe and Japan are absolutely dependent on overseas sources. Half of our oil is imported, but Europe imports 85 percent and Japan 100 percent. As for minerals, Western Europe imports 80 percent and Japan 95 percent. Minor interruptions of imports that would cause inconvenience and annoyance in the United States might create panic in our industrial allies. Thus they have even more reason than we to be concerned about the Soviet drive toward those "great treasure houses on which the West depends." But we too have a vital stake—both because we are also dependent on those treasure houses for strategic materials, and because the strength and unity of the Western alliance as a whole are essential to meeting the Soviet challenge. What weakens our allies weakens us.

The Soviet leaders have their eyes on the economic underpinnings of modern society. Their aim is to pull the plug on the Western industrial machine. The Western industrial nations' dependence on foreign sources of vital raw materials is one of our chief vulnerabilities. This, as well as the inherent instability of many of the producing nations, dictates Soviet strategy in such areas as the Middle East, Africa, and Latin America.

To most Americans, the map of Africa is as unfamiliar as that of Antarctica. Most would not know Mali from Malawi; nor would they have any idea where Somalia is, or Eritrea, much less why events there may be shaping the future of the world. Nor could they place such neighboring locales as South Yemen or Oman, or the Straits of Hormuz, Bahrain, or Qatar. Yet these places, and others like them, are vital to America's interests and those of the West. They are central to Moscow's drive for strategic dominance, and American ignorance or disinterest gives the Soviets one of their greatest advantages.

The ghosts of the colonial past haunt the leaders of many African nations today. Precolonial African politics were tribal; after the European conquest they became imperial; today they are a unique combination of the two.

The boundaries of most present-day African states make little sense from a nation-state point of view. They do not correspond to natural or tribal lines; they remain drawn where the armies of the colonial powers halted or where mapmakers in Paris or London chanced to place them. African countries often consist of twenty or thirty tribes, a mishmash of many mini-nations, while many tribes have been cut in two by inherited colonial boundaries. The resulting lack of national unity makes democracy almost an impossibility, economic development a distant dream, and internal tension a constant fact of life. Many African heads of state want only to maintain themselves in power and to keep their nations from disintegrating.

This is where the Soviets come in. They are masters of empire, virtuosos in the art of smashing nations and establishing totalitarian control over the remains. As Edward Luttwak, a senior fellow at Georgetown University's Center for Strategic and International Studies, has pointed out, postcolonial African politics are not the "politics of prosperity" that we are accustomed to, "but rather the politics of power accumulation." And in this respect the Soviets, experts at gaining and retaining power, have much more to offer than the United States.

When the leaders of African nations go shopping, the Soviets offer them a tempting grab bag. The Soviet military-industrial complex runs overtime, so they always have ample supplies of weapons to offer, sometimes at bargain prices, and without the delays occasioned by debates over the "morality" of trafficking in arms. The Soviet catalogue lists many other accessories for the dictator: East German "security" experts, Cuban troops, timely tips from the Soviet intelligence network, and, as Luttwak neatly puts it, "The broad support of Soviet propaganda, which will ceaselessly proclaim their virtues, even if they do have a weakness for executing people at random." Aggressive marketers, the Soviets have recently taken to shipping their clients whole proxy armies as well. They demand payment for their goods in the currency of power.

The Soviets have not made the naïve mistake of assuming that African leaders automatically care most about economic development for their people. From their own experience the Soviets know that the first priority of many of these leaders is to maintain themselves in power, and they, not we, offer the most effective "foreign aid" for this purpose.

They have been remarkably successful salesmen. Despite Russia's being a newcomer to the African continent, Moscow and its allies now supply more than 75 percent of the weapons going to Africa, and their sales quotas are surely being revised upward.

When they go to take a bite out of the world, the Soviets are not fussy eaters. It matters little to them whether an African or other client regime is "socialist," "communist," or, indeed, capitalist in the way it arranges its internal economic affairs. What does matter is that the regime exercise effective, preferably totalitarian, control over its people, and that it conduct its foreign and military policies in a way that serves the Soviet national interest. The key is *interest:* what matters is that the regime be a compliant client, whether or not it happens also to be doctrinaire communist. "Radish communists," red on the outside but white on the inside, taste as good to the Soviets as red tomatoes. Lately the Soviets have been seen picking their teeth in the Horn of Africa, sampling first one dish and then another. In the process, they have shown how rapidly their "friendships" can shift as new opportunities arise.

Until September of 1974 Ethiopia was a firm friend of the West. Under the rule of Emperor Haile Selassie, it had long been one of the closest U.S. allies in black Africa. Meanwhile, for years the Russians had watched eagerly as their allies in Cuba and others had fueled an armed secessionist movement in Eritrea—the strategically located northeastern province of Ethiopia, just across the Red Sea from Saudi Arabia.

Then, in the wake of a devastating famine in 1974, the military overthrew Selassie. A radical group within the military established its own dominance within the revolutionary government. The new rulers cut the country's Western ties and established Eastern ones. As Moscow's new friendship with Ethiopia warmed, its friendship toward the Eritrean rebels cooled; the Eritreans not only lost their Cuban support, but they soon found themselves fighting against Soviet-sponsored soldiers from that Caribbean country where they themselves had recently trained.

The abrupt change in its relationship with Ethiopia had its cost to the U.S.S.R. For years, neighboring Somalia had been Russia's chief base of influence in the area. Although it had not fallen completely into the Soviet orbit, Somalia had a treaty of friendship with Moscow and had been armed by the Russians, and it had been a loyal Soviet agent on the Horn of Africa. But Somalia had its own bitter territorial dispute with Ethiopia. Somalia claimed Ethiopia's Ogaden province. Moscow had supported that claim. Now Russia began retreating from that support, and Somalia's leader, Siad Barre, shopped for friends elsewhere.

In the summer of 1977, Barre launched an invasion of the Ogaden. At first, Barre's troops routed the Ethiopians. But then the Soviets sent nearly 20,000 Cuban troops to Ethiopia, which were deployed against Somalia as well as against the Eritreans; they also airlifted $2 billion worth of arms and 3,000 Soviet military technicians to Ethiopia. These turned the tide. In early 1978 Barre withdrew Somalia's troops from the Ogaden desert.

In terms of cold cost-benefit calculations, the Soviets had come out ahead. Barre retaliated against the Soviet help to Ethiopia by throwing the Russians out of Somalia; but the Soviets had created a political junkie out of Ethiopia. To survive, Ethiopia's regime needed a continuing "fix" of Soviet weaponry, as well as thousands of Cuban and Soviet personnel. The Soviets had traded a country of three million for one ten times its population. They had lost the naval base they had built in Somalia, at Berbera, but they had gained the Ethiopian port of Massawa, where a new and more strategically located base will soon be completed.

What kind of regime were the Soviets bankrolling? The *American Spectator* put it graphically:

A knack for imaginative and effective leadership is what the Soviets prize most in their African allies. In this respect, Colonel Haile Mengistu Meriam of Ethiopia—who in 1977 walked into a cabinet meeting and shot all of his erstwhile colleagues—is a model ruler.

Mengistu has not confined his attentions to Ethiopia. Sudan's borders have been violated, and it has had to absorb more than 300,000 Ethiopians who have fled Mengistu's "red terror." A new seed of unrest has been planted in African soil and nurtured by Moscow. The Soviet Union has gained potential bases, ports, a staging area for Cuban troops, and a strategically situated funnel to the rest of Africa. The only African country except Liberia that never lived under European colonial rule has fallen to communist imperialism. Of potentially even greater concern, Saudi Arabia is threatened: the Horn of Africa forms a claw with its pincers around the Arabian peninsula; the Ethiopian highlands look down menacingly on the desert sands of Saudi Arabia, just across the Red Sea.

Soviet activities in Africa underscore one of the great strategic changes of recent years: the emergence of the U.S.S.R. as a global power exerting direct pressure not just on contiguous territories, but wherever the opportunity presents itself.

Using Cuban troops transported in Soviet aircraft, Moscow has been leapfrogging national boundaries to strike deep in the heart of Africa. Now that European colonialism has disappeared from Africa, Soviet imperialism is moving to replace it. The new nations of Africa are particularly tempting because they control raw materials vital to a modern industrial society, and particularly vulnerable because of their instability and the priorities held by so many of their leaders.

In 1975, four centuries of Portuguese colonial rule ended in Angola and Mozambique. Now, instead of colonial ties to Portugal, both countries have "friendship treaties" with Russia; they bristle with modern Soviet weapons and threaten the whole of what Brezhnev so covetously referred to as the "mineral treasure house of central and southern Africa." Together, they border on every key country in that "treasure house." Just as the Soviets had their eyes on the oil of Arabia when they moved into Somalia and then Ethiopia, they had their eyes on these mineral resources when they moved into Angola and Mozambique.

It was in Angola that the Soviets first used Cuban troops to impose Russian rule in Africa. For more than a decade, during the independence struggle, Moscow had been funneling aid to the Popular Front for the Liberation of Angola (MPLA), a Marxist guerrilla force. When the Portuguese left, two other groups were also contending for power in the newly independent nation: the FNLA and UNITA. Fighting among them continued. In the final showdown the United States cut off aid to the pro-Western groups, while the Soviets airlifted in 15,000 Cuban troops to help MPLA. Not surprisingly, MPLA won. Angola became a Soviet outpost.

In late 1979 Jonas Savimbi, the leader of UNITA, was in the United States seeking support for his continuing guerrilla war against Angola's new masters. Savimbi earned his credentials by fighting for freedom from Portuguese rule; now he is fighting for freedom from Russian rule. Lamenting that in the United States "there is a total absence of resistance to Russian and Cuban aggression" in Africa, he complained that "a new form of imperialism is dominating our continent." The Russians and Cubans, he said, "who were supposed to be our friends and who did give us help in our struggle against the Portuguese, are now bringing us a new style of slavery."

Commenting acidly on the lack of American support for Savimbi, Francis X. Maier, editor of the *National Catholic Register*, noted that Savimbi is "a witness to the fact that, somewhere along the way, the United States has lost the ability to distinguish our natural friends from our natural enemies. It's another curious irony of the late twentieth century—and a hint of our moral disarray—that the only 'freedom fighters' we will *not* wine and dine are those who profess our own values."

In Mozambique, since 1978 East German military advisers have trained guerrillas for infiltration into Zimbabwe Rhodesia. Guerrillas are being trained in Angola for use in

Namibia to the south; already guerrillas from Angola have twice been sent north into Zaire, where they invaded Zaire's mineral-rich Shaba province. In their 1978 Shaba raid, the guerrillas slaughtered European technicians and their families in the key mining town of Kolwezi. Since then few Europeans have been willing to return to Shaba, leaving its copper and cobalt production 50 to 80 percent below normal. Copper is essential to Zaire's economy; cobalt, now critically scarce, is essential to jet aviation, and Zaire has 65 percent of the free world's supply.

Just as Ethiopia to the north, these former Portuguese colonies to the south are key outposts of Soviet empire. Like a cancer that gets into the system, Soviet influence spreads out from these and Russia's other African outposts. In Zambia, Tanzania, and elsewhere, Cuban troops and Eastern bloc "technicians" are becoming as familiar as Western colonialists used to be.

If the U.S.S.R. continues to succeed in its penetration of Africa, it will have come a long way in its larger strategy of encircling the world "city"—of cutting off the industrialized West from the resources without which it cannot survive. Even the resource-rich United States depends heavily on imports for several of the basic minerals vital to a modern economy. Chromium offers an example of the hidden dangers of this dependency.

Most people, when they think of chromium, think of the fancy trim on automobiles. But to strategic planners chromium means such things as ball bearings, precision instruments, and missiles. A single jet aircraft requires more than 3,600 pounds of chrome. As one expert has put it, "If you don't have chromium, you don't have top-quality aircraft engines." Stainless steel cannot be made without chromium. The National Research Council recently concluded that the U.S. long-term vulnerability in chrome is greater than in petroleum. Chromium is already in short supply, and we desperately need it to rebuild our armed forces. Our domestic supplies of chromium ore are small in quantity and low-grade in quality; 92 percent of our chrome must be imported. And our two principal sources have recently been South Africa (33 percent) and the Soviet Union (25 percent). Furthermore, of the world's known reserves of chromium, 96 percent are in the Union of South Africa and Zimbabwe Rhodesia.

This vital dependency illustrates why the Soviets have particularly targeted for interference that portion of the continent that intensely engages the emotions of many in the West: southern Africa. The Soviet Union seldom acts without a purpose, and its purposes are always strategic, never moral. Thus its persistent efforts to stir further the already troubled waters of southern Africa have to be viewed against the backdrop of the resources in that part of the world, and of the importance of those resources to the West. By one authoritative estimate, the Union of South Africa alone possesses a tenth of the world's asbestos, three fourths of the world's chromite ore, more than half of its platinum group metals, half of its gold, a third of its manganese ore, a fifth of its uranium, and a third of its diamonds: a mineral treasure of almost incalculable strategic and economic importance.

Zairean copper and cobalt, Rhodesian chrome, South African gold, diamonds, manganese, and platinum metals—these are among the economic stakes the Soviets are playing for in southern Africa. They already control the excellent ports in Angola and Mozambique flanking the Cape of Good Hope. If South Africa were to fall under their control, they would control the sea lanes around the Cape through which 70 percent of the strategic raw materials and 80 percent of the oil needed by European NATO powers flow. South Africa is also the continent's leading economic power. It alone provides 40 percent of the industrial production of all Africa and 25 percent of its agricultural production.

The Soviets want southern Africa. They also try to exploit its racial troubles, particularly those of the Republic of South Africa, in order to incite hostility toward the West; and, if they could, they would like to precipitate a military confrontation and a race war there, which would have incalculably tragic consequences for black and white alike, as well as for the whole continent of Africa and the whole of the Western world. It would leave a lot of shattered pieces for Russia to pick up.

South Africa's particular racial troubles are different, because that nation's history is different; but troubles between racial, ethnic, or tribal groups are not unique to South Africa. In northernmost Africa the Arabs rule. In the countries of the Sahel, the Arabs struggle with blacks for dominance. In Chad, struggles between Moslems in the north and Saharan people in the south have led to civil war for twelve years—an indication of the problems racial divisions can cause. In Africa south of the Sahara, blacks predominate, but this has not prevented violent tribalism, a sin just as bad as racism. Fierce intertribal rivalries and wars—the Katanga rebellion in the Congo; the civil war in Nigeria, which caused the death of probably more than a million Ibos in Biafra; the bloody war between the Hutu and the Tutsi in tiny Burundi in 1973, where 100,000 died; and many other conflicts—have occurred. Nor have black Africans been free of racism. In East Africa, those of Asian origin had their property expropriated and then were driven out, solely on racial grounds. In Equatorial Guinea a dictator supported by Russia, China, Cuba, and North Korea forced an estimated one third of that nation's population to flee into exile and many of those who stayed behind met their death in forced-labor camps or prison. For many Africans the benefits of "majority rule" have been so slight that, according to Amnesty International, eight black African countries are among the fifteen worst human rights violators in the world. Given the experience of the rest of Africa, instant majority rule, even if it were possible, would surely not be the best thing for the Africans of South Africa—black and white alike.

In the larger world struggle southern Africa is a key battleground—as vital in its way as the Middle East. We must not, out of a misplaced idealism, allow our policies toward southern Africa to become hostage to the parochial passions of African leaders who have no appreciation of or concern for the issues at stake there between East and West. We also must not, out of that same misplaced idealism, conspire in the destruction of societies that are moving forward, both economically and socially, and that do show signs of demonstrating how to succeed where others on the continent—including their most vehement detractors—have conspicuously failed.

Just as our own South changed dramatically after years of saying "never," South Africa now is changing. Prime Minister Botha has committed the government to a program of "adaptation to avoid revolution." One moderate member of Parliament recently commented that "more changes have taken place here in the last 18 months than in all the previous 320 years of this country's history."

Whether in the Union of South Africa or in Zimbabwe Rhodesia, those who are working for an evolutionary rather than a revolutionary solution to their countries' troubles should be given the world's sympathetic help, not be treated as international pariahs. It happens that the vital strategic interests of the West are bound up with the stability of those countries, and of that part of Africa; we should not be apologetic about defending those interests. Neither should we be apologetic about standing firmly with those who are committed to expanding freedom, even if gradually, as opposed to those who are extinguishing freedom, and doing so rapidly.

The real threat of white domination in Africa during the remainder of this century is not from the old order. The real danger is from the new order—the new slavery that Jonas Savimbi warns of, imposed and maintained by the new Soviet imperialism. In no Soviet-dominated state does *any* majority rule, whatever its color; minority rule is the essence of the Soviet system. Whatever the color of the local puppet, the strings are pulled from Moscow—and there are no black faces in the Politburo. The Soviets are not in Africa to "liberate." They are there to dominate, control, and exploit, and to replace the old white supremacy with a new white supremacy. White colonial rule is white colonial rule, whether exercised from London or from Moscow.

Throughout history many of the worst atrocities have been perpetrated in the name of the highest ideals. Passion is a poor guide to policy. The racist obsession of many black African leaders, while understandable in terms of their priorities, ought not to dictate ours. The sort of holy war they preach, to eradicate in southern Africa all vestiges of special privilege or even special protection for the white minorities, would be bloody even beyond the standards of Idi Amin; and it would destroy the economic and political structures on which both black and white depend for such freedom and prosperity as they have.

A race war against South Africa is not the way to end racism in South Africa, nor will economic warfare against the most economically advanced nation on the continent resolve the issue. Here in the United States we fought a civil war in part over the issue of slavery, and it took another century before even those racial discriminations sanctioned by law were wiped away. With our own history, we are hardly free enough of sin to cast the first stone—or even the second. Without condoning South Africa's racial policies, we should be more understanding of the need to change them peacefully over a period of time, and more sensitive to the other issues besides race that are at stake in the future of that tortured part of the continent.

The "Soft" Underbelly

With our eyes riveted on the successive crises in NATO Europe, the Middle East, Southeast Asia, and Africa, we have lost sight of the growing world of power to the south of us in Latin America. Geopolitically it has long been accepted that we are an "island nation," but if we maintain our past neglect of this area we may well awaken to find that the enemy is ashore on the "island continent" to the south of us. The Soviets already have outposts of influence on the offshore islands—in Cuba and some of the smaller Antilles. By the time this book appears, they may be ashore in Central America.

Latin America usually makes the front pages of our newspapers only when there is a revolution, an earthquake, or a riot at a soccer match. But it deserves attention equal to that we give Europe, Asia, and Africa, and in some ways even more because of its proximity to us.

Latin America is a prime Soviet target for three major reasons: it has enormous natural resources; by the end of the century its population will be substantially greater than that of the United States and Western Europe combined; and it is close to the United States—it is our soft underbelly.

The nations of Latin America won their freedom largely as a result of our example. They were able to keep that freedom during their early years because of the protective mantle the Monroe Doctrine spread over them. By allowing a Soviet client state in the Americas—Cuba—we seemed to them to have abandoned that doctrine. They see little resistance from us to the establishment of Cuban influence in the islands of the Caribbean and now on the mainland of Central America. They see us abandoning many of our friends on the grounds that they are not pure on the matter of human rights. They notice that the Soviets do not abandon their friends over matters of ideology, as long as interests coincide. They have watched as our friends in South Vietnam, Laos, Cambodia, Angola, Mozambique, Ethiopia, Afghanistan, and Iran have been defeated and overthrown, in some cases with the help of Cuba. They can hardly help wondering how firmly they can count on us in the future.

Many use the term "Latin America" as if it were an undifferentiated mass. But Latin America embraces an expanse far larger than Europe and contains an immense diversity of peoples. Each country has an old and proud tradition of independence and individuality. They all have a common religion. By the end of the century half of the Roman Catholics in the world will be in Latin America. Some countries, such as Argentina, Uruguay, and Costa Rica, have populations that are almost exclusively European in origin. Others, including Mexico, Peru, Colombia, and Ecuador, have a large Indian component. Many have large numbers of people with German, Italian, and other European backgrounds besides Spanish. In Brazil people of African and Portuguese origin have joined to produce a new civilization. There are wide differences in the degree of development and sophistication in these countries; in size, they range from the giant Brazil to such tiny countries as El Salvador.

Brazil, Mexico, and Argentina are rapidly becoming industrial nations. Brazil has more people than Britain and France combined, well over 100 million, and in some respects is already an industrial giant, with the tenth largest GNP in the world in 1978.

Mexico is taking great strides toward development. Revenues from its vast newly found oil reserves will enable it to move rapidly toward a better life for its 70 million people, but these riches also make it a tempting target for subversion.

Argentina, with a basically homogeneous and highly educated population, is keenly motivated and is engaged, like Brazil, in building vast new dams to provide electricity and power for its burgeoning industry. It needs only political stability to move forward even faster.

In Chile, the ruling junta has embarked on what has been labeled "a daring gamble . . . to turn the country into a laboratory for free-market economics." Investment has shot up, taxes have been cut, and tax reform enacted. Critics focus exclusively on political repression in Chile, while ignoring the freedoms that are a product of a free economy. In Cuba there are neither political nor economic rights. In Chile, the latter may well be the precursor of the former. Rather than insisting on instant perfection from Chile, we should encourage the progress it is making.

The Andean countries have shown promising signs of a growing ability to work together. Venezuelan oil wealth

Colombian diversity, Ecuadorian oil, and Peruvian minerals could be used to bring new hope to the underprivileged in the area.

Central America and the Caribbean are critical regions because of their strategic location, and because economically and militarily they are among the weaker areas of the hemisphere. Radical governments are now installed in Grenada and St. Lucia. Cuba has made efforts to ingratiate itself in Jamaica and Panama, and has intervened in Nicaragua. This could be the first step along a road that leads through Honduras, El Salvador, and Guatemala to the threshold of the great Mexican oilfields in the area of the Tehuantepec Isthmus. The Soviets and their allies may well try to repeat in Latin America the squeeze play they engineered in Afghanistan, South Yemen, and Ethiopia around the oil-producing lands of the Middle East. As Rowland Evans and Robert Novak have put it, the "Central American dominoes are falling." The primary reason for these reverses is one man on one island: Castro and Cuba.

If Soviet client regimes come to power in Central America, the western hemisphere will have been cut in two at its "slim waist." From their position in Central America such regimes would threaten the two largest oil producers in Latin America, Venezuela and Mexico, as well as the Panama Canal. We cannot afford to let this happen.

The Monroe Doctrine must be revitalized and redefined to counter indirect aggression, which was not a threat 150 years ago. The United States should make it clear that we will resist intervention in Latin America not only by foreign governments but also by Latin American governments controlled by a foreign power. Of the total of 10 million Cubans, more than 40,000 are now acting as proxies for Soviet expansion in Africa. This is the equivalent of sending an army of nearly 1 million Americans overseas to fight—almost twice the highest number we had in Vietnam. Tiny Cuba, under Soviet tutelage, has become a major imperialist power. Castro has made Cuba a disaster area. He must not be allowed, with Soviet support, to foist his discredited economic and political systems on other countries in Latin America. Any such effort at subversion should be firmly and unmistakably checked, and both Soviets and Cubans should be told in advance that any interference here will bring far more than a diplomatic protest from us.

At the same time, we must work with the nations of Latin America in building their economies and helping them to help their people escape the poverty that still is the lot of so many. As the dismal failure of the Alliance for Progress to achieve its grandiose goals demonstrated, a "war on poverty" in Latin America will not be won by primary reliance on government aid programs. Government aid is limited by budgets; private investment is limited only by opportunities. To attract the investments they need, Latin American countries will have to provide guarantees against expropriation and ensure that there are sufficient incentives. For their part, American and other private investors must come in as developers and not exploiters. As the Latin American countries industrialize, the markets of the West must be opened to their products. The United States, in view of our special relationship with these countries, should provide preferential tariff treatment for Latin American products.

Economic development will make Latin America an even more tempting target for Soviet expansionism. But by demonstrating that free economies produce progress, Latin American political leaders will enormously strengthen their hand against revolutionary leftist elements.

In everything that we do, we must remember that *how* we do it counts more with our proud and sensitive Latin friends than with any other people in the world. It is vital that we treat them as partners, not as patients; and, as the giants in this area grow, we must acknowledge their new status in the world. We must learn not only to take our Latin neighbors seriously, but to treat each nation individually, just as we do the nations of Europe. We must also remember that these are proud people, who will not be browbeaten into making our values their own.

Terrorism

If World War III is defined in one way by the tide of refugees, it is defined in another way by the tactic of terrorism. The first shows the human cost. The second shows the Soviets' inhuman contempt for even the most basic of civilized standards. In recent years the Soviets have stepped up their terrorism campaign with devastating effect.

Many of those who romanticize revolution prefer to view terrorism merely as one of the ills of modern society, or as an outraged response to intolerable social conditions. But "senseless" terrorism is often not as senseless as it may seem. To the Soviets and their allies, it is a calculated instrument of national policy.

An international fraternity of terrorists, with the Soviet Union as the chairman of the rush committee, has enabled the Russians to engage, as Senator Henry Jackson has put it, in "warfare by remote control" all over the world. Other members of the international club include North Korea, Cuba, South Yemen, East Germany, Libya, and the Palestine Liberation Organization. Malcontents from all over the world are trained by them—many at the appropriately named Patrice Lumumba Friendship University in Moscow—in the arts of kidnapping, assassination, sabotage, bomb making, and insurrection, and then sent off to ply their trade. Their tutors are careful to keep them well supplied with weapons and to provide sanctuary when they need it.

One of the most famous alumni recruited by the KGB for Patrice Lumumba Friendship University is the Venezuelan-born terrorist known as "Carlos"; or "The Jackal." The Venezuelan Communist Party footed the bill for Carlos' "education," and he has since used it to kidnap for ransom eleven participants in an OPEC conference of oil ministers in 1975, as well as to assassinate numerous businessmen, intelligence agents, and innocent bystanders. Carlos has won celebrity status, but there are many more like him who are less famous.

The Soviets, Libya, and the PLO were all heavily involved in the campaign to overthrow the Shah. The quasi-anarchy that followed his downfall in Iran provided the perfect culture medium in which fanaticism and terrorism together could flourish, and could be exploited by those whose calculated policy it is to exploit fanaticism and terrorism. The "students" who took over the American Embassy and seized the American hostages were clearly taught by experts in things other than the Koran, and the manipulators of that exercise gave international terrorism new dimensions of subtlety and effrontery. They also demonstrated what we invite when, like the baby and the bathwater, we mindlessly throw out authority along with authoritarianism. The guns are not put away; they simply are taken over by the mob.

Even as the American hostages were being held, across the Persian Gulf another terrorist team staged a meticulously prepared attack, breathtaking in its sheer audacity, on the holiest shrine of all Islam: the Grand Mosque at Mecca. The 500 who took part were led by a small group, apparently trained in South Yemen, the Soviet proxy state on the Arabian peninsula. Their cover story was religious fanaticism; their real intent was political: to undermine the stability of Saudi Arabia. The terrorists were so concerned with disguising their origins that they deliberately burned and mutilated the faces of their dead. Their leaders had been expertly schooled in guerrilla tactics, which enabled them to smuggle large quantities of food and modern weaponry into the Grand Mosque, take it over, and hold it for two weeks before finally being ousted with the help of 1,000 members of the National Guard, with hundreds killed in the fighting.

In Nicaragua the Sandinist offensive was aided by what British columnist Robert Moss calls "a miniature international Communist brigade, including 'volunteers' from West Germany's terrorist underground."

Fidel Castro was involved in terrorist activities in South America long before he came to power in Cuba, and he has sponsored them ever since.

Terrorism also plays a key role in communist "wars of liberation." The British expert on revolutionary war, Sir Robert Thompson, has pointed out that it is crucial to understand the relationship between the guerrilla cause and their organization. In most cases, the cause that originally draws people to the guerrilla organization is not love of communism but hatred of foreigners. Many people joined Mao Zedong's guerrilla forces in order to fight the Japanese invaders between 1937 and 1945, Tito's forces to fight the Nazis during World War II, and Ho Chi Minh's to fight the French from 1946 to 1954. The communists were, in all cases, only one of many groups fighting the foreigners; but they were the most ruthless and effective.

Thompson notes that once the original cause has been attained, the key issue is the remaining efficiency of the guerrilla organization. Once the French, Japanese, or Nazis are gone, how can the communists rally the population? Love of communism or hatred of rival national leaders is not enough; terrorism is necessary to maintain organizational discipline and preserve power for the leaders. A prominent German journalist, Uwe Siemon-Netto, recently provided a vivid illustration of how communist guerrilla groups use terrorism to effect their purposes. Siemon-Netto, who accompanied a South Vietnamese battalion to a village the Viet Cong had raided in 1965, reported: "Dangling from the trees and poles in the village square were the village chief, his wife, and their twelve children, the males, including a baby, with their genitals cut off and stuffed into their mouths, the females with their breasts cut off." The Viet Cong had ordered everyone in the village to witness the execution. "They started with the baby and then slowly worked their way up to the elder children, to the wife, and finally to the chief himself. . . . It was all done very coolly, as much an act of war as firing an anti-aircraft gun." He noted that this was no isolated case: "It became routine . . . . Because it became routine to us, we didn't report it over and over again. We reported the unusual, like My Lai."

This is how the North Vietnamese and the Vietcong

won the hearts and minds of the rural population—by cold-blooded butchering intended to intimidate those who were left.

Terrorism can strike at the heart of Western civilization as well. The Soviets secretly subsidized the Baader-Meinhof gang in West Germany. In Italy, in March of 1978 Aldo Moro, former Premier and the leading candidate for the presidency, was kidnapped and his five bodyguards shot in cold blood by the Red Brigades. Italy was traumatized as he was held captive for nearly two months before he was gruesomely assassinated, his body deposited in the back seat of an abandoned car in the center of Rome. There were more than 2,100 terrorist attacks in Italy in 1977, and the number rose in 1978.

Dr. Ray Cline—a former CIA official now with Georgetown University—points out that the current wave of world terrorism began after 1969, when the KGB succeeded in having the PLO accepted at the Kremlin as a major political instrument in the Middle East. The Soviets then proceeded to boost PLO terrorism by providing money, training, and weapons and by coordinating communications. What the Soviets and their equally conscience-free allies have done is to create an "international troublemaking system" that trafficks in wholesale murder for political purposes.

Terrorism threatens all governments except those engaged in it. All therefore must join together in developing tactics to deal with it. The number of international terrorist incidents nearly doubled between the first nine months of 1978 and the same period of 1979; according to one estimate, 60 percent of the terrorist incidents that have taken place in the last decade have occurred in the last three years. Not surprisingly, this huge upsurge in terrorism occurred immediately after the CIA was de-fanged and demoralized in the wake of sensationalized investigations by Congress. Restoring the ability of the intelligence community to protect us is essential if we are to deal with the problem of terrorism before it gets even further out of hand. But trying to put out the fire after it is blazing is not enough. It is necessary to go to the heart of the problem—those who support terrorism, the major culprit being the Soviet Union.

The Recipe for Revolution

While it has been relentless, the Soviet expansionist push has seldom been reckless. The Soviet leaders are aggressors, but they are cautious aggressors. They make most of their moves slowly and subtly, taking care to disguise them so as not to rouse the "sleeping giant" of the West from its slumber.

They try to strike where least expected, when least expected, in the least expected way. Their preferred method is to provoke disorder and chaos in a targeted country, and then to move in and pick up the pieces after the established order has collapsed.

They are professional revolutionaries, and one of the tenets of their professionalism is to stay out of sight while the old regime is being brought down, leaving the amateurs—the genuine patriots, the nationalists, the idealists—out front. Television shows us the amateurs storming into the streets; it does not reveal the professionals calling the shots from behind the scenes, plotting the capture of the new regime even while directing the overthrow of the old.

With seductive slogans designed to deceive, with a small but efficient cadre of ruthless terrorists, with cynical leaders willing to promise anything for the future as long as they can gain power now, the professional revolutionaries move like hot knives through butter in societies that have come untracked. As chaos spreads in the wake of upheaval, they alone are marching silently in lockstep—their eyes fixed on the armories, the secret police files, the key posts in the new government, the malcontents in the armed services, the labor unions that run crucial industries, the newspapers, the radio stations, the vacant police chief jobs. Positions are won, workers are stirred up, opponents are arrested, political rivals are assassinated, and when all is ready the *coup de grâce* is delivered.

This is the communist recipe for revolution. It enabled Lenin to depose the moderate Premier Alexander Kerensky only eight short months after Kerensky's forces had ousted the Tsar in the first Russian Revolution. Lenin himself summed up its essential cynicism when he declared privately that "we will support Kerensky as the rope does the hanged man." Since 1917 the Soviets have bottled their patented product and exported it to the rest of the world.

The Soviets thrive on chaos, confusion, fear; they know that in desperate circumstances people will reach for desperate means. Communism offers the slogan of "liberation," the promise of order; it tells the "outs" that it will put them "in," the underdogs that they will be top dog. It speaks in terms of passionate certainty, and this appeals to people awash in uncertainty.

The Soviets know that war, revolution, and economic depression can destroy the fabric of a society and make the siren song of communism sound sweeter. When people feel panic, tyranny can look attractive if it promises order. Chaos, war, and revolution are thus the natural allies of communism, just as famine, conquest and slaughter ride alongside the fourth horseman of the apocalypse, death.

Knowing this, the Russians try, by whatever means they can, to exacerbate tensions, to stir up discontent, to foment wars and revolutions. They do not want human needs met. They do not want problems between nations solved. They want to exacerbate the problems in order to seize the nation.

Because the Soviets are poised to exploit them, disorder and chaos are the greatest enemies of freedom today. Those who are unrealistically impatient for progress do the world a great disservice when they convulse vulnerable societies with non-negotiable demands; however pure their own intentions, the convulsion may open the door to a totalitarian regime. Looking back, we must ask ourselves: What would have happened if the Soviet Union had been on the scene during the American Revolution?

The American colonies fought a war of independence for seven years. It took six more years before the Constitution was adopted, and two more after that before the Bill of Rights was added. Even then, tensions and inequities persisted that eventually led to a brutal civil war. Our country had time to sort out its problems, protected as it was by two oceans from the outside world. People striving for liberty today do not have the same luxury. The road for them will be much more difficult. They too need time. They too need protection.

The Danger: Defeat by Default

The Russians play chess. In chess a player gains an advantage by eliminating as many of his opponent's men as possible. But chess masters know that the game can be won when there are still many pieces left on the table. All that is necessary is that the opponent's king be immobilized, hemmed in by threats on all sides so he cannot move.

The king in the Western chess set is the United States. We are the principal obstacle between the Soviet Union and its goal of world domination. The Soviets know they will never be able to outproduce us economically. They also know they can only hope to overwhelm us militarily if our guard remains down long enough to let them get a decisive advantage. But in our will they sense a weakness that could offset the margin of safety our other strengths give us. The Soviets know their multiplication tables. Looking at Sir Robert Thompson's equation, national power equals manpower plus applied resources, *times* will, they understand that if the will factor is zero the whole equation is zero.

As British military historian B. H. Liddell Hart has noted, "Lenin had a vision of fundamental truth when he said that 'the soundest strategy in war is to postpone operations until the moral disintegration of the enemy renders the delivery of the mortal blow both possible and easy.'" This is the Soviet strategy. They seek first to demoralize us so that they can then destroy us. They want to end World War III not with a bang, but with a whimper.

They do this in three ways. First, they try to deceive us,

in order to disguise their intentions and make us relax our will; second, they try to make us feel guilty and defensive, even about our most dramatic successes, so that our will is paralyzed; third, they try to break our will by bullying us with threats and bluffs,

I vividly recall my old friend, NATO Secretary General Manlio Brosio, who had served for five years as Italy's ambassador in Moscow, emotionally telling me in 1967, "I know the Russians. They are great liars, clever cheaters, and magnificent actors. They cannot be trusted. They consider it their duty to cheat and lie."

To the Soviet Union, the United Nations is not a place where differences between nations can be settled amicably; it is a place where propaganda points can be scored, where the West can be condemned, where the jailers can parade as the justices. This elaborate masquerade is performed in order to deceive others and to make us doubt ourselves. Over the course of many years even the most absurdly misapplied words, if repeated often enough, have an effect. Some begin to believe that "Democratic" Kampuchea is actually something besides the contemporary equivalent of Hitlerian genocide, or that "People's Liberation" forces actually liberate people.

A refugee who fled from South Vietnam in 1979 after he had stayed to greet the communists said he had learned the hard way that the communists consider the lie "a weapon, a legitimate and honest weapon, to be used by the weak to defeat the strong." If the Soviets can, by their lies, make us forget who they are and doubt who we are, this weapon in World War III will have served its destructive purpose.

One of the Soviets' favorite tactics is bluster. Even when they were vastly inferior to us in power, Nikita Khrushchev would rattle his nuclear sabers, hoping to instill in the West a fear of Soviet might. Our leaders at the time were not fooled; they knew that Khrushchev had no intention of committing national suicide, but public opinion was strongly affected.

During the Cuban missile crisis Khrushchev overplayed his hand, Kennedy called his bluff, and the Soviet leader backed down. But since that time the Soviet Union has pressed forward with a sustained and intensive military buildup while the United States has let its nuclear superiority wither away. If in the future the Soviet leaders feel they have attained clear nuclear superiority, they will try once again to break our will, only this time it will be a substantive threat rather than a bluff.

The greatest danger we face in World War III is that we will lose it by default.

In 1975 the North Vietnamese went unopposed by a war-weary United States in their invasion of the South; in 1978 they invaded Cambodia. In 1975 and 1976 the Cubans met only a feeble response from the West when they went into Angola; in 1977 they showed up in Ethiopia. In April of 1978 the pro-Soviet coup in Afghanistan brought hardly a murmur from Western leaders; in June there was one in South Yemen. Then on Christmas Eve, 1979, the Red Army rolled into Kabul to suppress an anti communist revolt in Afghanistan. The dominoes have always taken the "domino theory" seriously—only in the fashionable salons of the West was it scoffed at.

As social critic Irving Kristol has pointed out:

> The nations of this world admire winners, not losers—not even 'nice' losers. . . . When a democratic nation . . . and most especially the leading democratic nation, engages interminably in Hamlet-like soliloquies on the moral dilemmas of action, the world will seek its political models elsewhere. . . .
>
> We know that power may indeed corrupt. We are now learning that, in the world of nations as it exists, powerlessness can be even more corrupting and demoralizing.

In World War III, as in other human activities, small problems neglected have a way of growing into large ones. The old adage that a stitch in time saves nine is as true in diplomacy as it is in the household. Acquiescence in one aggressive move invites another. A timely response at one level can avert the need for an escalated response later. Momentum is a powerful force among nations. Wavering leaders sense a shift in the balance of power and the direction of history, and they accelerate that shift by joining it. The key to winning World War III is to shift that balance, that momentum, in our direction.

3
The Visible Hand

There are, at the present time, two great nations in the world which seem to tend towards the same end, although they started from different points: I allude to the Russians and the Americans. Both of them have grown up unnoticed; and whilst the attention of mankind was directed elsewhere, they have suddenly assumed a most prominent place amongst the nations; and the world learned of their existence and their greatness at almost the same time. . . .

The American struggles against the natural obstacles which oppose him; the adversaries of the Russian are men; the former combats the wilderness and savage life; the latter, civilization with all its weapons and its arts: the conquests of the one are therefore gained by the ploughshare; those of the other by the sword. The Anglo-American relies upon personal interest to accomplish his ends, and gives free scope to the unguided exertions and common-sense of the citizens; the Russian centers all the authority of society in a single arm: the principal instrument of the former is freedom; of the latter servitude. Their starting-point is different, and their courses are not the same; yet each of them seems to be marked out by the will of Heaven to sway the destinies of half the globe.

—*Alexis de Tocqueville, 1835*

Communism became the force it is today largely by historical accident—because the first state whose system took its name was Russia. Soviet Russia is a peculiar, fascinating amalgam of past and present, and an insight into its past is essential to an understanding of its present.

Fifty years ago I saw Russia for the first time—through the eyes of Leo Tolstoy. At the urging of Dr. Albert Upton of Whittier College, I spent the summer between my junior and senior years reading everything Tolstoy had written. I came away with a feeling of sympathy, respect, and affection for the Russian people and with a profound dislike for tsarist imperialism and despotism.

During World War II I became strongly pro-Russian as the Soviet Union fought alongside us in the war against Hitler. My attitude began to change in 1946, in part because I was impressed and disturbed by the warning to the West that Winston Churchill delivered that year at Fulton, Missouri—his "Iron Curtain" speech. At first I thought that Churchill might have gone too far, but these doubts were soon removed by Stalin's actions. When President Harry S. Truman asked for aid to Greece and Turkey and initiated the Marshall Plan, I strongly supported both in Congress.

In 1948 the Alger Hiss case brought me face to face with the ugly realities of Soviet subversion in the United States.

In my travels as Vice President, I saw tens of thousands of refugees from communism in all areas of the world. In 1958 Mrs. Nixon and I were almost killed by a communist-led mob in Caracas, Venezuela.

In July of 1959 I became the first U.S. Vice President to visit the Soviet Union. In what was in effect a two-month cram course, I read books on Russia and thousands of pages of analyses of the Soviet Union prepared by the State Department, the CIA, and the Defense Department. Among those from whom I received briefings on Nikita Khrushchev and the other Soviet leaders were British Prime Minister Harold Macmillan, Secretary of State John Foster Dulles, two former ambassadors to the Soviet Union, William Bullitt and Charles E. Bohlen, journalist Walter Lippmann, New York *Times* editor Turner Catledge, and publisher William Randolph Hearst.

But no amount of briefing could have prepared me for what I encountered when I arrived in Moscow. Khrushchev was tougher and smarter than most of the briefers had indicated. All the Soviet leaders I met were communist to the core, but at times they were more Russian than communist. They pointed with pride to what they claimed communism had achieved in the Soviet Union. But they also showed pride in the glories of Russia's past as they escorted me through the Kremlin, the Winter Palace in Leningrad, and other points of historic interest.

Khrushchev was at his vociferous communist best, or worst, in an impromptu no-holds-barred debate between the two of us at the American National Exhibition in Moscow. But at a luncheon in an ornate room in the Kremlin immediately afterward he was all Russian—directing his guests to throw their glasses into the fireplace after we had had our vodka and champagne.

The Russian people impressed me tremendously with their strength and warmheartedness. In the heart of Siberia, in Novosibirsk, away from the tight control of the central government of Moscow, thousands of Russians swarmed around us shouting *"Mir y druzhba"*—"Peace and friendship." Schoolchildren stopped our car as we traveled through the Ural Mountains and threw flowers into it, shouting "Friendship." My Russian host told me that *friendship* was the first word in English that Russian children were taught in school. The people wanted friendship; the leaders, however, made no bones about the fact that they wanted something different. As Khrushchev put it coldly, "Your grandchildren will live under communism."

After our visit to Moscow we went to Poland. Over 200,000 cheering Poles gave us a tumultuous welcome, shouting *"Niech zyje Ameryka"*—"Long live America." Polish soldiers clapped and held up the "V" sign. In Moscow Khrushchev had bitterly assailed the Captive Nations resolution that had just been passed by Congress. The Polish people were vividly demonstrating why, and the Kremlin leaders must also have had doubts about the loyalty of those within the Soviet Union itself.

•   •   •

In 1972 I became the first U.S. President to visit the Soviet Union. Leonid Brezhnev was different from Khrushchev. Brezhnev's humor was earthy whereas Khrushchev's had been vulgar. Brezhnev wore tailored shirts with French cuffs instead of the plain-sleeved shirts Khrushchev preferred. He sat in the back seat of a limousine rather than the front seat with the chauffeur as Khrushchev had done. He was outwardly cordial while Khrushchev had been blustery and aggressive. But though the players had changed, the game remained the same. Brezhnev's goals were the same as Khrushchev's: the increase of Soviet power, the extension of Soviet control, and the expansion of communism throughout the world. He did not have the obvious inferiority complex that Khrushchev had had because, from a position of overwhelming inferiority thirteen years before, the Soviet Union had now virtually caught up with the United States in military power. But catching up was not enough for Brezhnev. He wanted unquestioned superiority. Neither Brezhnev nor his predecessors engaged in negotiation to achieve peace as an end in itself. Rather they sought peace so that they could use it to extend communist domination without war in all areas of the world.

This time Mrs. Nixon and I stayed in a splendid apartment once used by the Tsars of Imperial Russia. Now even more than in 1959 our Soviet hosts emphasized the glories of Imperial Russia's past rather than communism's achievements in the present. Both in 1972 and again in 1974, when I returned to Moscow, I was a guest at musical performances in the ornate, gilded splendor of Moscow's Bolshoi Theater, where I sat with the Soviet leaders in the Imperial Box. Premier Alexei Kosygin confided to me that he preferred the Bolshoi to the sterile, modernistic new auditorium that had been built within the Kremlin walls. The Soviet leaders clearly were still dedicated communists but it seemed that they had also become more Russian.

My views have changed since that time fifty years ago when I first saw Russia through the eyes of Tolstoy, and

Russia itself has changed since Tolstoy's time. But understanding the Soviet challenge requires an understanding of how Russia has *not* changed as well as how it has. The answer to many puzzles of Soviet behavior lies not in the stars, but in the Tsars. Their bodies lie buried in Kremlin vaults, and their spirits live on in the Kremlin halls.

In many respects the revolution that brought the communists to power in Russia was less a change from the tsarist ways than it was a refinement and reinforcement of those ways. Russia has never *not* been an expansionist power. Nor, except for a few brief months in 1917, has it ever *not* been either an authoritarian or a totalitarian state. There simply is no tradition in the Soviet Union of freedom internally or of nonaggression externally. Territorial expansion comes as naturally to Russia as hunting does to a lion or fishing to a bear.

If we take the trouble to study it, the past is a highly visible hand pointing the directions of history. It shows the courses along which nations are propelled by their particular combinations of interests, tradition, ambition, and opportunity. It shows the directions in which the momentum of past events continues to move us today.

Seven centuries ago two great events took place that set the courses of two civilizations. These are the courses Alexis de Tocqueville described a century and a half ago.

In England, in 1215, rebellious nobles forced King John to sign the Magna Carta. From this document grew the concept of constitutional monarchy, and eventually the structure of individual liberties and democratic self-government that was transported to the New World, where it flourished in the birth and development of the United States.

As this first step toward democracy was being taken in England, the grandsons of Genghis Khan were sweeping westward across the vast Eurasian plain, which stretches nearly halfway around the world from the eastern parts of Siberia to the shores of the English Channel. The Mongol hordes were stopped short of the heart of Europe, but they laid waste to Russia. They sacked its major towns and reduced Russian civilization to a barbarous level. For almost 250 years the Mongols imposed their rule and impressed their harsh brand upon the Russian soul, exacting a crippling tribute—the "Tartar yoke"—that kept the Russians impoverished and in bondage.

These two events, the signing of the Magna Carta and the subjugation of Russia by the pillaging Mongols, marked the starting points of two drastically different chains of historical development. The Bill of Rights traces its lineage to the Magna Carta. The Soviet police state traces its lineage to the Tartar yoke. The contrast is aptly summed up by an ancient Russian saying: "Despotism tempered by assassination—there is our Magna Carta."

The Mongols ruled by ruthless terror, a complex bureaucracy, and adroit manipulation of local rivalries; they imposed a crushing tax as tribute. With what one nineteenth-century writer called the "Machiavellism of the usurping slave," the native rulers of Moscow began to adopt the Mongol techniques, first by taking on the role of local tax collectors for the Mongols. Gradually they brought more and more lands under their own control, even while slavishly kowtowing to the Mongol Khans. Finally, after almost 250 years of bondage and humiliation, in 1480 Ivan the Great threw off the Tartar yoke and ended the Mongol rule. But its imprint remained. In the words of that same nineteenth-century writer:

> The bloody mire of Mongol slavery . . . forms the cradle of Muscovy, and modern Russia is but a metamorphosis of Muscovy. . . . It is in the terrible and abject school of Mongolian slavery that Muscovy was nursed and grew up. It gathered strength only by becoming a virtuoso in the craft of serfdom. Even when emancipated, Muscovy continued to perform its traditional part of the slave as master.

The author of those words was Karl Marx.

Even after the Tartar yoke was thrown off, the Mongo

error continued. With the defensible frontier often not
more than one hundred miles from Moscow, waves of Tartar cavalry swept in from the steppes every year, leaving
devastation. They came to seize slaves. The word "Slav" is
itself related to the word "slave."

To fight off the Tartar slavers, Russian men were called
up every spring to take their battle places on the frontier,
and were kept there until fall, when the steppes became im-
passable. This was repeated each year for a man's entire lifetime. Russia's struggle with the Tartars, historian Tibor
Szamuely argues, "comes nearer to the modern concept of
total war than anything else in pre-twentieth-century European history."

The brutal exercise of total power, the subjugation of
the individual to the state, the ruthless marshaling of all resources for the purposes of the state, the idea of constant,
unremitting war—these all have their roots deep in the Russian past, in the terrors of Mongol-rule and in the bitter ne-
cessities of fighting the Tartar hordes.

Constant expansion also has roots deep in the Russian
past. The Duchy of Muscovy spent two centuries expanding
its power over its neighbors before Ivan the Great was able
to throw off the Tartar yoke in 1480. He more than tripled
the lands under Moscow's rule, extending its reach from the
Baltic Sea to the Ural Mountains.

It was another Ivan, Ivan the Terrible, who a century
later was crowned the first "Tsar of all the Russias." Tsar
is the Russian word for Caesar; his reign marked the beginning of Russian imperial rule.

In the seventeenth century Russia conquered Siberia.
Cossacks and fur traders swept 2,500 miles across the wilderness in fifty-five years, reaching the Pacific in 1639.
From the frozen north, the Russians pushed south across
the steppes of Central Asia in the eighteenth and nineteenth
centuries toward China, Persia, India, and Afghanistan.
Millions of Moslems fell under the sway of the Tsars as the
ancient cities of Samarkand, Bukhara, Tashkent, and

Ashkhabad felt the alien hand of a European conqueror for the first time.

But two continents were not enough; Russia raced to occupy a third: North America. In 1741 Captain Vitus Bering, a Danish navigator in the service of Russia who gave his name to the Bering Straits, led an expedition which sighted Alaska. Russian settlements were established in Alaska. Until 1867, when the United States bought it, Alaska was known as Russian America. The local authority, the Russian–American Company, had been chartered in 1799 and empowered to discover and occupy new territories for Russia. Venturing south, the company established a settlement and built a fort sixty miles from present-day San Francisco, near what is now called the Russian River. Fortunately the fort was sold to John Sutter only seven years before the discovery of gold on his land launched the great California gold rush. The Russian–American Company also tried to gain a foothold in the Hawaiian Islands, but failed.

Meanwhile, Russia was pressing its expansion in two other directions. In the nineteenth century it conquered the Caucasus, the gateway to Persia, Turkey, and the Middle East. It also pushed westward against Europe, where it encountered its most sophisticated and formidable foes.

In terms of territory Russia dwarfs the countries of Europe, but for centuries it has found itself threatened and at times overwhelmed by these smaller but technologically more advanced powers. Russia was invaded by Poland in the seventeenth century, by Sweden in the eighteenth, by France under Napoleon in the nineteenth, and twice by Germany in the twentieth. Against each foe the Russians suffered staggering defeats, but they held on, regained the initiative, and eventually triumphed.

Just as the Tartar conquest led Russian rulers to adopt Oriental political techniques, the threat from the West led them to "Westernize." This has chiefly meant the industrialization and modernization of Russia's military.

Italian architects had been imported to build the Kremlin. German military engineers helped Ivan the Terrible capture the Tartar city of Kazan by blowing up its walls, thereby clearing the way for the conquest of Siberia. But it was Peter the Great, the Tsar from 1682 to 1725, who systematized the importation of modern techniques from the West and made Russia a modern power on a par with the countries of Europe. Peter wanted "Western technique, not Western civilization," according to Russian historian Vasily Kliuchevsky; the techniques of manufacture, particularly of arms manufacture, not the techniques of self-government. "For a few score years only we shall need Europe," Peter said. "Then we shall be able to turn our backs on her."

Peter used his "Westernization," not to enlighten the people, but to advance the interests of their rulers. The Tsars who have been given the title "the Great" in Russia have earned it not for benevolence but for their military conquests. Peter was no exception. After he got what he wanted from the West, he warred with Sweden, Turkey, and Persia for twenty-eight consecutive years, from the age of twenty-four to a year before his death. He was hailed for defeating Sweden in the Great Northern War. But his greatest accomplishment was not in the lands he himself conquered but in those he made it possible for his successors to conquer. He has been called by some "Russia's most important industrializer before Stalin." This was his genius: he wedded Western industry to Russian expansionism. After his reign Russia's army was able successfully to assault the West.

The next "Great," Catherine, who ruled from 1762 to 1796, subjugated the Crimean Tartars and secured for Russia a permanent place on the Black Sea. It was one of Catherine's ministers who delivered the classic warning: "That which stops growing begins to rot." She partitioned Poland three times with Prussia and Austria, until in 1795 there was nothing left of it. The Russian move toward Central Europe had begun.

Next, Russia took advantage of the chaos caused by the Napoleonic wars to seize Finland. Russian armies drove deep into Central Europe, extending Russia's borders to within 200 miles of Berlin. When the dust had settled, Russia was the predominant military power on the continent.

In the mid-nineteenth century Russia's relentless expansion drew a baleful notice from a New York *Tribune* correspondent in Europe, who little imagined that future Russian expansionism would be pursued in his name: Karl Marx. On June 14, 1853, Marx wrote a piece for the *Tribune* in which he pointed out that in just the past sixty years, the Russian frontier had advanced toward Berlin, Dresden, and Vienna 700 miles; toward Constantinople 500 miles; toward Stockholm 630 miles; and toward Tehran 1,000 miles. The pace was relentless. It did not stop with the Tsars.

What today is called the "Union of Soviet Socialist Republics" is the product of seven centuries of conquest, first by the Dukes of Muscovy as they subjugated what became Russia, then by the Tsars and their twentieth-century successors as they expanded the Russian empire. Fifteen "Soviet Socialist Republics" make up the U.S.S.R.; fourteen of those are essentially separate nations that were conquered by the fifteenth, Russia.

The Russian general who conquered Turkestan and captured Tashkent, General Skobelev, tersely summed up the Russian theory of conquest: "In Asia he is master who seizes the people pitilessly by the throat." That, not a Continental Congress or a Constitutional Convention, is the way what now are the "socialist republics" were formed into a "union."

America is made up of people of many nationalities who came here voluntarily. Whole *nations* were absorbed into the Russian empire and are kept there by force. We have Armenians and Lithuanians; they have Armenia and Lithuania.

Except for the opening of Siberia, these were not settlements of empty lands. Nor were they an extension of colonial rule over primitive peoples. They were the conquest and subjugation of ancient nations with highly developed cultures, distinct identities, and long histories. In the process the most extensive land empire of its time was created. Imperial methods were needed to acquire and rule it. These came naturally to the heirs of the Mongols, sovereigns over a vast, harsh land where serfdom was the rule, where freedom was unknown, and "human rights" unheard of.

The tsarist tradition is one of brute, autocratic rule. Only a very powerful state could organize the conquest of so many nations, and then preserve Russian imperial rule over them after the conquests.

Bondage for the people was the price of conquests for the state. Military conquest was the first imperative of the state; the greater glory of the rulers was the *raison d'être* of the ruled. The people were resources, to be harnessed along with all other resources to the systems of the state. In effect, the people became the property of the state, to be used for its purposes.

The first "Tsar of All the Russias," Ivan the Terrible, was also the first Tsar to make the use of terror a state policy; the origins of both the tsarist secret police and today's KGB can be traced to him. Ivan used his own private secret police to eliminate rivals for power, especially among the Russian nobility. He crudely but effectively ensured that they would never limit his power with a Russian Magna Carta.

At one point Ivan attacked Novgorod, one of his own cities, and put to death thousands of his own subjects by such bizarre means as "impaling, flaying alive, boiling, roasting on spits, frying in gigantic skillets, evisceration, and most mercifully, drowning." For a time, he actually put half of Russia under the direct rule of his secret police, establishing, quite literally, a police state under his personal control, a method later favored by Stalin. Stalin admired Ivan the Terrible and made a point of having his reputation rehabilitated in Soviet history books.

Peter the Great, remembered as the great modernizer for his openings to the West, was one of the most despotic rulers at home. He described himself as "an absolute monarch who does not have to answer for any of his actions to anyone in the world." It was he who instituted the hated internal passport system, which made it illegal for most people to move about their own country without permission.

In our own century Joseph Stalin personified Russia's tsarist heritage. The dynasty he represented was a party, not a family, but like the "great" Tsars before him, he extended Russian rule over vast new areas. Countries that had broken free from the Russian empire in the aftermath of the Russian revolutions were reconquered by Stalin. In 1940 he retook the Baltic states—Latvia, Lithuania, and Estonia—and seized Bessarabia and Northern Bukovina from Romania. At the end of World War II he captured Poland, this time all of it, and part of Germany as well. Hungary, Czechoslovakia, Bulgaria, and Romania all fell under Russian rule for the first time.

Like Ivan the Terrible, Stalin created his own private secret police and employed terror as a basic instrument of state policy. Like Peter, he appreciated the value of Western technology in fashioning a modern fighting machine. Also like Peter, he cemented his power over the people with an internal passport system.

Stalin will never be known as "the Great" or "the Terrible," but people in the Soviet Union have their own wry way of noting the continuity between the tsarist past and the communist present. It was perhaps best expressed by a Russian youth who said to an American visitor, "You have Jesus Christ Superstar, we have Lenin Super-Tsar."

Russia Encounters China

As the Russian conflict with the West has its roots deep in the past, so does its conflict with China. It goes back to the mid-1600s when Russian expansionism first encountered the might of the Chinese empire. The Chinese and the Russians fought their first battle in 1652. Whether ironically or prophetically, it was at the mouth of the same Ussuri River that was to be the site of violent border clashes three centuries later, in 1969, after I became President. It was at the negotiating table that the Chinese won that first test, in the process giving the Russians a good lesson in the value of negotiating from a position of strength.

After thirty-five years of intermittent warfare the two sides finally agreed to hold peace talks. The Russians sent a negotiating party of 2,000 soldiers, diplomats, and servants to the faraway border. But the Chinese, being much closer, arrived with 15,000. When the talks bogged down, the Chinese delegates resolved the impasse by threatening to attack their Russian counterparts. Faced with superior force, the Russians backed down and withdrew from the disputed lands, leaving the Chinese in peace for the next 150 years.

By the middle of the nineteenth century, however, China had weakened. The Russians seized two huge chunks of land from China—about 650,000 square miles, an area as large as all the states of the East and West coasts of the United States combined. In 1860 the Treaty of Peking gave them undisputed title to a seaport in their new territory, which they named Vladivostok—meaning Rule of the East. The chief foreign affairs counselor to the Emperor of China warned that "Russia, with her territory adjoining ours, aiming to nibble at our territory like a silkworm, may be considered a threat at our bosom." At the turn of the century the Finance Minister of Russia agreed, declaring that "The absorption by Russia of a considerable portion of the Chinese Empire is only a matter of time." By the eve of the Russian Revolution Sun Yat-sen, the father of modern China, estimated that the Russian sphere of influence in his country included 42 percent of its territory.

After the Russian Revolution the Chinese looked with hope to the new communist regime which repudiated the expansionism of the Tsars and promised to treat all nations with a new respect. In 1919 the young Soviet state issued the Karakhan Declaration, which "renounced the conquests made by the Tsarist Government, which deprived China of Manchuria and other areas," promised to annul all unequal treaties that the Tsars had made, and pledged to "return to the Chinese people everything that was taken from them by the Tsarist Government. . . ." China was ecstatic, but soon the Soviet commissars showed that they were no more generous than the Russian Tsars had been.

In 1921, Russia's encroachments on China resumed in a way that foreshadowed its invasion and satellization of Afghanistan in 1979. The Russians sponsored a few Mongolians who formed a Mongolian People's Revolutionary Party, proclaimed a Provisional Revolutionary Government, and "appealed" to Moscow for "help." The Red Army marched in, and Mongolia, which had been part of China for centuries, became the first Soviet satellite. The Karakhan Declaration was repudiated. In 1929 the Soviet Union and China fought an undeclared war in Manchuria in which 10,000 Chinese were killed. Farther to the west, the Chinese province of Sinkiang became, in the words of one observer, "virtually a Soviet colony" during the 1930s.

The brief period of friendship between China and Russia in the 1950s was the exception rather than the rule; through the centuries their relations have been characterized by rivalry, hostility, and Russian territorial expansion.

Renaissance and Reaction

The "visible hand" of history not only shows the directions in which we are traveling. It also points to what might have been, if at critical junctures those who had the power to make a difference had used that power differently.

The most costly failure in history was the failure to prevent Lenin's seizure of power in Russia in 1917. That failure was as much a tragedy for the people of Russia as it was for the world. Long before the last Tsar was overthrown, the forces of liberal change were powerfully at work and Russia was beginning to absorb more from the West than military technology. If the process had not been interrupted and diverted, Russia might, like Japan, have become a free and prosperous part of the Western world.

Early in the nineteenth century the ideals of the French

Revolution penetrated Russia as Napoleon's army marched to Moscow and the Russian army pursued it back to Paris. Western ideas stirred the Russian soul, bringing a flowering of culture and an era of enlightenment to this hitherto sullen land. A liberation of the mind occurred, leading to outstanding accomplishments in science, literature, the arts, and industry. Pushkin, Dostoevsky, Tolstoy, and Chekhov took their place among the greatest writers in the world. One student of the era wrote that "long-mute Russia found her voice," and "suddenly full-throated, it astonished the world."

In politics far-reaching changes began ushering in a new era. Tsar Alexander II, the Liberator Tsar, abolished serfdom in 1861. Censorship was eased, trial by jury was introduced, and representative self-government at the local level was begun. The term of duty in the army was shortened from twenty-five years—a virtual life sentence—to six. The seeds of a new society had been planted in Russia. The first spring shoots of a new order began to crop up, but tragically, they were soon plowed under.

The first breaths of freedom are the most exhilarating—and the most intoxicating. As liberalization began in Russia, so did revolution. Along with those who wanted to build a new society were those whose only thought was to destroy the old one. In the process the revolutionaries destroyed the budding new one as well.

In 1881 Tsar Alexander II was assassinated by a group calling itself Narodnaya Volya—the People's Will. Then, in 1887, several young dissidents plotted the assassination of the new Tsar. They were discovered and one of them nobly stepped forward at their trial and attempted to take the blame for all. He was a twenty-one-year-old named Alexander Ulyanov. Officials were impressed by his courage and suggested that he petition the Tsar for mercy. Alexander refused, and was hanged; his family was shamed and thereafter shunned by the liberal society of the day. Alexander Ulyanov had a sixteen-year-old brother who was seared by these events and especially stunned by his family's sudden ostracism by respectable society. That younger brother was named Vladimir—Vladimir Ulyanov. Years later he took another name: Lenin.

The experience, Bertram Wolfe writes, opened "an unbridgeable gulf between [Lenin] and the regime that had taken his brother's life. And it inoculated him with a profound contempt for the 'liberal society' which had abandoned the Ulyanov family in its time of trouble." When Lenin came to power, all the impressive gains that the liberalizing forces had made in the final days of tsarism—a parliament, land reform and extensive individual land ownership, the economic and political building blocks of a new society—were swept away.

Lenin's Bolsheviks abandoned what was best in Russia and embraced the worst. Russia's liberalization, its frail new democracy, its brilliant new culture, and its willingness to learn from the world were all jettisoned. The communist rulers reached back to the terrorism of Ivan the Terrible, the despotism of Peter, and the ruthless expansionism of Catherine to create their new society. They uprooted all the liberal changes that had taken hold in the century between Napoleon's invasion and World War I, turning the clock back a hundred years or more for the Russian people.

The Spanish painter Goya once said, "The dream of reason produces monsters." So it was with the dream of Marxism. The monsters it produced did things the old Tsars would never have dreamed of doing, and the techniques they adopted have been copied by every Communist party that has come to power since.

The New Tsars

The suffering the Russian people have undergone under communist rule is staggering. Citing an official document published in 1920 by the Cheka, the forerunner of today's KGB, Alexander Solzhenitsyn estimates that the communists executed more than 1,000 people per month in 1918–1919—before Stalin came to power. Twenty years later, at the height of the terror in 1937 and 1938, Stalin executed 40,000 people per month—over 1,000 a day for two full years. Robert Conquest, a renowned expert, estimates that executions during the first fifty years of Soviet rule—under Lenin, Stalin, Khrushchev and Brezhnev—"were at least fifty times as numerous as over the last half century of Tsarist rule."

These figures tell only part of the story. There were many more deaths in the forced-labor camps, which held an average 8 million people during the 1930s, and between 12 million and 15 million after World War II. In addition, during the artificially created famine in the Ukraine in the early 1930s, 3 million to 5 million people are believed to have died, perhaps more. While millions starved, the communist leaders shipped grain abroad to pay for their industrial trade with the West.

In one personal account a former Communist Party official recalls entering a village where people were cooking horse manure and weeds to survive, where the bark had been stripped from the trees for food, and where all the cats, dogs, birds, and field mice had been eaten. In this town he found a state butter plant in which milk was hoarded so that butter stamped "U.S.S.R. Butter Export" could be shipped overseas. In the same town the Soviet official discovered a granary of "State reserves" stocked with thousands of pounds of grain from the previous year's harvest—all in a village where in the mornings the wagons rolled to pick up the dead.

A man who heard V. M. Molotov, later Stalin's Foreign Minister, explain the reasons for initiating the "collectivization" drive that created the famine recalled:

> Comrade Molotov called the activists together and he talked plainly, sharply. The job must be done, no matter how many lives it cost, he told us. As long as there were millions of small land-owners in the country, he said, the revolution was in danger. There would always be the chance that in case of war they might side with the enemy in order to defend their property.

During the 1930s, 70 percent of the senior officers in the Russian Army were executed. No one was exempt from Stalin's terror, not even those on the highest levels of the Communist Party; 98 out of 139 Central Committee members in 1934 were later killed. After World War II millions of former POWs were sent directly to forced-labor camps because they had seen the West. Stalin, the student of Russian history, was taking no unnecessary chances. He knew his two greatest enemies were the same enemies the Tsars had fought—Western armies and Western ideas—and he was as determined to shut out the latter as he was to defeat the former. It is conservatively estimated that he killed 20 million Russians, and the killing did not start or stop with him.

In addition to the destruction wrought by their communist leaders, the Russian people have also suffered two great German invasions in the twentieth century. In World War I the Russians lost half their men under arms—1,650,000 were killed, 3,850,000 wounded, and 2,410,000 captured. In World War II half were lost again—this time 5 million were killed and 11.5 million wounded. Total Russian deaths in World War II are estimated at 20 million.

The combat on the Eastern Front in World War I, and again in World War II, was cataclysmic. Winston Churchill wrote of the first war:

> In its scale, in its slaughter, in the exertion of the combatants, in its military kaleidoscope, [the struggle on the Eastern Front] far surpasses by magnitude and intensity all similar human episodes. . . . Here all Central Europe tore itself to pieces and expired in agony, to rise again, unrecognizable. . . .

Both in war and in peace merciless slaughter has been an ever-present part of the Russian experience. Together, the capacity to endure slaughter and the capacity to endure suffering can make a nation both ambitious and formidable. The Marquis de Custine visited Russia in the 1830s and remarked, "An inordinate, a boundless ambition, the kind of ambition that can take root only in the soul of an oppressed people and be nourished only on the misery of an entire nation is astir in the hearts of the Russians. ... To cleanse himself of his impious sacrifice of all public and personal liberty, the kneeling slave dreams of world domination." And he went on to prophesy, "The Russian people will surely become incapable of anything except the conquest of the world. I always return to this expression, because it is the only one that can explain the excessive sacrifices imposed here upon the individual by society."

In his book *Ideology and Power in Soviet Politics*, Zbigniew Brzezinski wrote:

> The triumphant assertions that the Soviet leaders are abandoning their Marxism or Communism, voiced in the West with such monotonous regularity and persistent ignorance, might possibly be dismissed more quickly if the usual image of an abstract and arid Marxist dogma were to give way to a better appreciation of the inextricably close linkage between the Soviet social environment and the Soviet ideology. It is precisely because the ideology is both a set of conscious assumptions and purposes and part of the total historical, social, and personal background of the Soviet leaders that it is so pervading and so important.

What threatens the world is not theoretical "communism," not philosophical "Marxism," but rather an aggressive, expansionist totalitarian force that has adopted those names for an ideological fervor it has grafted onto the roots of tsarist expansionism and tsarist despotism. Karl Marx died in 1883, thirty-four years before "Marxism" became the official religion of the Russian state. The authors of *The Communist Manifesto* never saw their teachings "interpreted" into a rationale for Soviet conquest: Marx and Engels had no idea that the red flag would fly over the Kremlin, or that the armies of the Russian empire would march into battle under its colors.

The doctrines of Marx are to today's communist regimes what Christianity was to the secular rulers of the Holy Roman Empire: convenient as a banner, but irrelevant as a guide. Marx would not recognize "Marxism" today, but

Ivan the Terrible or Peter the Great would be at home with it. And it was from Lenin's and Stalin's Kremlin fortress, not from Karl Marx's London garret, that communism spread across the world. The tightly controlled Communist parties of other nations answered to the living Stalin, not to the ghost of Marx: they served the interests of the twentieth-century Soviet empire, not the teachings of a nineteenth-century German philosopher.

If the spiritual heritage of today's communism derives less from Marx than from the Tsars, the reverse of that coin is that the new Russian empire differs from the old in the intense missionary zeal, the ideological fervor, of Marxism as reinterpreted by Lenin and his heirs. These provide a rationale for tyranny, a banner under which to rally the desperate and the discontented.

The ideological fervor and framework with which Soviet leaders approach the world provides a historical rationale, a dialectic, that is a mandate for change. According to it, "stability" or "normalization" of relations is a contradiction. It combines with a totalitarian political regime to make "forward progress" of socialism mandatory; for socialism to succeed, and to be compatible with the security of the Soviet Communist Party and state, it must be advanced and controlled by the Kremlin. All of this tends toward a preoccupation with change in the world.

Communism has created a new alliance between Russian imperialism and "revolutionary" movements worldwide. It disguises despotism in the language of radical idealism, thus entrancing idealists. The banner of revolution gives despotism a new semblance of legitimacy, and despotism gives the "revolutionary" movement arms, money, membership in a global club, and a full array of modern techniques of conquest and control.

After 1917 the techniques of the tsarist secret police were taken over by the communist revolutionaries and a vastly more powerful entity, the KGB, was created. The Russian tradition of militarism was wedded to communist techniques of subversion and the marriage produced a new danger to sovereign states—unscrupulous Communist parties controlled by Moscow. The traditional Russian fear of invasion was redoubled as the entire world automatically became Moscow's ideological enemy. Finally, the Russian habits of expansion and conquest were given a new lease on life when Moscow proclaimed that it was Russia's holy duty under Marxism to liberate the doomed "capitalist" world. Tsarist imperialism was fused with communist revolution and a terrible new force entered on the world's scene: the "imperialist revolutionaries."

Lenin ruled the Soviet Union for barely six years before his death in January 1924; Stalin ruled for more than a quarter century before his death in March 1953. Lenin set the course, but Stalin established the iron rule. Stalin massacred the small landholders, collectivized the farms, built the secret police, conducted the purges of the thirties, and spread the terror of the Gulag Archipelago.

The post-Stalin leaders have moderated some of the earlier brutalities, introduced some individual freedoms—which would not be recognized as freedoms in the West, but that by contrast with what prevailed before are a step forward—and become a more polished, more sophisticated, at times more mannerly force in the world. But the power structure remains. The absolute dictatorship remains. The totalitarian state remains, because this is the essence of the neo-tsarism on which the whole authority of the Soviet state is built. The relentless drive toward expansion remains. The Soviet leaders have a military machine beyond the dreams of the Tsars, and they have spread their power beyond the farthest reach of tsarist ambition.

Russia Encounters America

At the start of the twentieth century the relentless outward thrust of Russian expansion was blocked chiefly by five great containing powers. The gates were guarded by Germany and Austria-Hungary in Europe, by the Ottoman

Empire to the south, and by Japan in the Far East. Throughout the heartland of Asia, in Persia, Afghanistan, India, Tibet, and the rest, the British played what Kipling called the "Great Game" with Russia, strengthening local powers so that they could stand up to the Russians, stepping into the breach themselves when necessary. These powers managed to keep the restless Russian giant confined; they kept it a continental rather than a global power, extending its rule to the edges of the Eurasian continent only in its forbidding northern and eastern reaches.

World Wars I and II destroyed the European-made world order. They brought the communists to power in Russia and China. They destroyed the five great containing powers that had kept Russia penned in. They catapulted the United States to the center of world politics before it was ready.

For the United States the twentieth century has meant the end of innocence. For Europe it has meant the end of empire. For the peoples of Russia, China, and more than a dozen other countries it has meant the horrors of communist rule. For the rulers of the Soviet Union it has meant the end of the great power constraints that had previously kept Russian expansion in check.

In World War I Germany was struck down and its empire reduced. Austria-Hungary was split apart, vanishing from the map. The Ottoman Empire disintegrated. Britain and France, although nominally victors, were gravely weakened.

What World War I began, World War II completed. As Charles de Gaulle told me in 1969, "In the Second World War all the nations of Europe lost, two were defeated." Germany was partitioned, Japan was disarmed, and Britain was so weakened that the dissolution of its empire began almost immediately. In thirty years' time the powers that had contained Russia in the nineteenth century either had been crippled or had vanished from the world scene.

Americans paid little attention. True to our isolationist past and to the naïve idealism that infused our approach to world affairs, we approached World War II as if it were a sporting match with no other goal but victory. Churchill and Stalin, by contrast, were aware of the cataclysmic changes taking place and had their eyes less on the immediate military task than on the political aftermath. On the Western side, Churchill was overruled. Stalin was able to make a clean sweep through Eastern Europe, getting his armies in place to begin the new conquests that would follow the defeat of Nazi Germany. We soon had to pay for our carelessness. The failure of the United States to block Soviet expansionism during the war led to a situation in which we had to scramble to do so after the war, when much territory had already been lost.

In Greece and Turkey, where the power of the Ottoman Empire and then Great Britain had previously held Russia in check, a power vacuum emerged in 1947 that the Soviets were eager to fill. We were obliged to respond with the Truman Doctrine. In Europe, where Germany, Austria-Hungary, and the other great European powers had once stood, there was now chaos. We came up with the Marshall Plan and NATO to replace the former containing powers there. In the Far East we replaced the former containing power of Japan when we stopped the Korean invasion in 1950 in concert with the U.N.

Finally, with the worldwide retreat from empire by Britain and France and the other European powers, we picked up many of their former obligations in the Middle East, in South and Southeast Asia, in Africa, and in the Persian Gulf. At the same time, we continued to play our traditional protective role in Latin America. We had become the world's gyroscope, single-handedly maintaining the balance of power all across the globe, taking over the responsibilities that five great empires had previously borne both in containing Russia and maintaining world order.

This unprecedented burden would not have been easy even if the United States had been well prepared to assume its new responsibilities. As it was, Americans were unfamiliar with many of the subtleties of dealing with the various peoples of the world and unaccustomed to power on a global scale. The end of innocence has been a long, confused, and sometimes difficult process for us.

For all the vigor of its frontier spirit, and for all the harsh obstacles it had to overcome in taming a continent, in international terms the United States grew up in a protected environment. As the modern world's first democracy, America was nurtured on the faith that, in the words of one observer, "the United States was not merely to be a beacon of a superior democratic domestic way of life. It was also to be an example of a morally superior democratic pattern of international behavior. The United States would voluntarily reject power politics as unfit for the conduct of its foreign policy."

Shielded by 3,000 miles of ocean from the wars and intrigues of Europe, America was well able to avoid those "entangling alliances" against which Washington warned. While European nations vied with one another to establish dominion over vast reaches of Asia and Africa, the United States—with a few exceptions, as when it took the Philippines as spoils of war from Spain—bent its efforts toward linking its Atlantic and Pacific coasts and developing the land between.

The result was a continental power with a continental, even an insular, outlook. In sharp contrast Britain, from its small "sceptered isle" off the coast of Europe, had in its heyday ruled more than one-fifth of the world's land mass and one-fourth of its population. For the British and their rivals in the colonial race, empire was a source of power. It was also a consequence of power, a reason for power, and an arena for its exercise—and they developed a natural familiarity with the uses of power.

Generations of British statesmen learned to think naturally, automatically, in global terms. What happened halfway around the globe was news in Britain because it mattered in Britain. To the British mind, empire was not "exploitation," it was destiny. Britain stood at the head of a Europe that was, as historian Hajo Holborn put it, "the center of the expanding world economy as well as the heart and brain of Western civilization, which was thought to be destined to transform all the other civilizations after its own image." Victoria reigned, Britannia ruled, and if soldiers died on dusty fields in distant places, the British saw that as the price not only of progress, but also of peace. Those who administered the empire sought to curb ancient rivalries and check tribal wars, often with considerable success. And Britain itself shifted its weight now one way, now another, to maintain a stable balance of power in Europe and thus to maintain the peace.

Americans, by contrast, regarded involvement in the affairs—and the wars—of Europe as an aberration, a burden to be borne only for as long as necessary and then to be cast aside in a return to the normality of its western hemisphere isolation.

Veteran diplomat Charles E. Bohlen wrote that

> when I joined the foreign service on March 1, 1929—the United States had had about as safe, secure, and easy a position as any great nation on the face of the earth. We had neighbors to the north and south of us who constituted no conceivable threat. We were protected by two wide oceans, which in those days meant that no foreign nation could reach us. To the south we had Latin America, where we had relations that were on the whole friendly and even protective in continental terms. But more importantly, vast areas of the world were held by the two democracies who had been allied with the United States in World War I, namely, England and France. . . . At the end of the 1920s we were totally protected, and we acted accordingly.

At that time the nation's total military budget was less than $1 billion, and that of the State Department was only $14 million.

In the 1930s American isolationism was so strong that in 1938 the House of Representatives came within twenty-one votes of passing the Ludlow Amendment, which would have required a national referendum before war could be declared. A Roper poll in September 1939 showed only 2.5 percent in favor of any form of intervention in the war in

Europe. In October 1940, campaigning for reelection to a third term as President, Franklin Roosevelt drew cheers with his declaration that "I have said this before but I shall say it again and again and again, your boys are not going to be sent into any foreign war."

During World War II America's naïveté about the nature of the postwar world was epitomized by Secretary of State Cordell Hull's declaration to Congress that with the creation of the United Nations, "there will no longer be need for spheres of influence, for alliances, for balance of power, or any other of the separate alliances through which in the unhappy past the nations strove to safeguard their security or promote their interest."

World War II radically changed the world situation without radically altering the attitudes of most Americans. After the war only America was left to lead, but Americans had little taste for leadership. It was difficult. It was a burden. It required sacrifices.

World leadership also requires something that is in many ways alien to the American cast of mind. It requires placing limits on idealism, compromising with reality, at times matching duplicity with duplicity, and even brutality with brutality. After a century and a half of holding the world at arm's length, of declining to be contaminated by contact with its intrigues and its tyrannies, it requires marching onto the field and playing the game of power diplomacy as a contact sport—no matter who is in the lineup on the other team. And it requires doing so even when the rules imposed on the game are rules that we would not have chosen.

Moralizing is always easier from behind the lines than it is at the battlefront, and many have a way of ascribing their good fortune to their own high virtue. Growing up with two oceans to protect it, America could look with disdain on the conflicts of Europe, while cherishing the illusion that its own security derived somehow from its democratic system. In fact, the United States in its younger days was one of the chief beneficiaries of the British Navy. As long as Britain ruled the seas, the "island continent" was secure.

The lessons of world leadership come hard. In earlier days we could look with curious fascination at the alien ways of distant Russia. Now we have to cope with the massed power of the Soviet Union. In earlier days we could take pride in our democratic tradition, secure in our splendid isolation. Now we have to defend that tradition, not only for our own sake but also for that of all others who share this tradition. In his prescience de Tocqueville defined the challenge. But we have to provide the answer. Of the two nations, each "marked out by the will of Heaven to sway the destinies of half the globe," which will prevail?

4
The Oil Jugular

No arm of the sea has been, or is of greater interest alike to the geologist and archeologist, the historian and geographer, the merchant, and the student of strategy, than the inland water known as the Persian Gulf.

—*Sir Arnold Wilson*

The area south of Batum and Baku in the general direction of the Persian Gulf [is] . . . the center of the aspirations of the Soviet Union.

—*Soviet Foreign Minister*
Vyacheslav M. Molotov

Events in the Persian Gulf show dramatically how places that until recently seemed remote and exotic can suddenly present us with crises of surpassing urgency; how we can awake to find that a region once celebrated largely in romantic fantasy now holds the fate of the world in its hands—or, more precisely, in its sands.

The story of the Persian Gulf stretches back thousands of years, to the early stirrings of Western civilization. The complex, often strained and sometimes bitter relationships among its various cultures and religions span the centuries to shape the present. But its strategic significance today centers on two factors: its location and its oil.

Both military and economic power now depend on oil

This basic fact makes the Persian Gulf the eye of the global storm in these final decades of the twentieth century. If the Soviet Union gains the power to turn off the oil spigots of the Middle East, it will gain the power to bring most of the industrialized West to its knees. To achieve this, it is not necessary that the Soviets actually take over the nations of the Persian Gulf, as they took over Afghanistan. Their purpose can also be served by external pressures or internal upheavals that deny those countries' resources to the West.

The Soviets have long been aware of this. Dissident Soviet physicist Andrei Sakharov recalls a talk given at the Kremlin in 1955 by a high Soviet official, who explained that the long-range goal of Soviet policy in the Middle East was "to exploit Arab nationalism in order to create difficulties for the European countries in obtaining crude oil, and thereby to gain influence over them." This was eighteen years before the 1973 oil embargo.

Sometime in the twenty-first century nuclear, solar, geothermal, and other energy sources may be sufficiently developed to meet most of the world's energy needs. But for now we live in an age of oil. In the decades just ahead this gives extraordinary strategic significance to the region of the Persian Gulf. This means that one of the world's most troubled, unstable, and imperiled areas is also one of its most vital.

In the industrial age energy is the lifeblood of the economic system, and economic power is the foundation of military power. Great Britain was the first great industrial power, and in the nineteenth century it became the world's leading political and military power. Britain got a head start on the world because it was virtually an island made of coal, and because coal powered the industrial revolution.

As the age of coal gave way to the age of oil, Britain, the world's first coal superpower, gave way to the United States, the world's first oil superpower. The first oil well in the world was drilled in Titusville, Pennsylvania, in 1859. John D. Rockefeller's Standard Oil Trust was the OPEC of its day, the United States the world's largest oil exporter.

Oil fueled the automobile. Since it also made possible the airplanes, ships, tanks, and trucks of twentieth-century warfare, access to supplies of oil became a military necessity. In World War I the French statesman Georges Clemenceau declared that "Oil is as necessary as blood." Marshal Foch warned, "We must have oil or we shall lose the war." Lord Curzon later claimed that "The Allies floated to victory on a wave of oil." In the first few weeks of the war Marshal Joffre won the Battle of the Marne by rushing French reinforcements to the front in gasoline-powered taxi cabs commandeered from the streets of Paris.

In World War II, when General George S. Patton was streaking across France, Texas pipeline specialists followed in the wake of his tanks, laying pipe at a fifty-mile-a-day clip. One of the Allied powers' principal strategic advantages in World War II was that they controlled 86 percent of the world's oil.

Oil After World War II

The guns of World War II were barely silenced when Stalin made his first push toward the Persian Gulf. After their wartime occupation of the northern part of Iran, the Soviets brazenly refused to remove their troops, set up an "Autonomous" Republic of Azerbaijan and a Kurdish People's Republic under their control, and demanded creation of a "joint company" to exploit the oil reserves of northern Iran, with 51 percent of the shares to be held by the U.S.S.R.

Harry Truman, President at the time, later wrote:

> The Soviet Union persisted in its occupation until I personally saw to it that Stalin was informed that I had given orders to our military chiefs to prepare for the movement of our ground, sea and air forces. Stalin then did what I knew he would do. He moved his troops out.

The next Soviet threat to the Persian Gulf, "the center of the aspirations of the Soviet Union," came in the eastern

Mediterranean, in Greece and Turkey, where Britain was cutting back on its foreign commitments.

President Truman again responded, going before a joint session of Congress to seek American aid for the two countries. The Truman Doctrine was born; American power would seek to restrain Soviet power in the eastern Mediterranean. By mid-1948 the Sixth Task Force, forerunner of the U.S. Sixth Fleet—the Navy's Mediterranean fleet—had been formed, and U.S. planes were soon using bases in Libya, Turkey, and Saudi Arabia. An American military presence had been established in the Middle East.

In those desperate and decisive postwar years oil became, in the words of one observer, "the link between the Truman Doctrine for the Middle East and the Marshall Plan for Europe." For a Europe struggling to rebuild its industries, oil was crucial, and it was oil from the Middle East. In 1948 Secretary of Defense James V. Forrestal sent a memo to President Truman declaring, "Without Middle East oil the European Recovery Program has a very slim chance of success."

Europe's shift in basic energy source from its own coal to imported oil dramatically changed the geopolitical structure of the world. The Middle East had long been the crossroads where Asia, Africa, and Europe met. Now its oil is the lifeblood of modern industry, the Persian Gulf region is the heart that pumps it, and the sea routes around the Gulf are the jugular through which that lifeblood passes.

Japan relies on what columnist James Reston has called a "bridge of oil tankers—one every 100 miles from the Gulf every day of the year." The Gulf supplies 70 percent of Japan's oil needs as well as over half of Europe's.

The United States has become increasingly dependent on oil as a source of energy, and increasingly dependent on imports as a source of oil. Oil now supplies nearly 50 percent of our energy, and while we depended on imports for a third of our oil in 1973, we now import half of it. Further, Canada was one of our leading suppliers in 1973; five years later the Organization of Petroleum Exporting Countries (OPEC) provided more than 80 percent of our imports. The

United States, once the world's principal supplier of oil, has become the largest purchaser from OPEC, taking a fifth of its oil.

More than ever, the question of who controls what in the Persian Gulf and the Middle East is the key to who controls what in the world.

The British saw this coming a long time ago. In the early 1950s they tried to convince the United States that the problems of the Gulf were "highly strategic and political, not just economic." The British were more vulnerable than the Americans, so they needed to see these problems more clearly; but they were also more experienced, especially in the Gulf, and were therefore able to see them more clearly.

Although most of the world did not become aware of the small Gulf sheikhdoms until after the Arab oil embargo of 1973, British rulers had been paying attention to the minutest details of their affairs for 150 years.

The British first moved into the Gulf in the early 1800s in order to prevent pirates from disrupting their trade. From then until the early 1970s British military power kept order, provided protection, and settled disputes in the various sheikhdoms dotting the Gulf's coastline.

Throughout the Gulf and around the Arabian peninsula, Britain reigned supreme. In Aden, Oman, Qatar, Bahrain, Kuwait, and the United Arab Emirates, a group of sheikhdoms that used to be known as the Pirate Coast, the British were the link between the sheikhs and the rest of the world. They handled their task with tact, thoroughness, and toughness. In 1934, in a campaign to safeguard their port of Aden, the British used flattery, bribery, and well-calculated shows of force to conclude no less than 1,400 "peace treaties" with the various rulers in the hinterlands of what is now South Yemen. It was under the umbrella of British protection that the great multinational companies began to explore the region in their search for oil.

Britain controlled not only the Gulf but also access to it from all areas of the Indian Ocean—from Singapore, Malaya, Burma, India, Ceylon, Aden, Suez, Kenya, South Africa, Australia, and from Diego Garcia and other islands in the Indian Ocean—all British possessions at one time or another. Both the Persian Gulf and the Indian Ocean that led to it were "British lakes."

Britain maintained its presence in the Gulf until 1971. But its phased withdrawals from responsibility "East of Suez" after World War II created a series of power vacuums that were filled by anti-British nationalists, egged on by the Soviets.

Iran: Foretaste of Trouble

Another foretaste of later troubles in Iran came in 1951, when Mohammed Mossadegh pushed through the Iranian legislature a measure nationalizing the Anglo–Iranian Oil Company, and then himself became Prime Minister. Under the highly emotional, anti-Western Mossadegh, Iran tumbled into chaos. Oil production virtually ceased. Economic development plans were crippled. Land reform, previously begun by the Shah, lagged. Discontent spread, the communist Tudeh party thrived, and it looked as though Iran might fall into the Soviet orbit.

In 1953 Mossadegh attempted to overthrow the Shah. The CIA and other allied intelligence agencies gave covert help to General Fazollah Zahedi in his successful effort to put down Mossadegh. Mossadegh was ousted and the Shah was restored securely to his throne; from then on, the Shah took personal control of Iran's affairs. Much later—during my administration—General Zahedi's son, Ardeshir, became Iran's ambassador to the United States.

With Iran once again in the pro-Western camp, it was possible to unite the "northern tier" countries, Turkey, Iraq, Iran, and Pakistan, in a military alliance with Great Britain called the Baghdad Pact, and later the Central Treaty Organization (CENTO). This effectively blocked Russia's direct thrusts toward the Gulf.

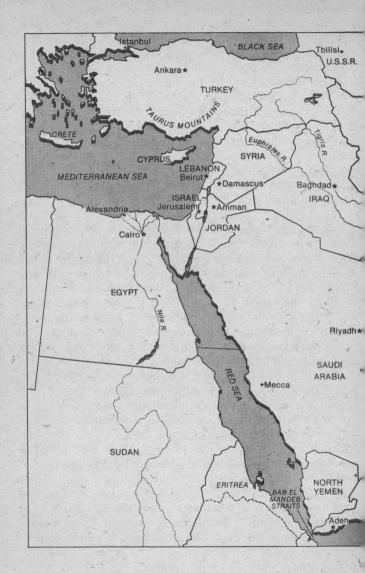

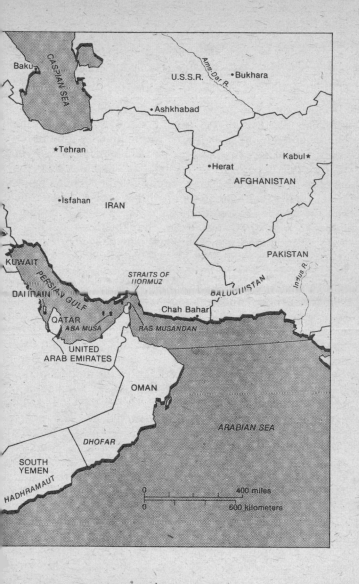

The Suez Crisis

The next warning shot came from Egypt. President Gamal Abdel Nasser, a charismatic, left-leaning nationalist, touched off a worldwide furor in 1956 by nationalizing the Suez Canal.

Far more was at stake in the Suez takeover than the economic interests of the canal's shareholders. The canal had been operated in trust for all nations. Europeans depended on it both for their life-sustaining trade and for the transport of 70 percent of their oil. They had little faith that its operations would be secure in the volatile Nasser's hands. Israel soon struck across the Egyptian border, and France and Britain then moved immediately with air, sea, and land forces to seize the canal. From the American standpoint, their timing could not have been worse. The British and French forces landed just as the United States was condemning the Soviet Union for its brutal suppression of the Hungarian revolution, and on the eve of a presidential election in which Eisenhower's slogan was "peace and prosperity." With the anticolonial movement gathering force, and with the Soviets threatening to intervene, rather than joining its allies the United States brought heavy pressure on them and caused them to withdraw.

Far more than the canal was lost. This humiliating defeat in Suez had a devastating effect on the willingness of Britain and France to play a major role not only in the Mideast but in other areas of the world as well. The U.S. action, rather than winning Nasser's friendship, gained his contempt and increased his hostility toward Israel, other Arab countries, and the United States itself. Years later Eisenhower was to reflect that the U.S. restraint of Britain, France, and Israel when they were trying to protect their interests in Suez was a tragic mistake.

Stirred up by the Suez crisis, radical workers set fire to many of Kuwait's wells and pipelines. Tough, fast action by the Kuwaiti security forces prevented further serious damage: 100 time bombs, set to blow up the sheikhdom's pipelines, were discovered. Some of the radicals involved were

Palestinians. The Iranian crisis, Suez, and the flare-up in Kuwait had shown the world that in the Middle East oil and politics can mix explosively.

New discoveries of oil in the late 1950s made the supply again seem secure. Oil became so plentiful that in 1960 Exxon cut the price it was willing to pay the oil-producing countries by 14 cents a barrel, an amount that seems minuscule now but was significant then. The oil-producing countries were distraught. Five of them banded together in an organization that got little attention at the time, but has gotten a great deal since: the Organization of Petroleum Exporting Countries.

In its first years OPEC managed to make only a minor impact on prices. At the time of the 1967 Arab-Israeli Six-Day War OPEC's Arab members declared their first oil embargo against the West. It quickly collapsed, however, when non-Arab producers, led by Iran and Venezuela, filled the gap and those who had attempted the embargo found they were hurting themselves more than anyone else.

But changes were occurring, and the balance soon shifted.

In 1967 the combined oil production of Iran, Iraq, Kuwait, and Saudi Arabia—now the top four producers in OPEC—exceeded that of the United States for the first time. In 1970 U.S. oil production peaked at 11.3 million barrels per day and thereafter began to drop. Europe and Japan were rapidly increasing their oil imports, and U.S. consumption was growing. The buyer's market was turning into a seller's market, and the sellers were getting more wily.

A twenty-seven-year-old firebrand named Muammar el-Qaddafi seized power in Libya in 1969 and began to put pressure on the small oil companies there. He got one producer to break ranks and post a 30-cents-a-barrel price hike. The genie was out of the bottle. The other Libyan producers soon fell in line, and then the other OPEC members matched Qaddafi's price boost and upped the ante in turn. A "leapfrogging" of prices between Libya and the Gulf states had begun.

From World War II until 1970 the price of oil had held fairly constant, rising in 25 years from about $1.45 to $1.80 a barrel. By 1971 the major producers were paying $3.30 for high quality Libyan oil. The OPEC nations were learning to use their muscle, and they enjoyed the exercise.

The 1973 Arab Oil Embargo

In the fall of 1973 the West had a stunning, dramatic, and extremely painful lesson in the new realities of the age of oil. Against the backdrop of renewed Arab-Israeli fighting, Arab oil producers in the Middle East declared a selective boycott against consuming countries, including the United States. And OPEC, feeling its strength, decreed a quadrupling in the price of oil. Oil that sold for $3.00 a barrel in September was raised to $5.12 in October, and to $11.65 in December; the same oil had sold for $1.80 three years earlier. Overnight, the economic structure of the world was turned upside down.

It was made transparently clear that the economies of Western Europe and Japan could be devastated almost as completely by an oil cutoff as they could be by a nuclear attack. It became embarrassingly obvious that the consuming countries had become so dependent on OPEC—and the OPEC governments had assumed so commanding a position in oil decisions—that in the short run, at least, the West was virtually helpless in the face of whatever demands those governments might choose to make. The control over Mideast oil had shifted from the multinational companies to the host countries and statesmanship and restraint on the part of Arab leaders suddenly became the key to Western survival.

Neither the oil companies nor the Western governments could dictate terms to the OPEC countries any longer. The best the Western nations could do was try to persuade the producing nations that their own long-term interests were tied up with those of the West; that if their actions wrecked the Western economies, or destroyed the dollar, or so weakened the West that it could no longer protect their interests as well as its own, then those actions would be ultimately self-defeating.

Some of the leaders of the OPEC nations saw the logic of this argument and were able to restrain their colleagues from taking what might otherwise have been even more drastic measures. But the West had discovered its Achilles' heel. Oil, being so cheap to produce and so versatile to use, had so widely replaced other energy sources that the industrial economies had become dependent on it; and now the sources of oil were no longer secure.

In the immediate crisis of the 1973 embargo, as factories went dark in Europe, as lines lengthened at gas stations in America, and as prices soared worldwide, most people saw the problem as primarily an economic one. Although the economic impact was serious, however, this was by no means the whole of it. The political and strategic problems the British had referred to twenty years earlier now made themselves evident with a vengeance.

The nations of the Persian Gulf were becoming more powerful—and enormously rich—but they were also becoming more vulnerable. Britain's withdrawal from "East of Suez" had been announced in 1968 and completed in 1971. When Britain had stated that it could no longer serve as the support for Greece and Turkey, Truman had filled the vacuum thus left in the eastern Mediterranean with U.S. power in order to keep the Soviets out. Now this latest retrenchment threatened to leave another vacuum, which the Soviets would again be only too ready to fill if given the opportunity. In fact, within two months of Britain's January 1968 announcement of its intention to withdraw, the Soviet Union began introducing naval power into the area: a Soviet naval flotilla has been on permanent duty in the Indian Ocean since March 1968.

Unfortunately, this came at a time when outcries against the war in Vietnam raised serious questions about whether the American public would support another major American commitment in a distant trouble spot such as the Persian Gulf.

Rather than replace the British presence with a direct American presence, therefore, the United States chose to rely on local powers, primarily Iran and Saudi Arabia, to provide security for the Gulf, while we assisted by making arms and other supplies available. This "two-pillar policy" worked reasonably well until one of the pillars—Iran—collapsed in 1979.

In addition to the threat presented by their naval presence, in recent years the Soviets have been converging in a bold pincer movement on the Gulf. They are making two wide flanking movements, trying to sweep in close for the kill, in an attempt to cut the West's oil jugular.

The first pincer came across Africa, up through the Horn, right into the Arabian peninsula. It started in Angola, where the Soviets ferried in more than 15,000 Cubans in order to install the regime of their choice. It continued in Ethiopia, where nearly 20,000 Cubans landed, this time just across the narrow Red Sea from Saudi Arabia. In 1978 the pincer movement swept onto the Arabian peninsula itself as a pro-Soviet group in South Yemen, formerly the British colony of Aden, purged its opponents and soon afterward launched a war on North Yemen, the source of much of Saudi Arabia's labor force and one of its most sensitive national security concerns. In late 1979 terrorist groups, some of them armed and trained in South Yemen, struck at Saudi Arabia itself when they seized the holiest shrine in Islam, the Grand Mosque at Mecca, in what was apparently an effort to undermine the Saudi regime.

Unopposed in their whirlwind move across Africa and onto the shores of the Arabian peninsula, the Soviets set into motion a second pincer movement from the north. In 1978 a pro-Moscow group seized control of Afghanistan and eagerly accepted Soviet offers of aid. And then, between the pincers, the Shah of Iran was driven from his throne. In the final days of 1979, with the Shah gone, with Pakistan in turmoil and shunned by the United States, the Soviets brazenly moved the Red Army itself into Afghanistan, bringing Russian planes and armor within easy striking range of the narrow entrance to the Persian Gulf.

Henry Kissinger commented late in 1978 that "one cannot look at what has happened in Afghanistan, Aden, Ethiopia, and Angola and draw a line between these various countries without coming to certain geopolitical conclusions." A line drawn through these countries passes directly through Saudi Arabia, Iran, the United Arab Emirates, and the Straits of Hormuz, the strategic choke point through which 40 percent of the free world's oil passes—20 million barrels each day, 800,000 barrels every hour. Like a lion stalking its kill, the Soviets are moving closer to their prey. In 1979 Lloyd's of London announced that shipowners sending tankers through the straits would need special warzone insurance.

The downfall of the Shah was a stunningly ominous event for the remaining monarchs of the Gulf as well as for the countries of the industrial West. After the British withdrew in 1971 Iran had taken their place as the military power that guaranteed stability in the Gulf. On the eve of the British withdrawal Iranian forces occupied the strategically located islands of Abu Musa and Tumbs overlooking the Straits of Hormuz. In 1973 the Shah sent Iranian troops to Oman's Dhofar Province, where Marxist guerrillas supplied by neighboring South Yemen were threatening the Sultan of Oman's regime. The Shah ordered work begun on a naval base at Chah Bahar in Iranian Baluchistan to guard the entrance to the Straits of Hormuz.

In addition to refusing to participate in the Arab oil embargos of 1967 and of 1973, the Shah had continued to recognize Israel, provided oil for our Mediterranean Fleet, and kept Iraq from playing any significant role in the Yom Kippur War by moving troops to the Iran-Iraq border and by giving covert support to rebellious Kurdish forces, thus tying down the Iraqi Army. During that war his was the only country in the area to prohibit Soviet overflights; he also rushed oil to an American carrier force in the Indian

Ocean to keep it in operation. When our allies were asked to send arms to South Vietnam before the Paris accords forbade it, the Shah stripped himself of F-5's to accommodate us.

The Shah provided the muscle that protected the rich but vulnerable Saudis. He settled territorial disputes with Bahrain and Iraq. He encouraged arrangements for regional security with other Gulf states. When the first communist coup in Afghanistan interrupted his efforts, he was wooing that country away from its reliance on the Soviets for military and economic aid.

Now that the Shah's rule is over, all these efforts have ended. And the eventual political direction of that conflict-ridden country—even its continued existence as a unified nation—is uncertain. As former CIA official Cord Meyer put it in early 1979:

> . . . the disintegration of the Iranian army is seen as an accomplished fact that has already caused a seismic shift in the power balance throughout the entire region. For many years, Iran's army served to keep in check Iraqi ambitions against Israel and Kuwait, protected the sultan of Oman against the Dhofar guerrillas armed by South Yemen and reassured Sadat in Egypt and the Saudi princes. A tempting vacuum now yawns where once the Shah's army stood.

When the British left in 1971 only Iran had the trained manpower, the resources, and the will to take over Britain's stabilizing role. With the fall of the Shah, the disintegration of the Iranian Army, massive cutbacks in Iran's military budget, and Iran's descent into chaos, all the forces that the Shah held in check are free to press forward unrestrained. The new Iranian regime has made enemies of its neighbors by pitting Shiite Moslems against Sunni Moslems and reopening territorial disputes the Shah had settled.

The Shah's successors have abandoned work on the Chah Bahar naval base and canceled most of his billions of dollars of projected arms purchases. Dhofari guerrillas based in South Yemen have vowed to rekindle their attempt to bring down the Sultan of Oman. The Russians have invaded Afghanistan, which they might not have dared do if the Shah were still on his throne, allied with the United States and in control of the once formidable Iranian Army. Pakistan now feels the hot breath of the Russian bear on its own border, and has to expect that the Soviets will soon try to subvert it by encouraging and directing Baluchi and Pushtun rebellions, which could lead to the disintegration of what is left of that country. The whole area is in turmoil and the question on everybody's mind is: Who will replace Iran? Saudi Arabia, with nearly a fourth of the world's known recoverable oil, has a special interest in this question.

Radical Iraq is now the most powerful military force in the Gulf. Its military strength is overwhelming in strictly regional terms. It has 4 armored divisions and 2 mechanized divisions, with over 3,000 Soviet and French tanks and armored fighting vehicles, plus 4 infantry divisions. Even without any further Soviet support, the Iraqis could move with impunity anywhere they decided to: in Kuwait, Saudi Arabia, or Iran.

Iraqi military forces have already been deployed against Kuwait—in 1961 and again in 1973. In the 1961 incident the British and the other Arabs forced the Iraqis to pull their massed troops back from the Kuwait border. In the 1973 incident, however, the Iraqis did not back down, but took some Kuwaiti territory. Iraq has since settled its border differences with Kuwait, but the possibility of future problems remains.

The vast majority of the crude oil reserves in the Persian Gulf are within a few hundred miles of the Iraqi border—in the nearby areas of Iran, Kuwait, Saudi Arabia, and the United Arab Emirates. The payoff for a successful Iraqi move into any one or all of these areas would be an enormous transfer of assets.

Iraq is now making a determined bid for political dominance in the Gulf. Although its leftist authoritarian regime has been anti-American, it does not want to see the Russians establish hegemony in the Gulf, and therefore may become willing to moderate its past stance. We therefore have reason to seek improved relations with Iraq. For their part, the

Soviets remain interested in gaining control of Iraq, although the Iraqis have been vigilant in cutting back the growth of the Iraqi Communist Party. In 1977 and 1978 communist attempts to form party cells in the army were smashed and the organizers executed. Though these attempts failed, the history of faction-ridden Iraq in the last twenty years has included many coups and attempted coups by a variety of groups; the Soviets can be expected to continue trying to increase their influence by any and all means, meanwhile benefiting from Iraq's efforts to pull the rest of the Arab world in a more radical, more anti-Western direction.

The Big Enchilada

With their enormous oil riches, their vast, sparsely populated lands, and their small army, the Saudis have been aptly described by columnist John P. Roche as "coup-bait." Their situation was well summed up by one U.S. official, who commented, "Suppose you were a rich woman living alone in a tiny town surrounded by hoodlums. Everyone knows you have millions in diamonds under your bed and no police to protect you. Occasionally the sheriff comes by, siren blaring, hops out, gives you a big kiss and roars off. Would you feel safe?"

Geographically, there are four approaches to Saudi Arabia: (1) from the "front-line states" in the Arab-Israeli conflict—Egypt, Jordan, Syria, and Israel; (2) from the direction of the Persian Gulf—Iran, Iraq, or one of the small sheikhdoms on the Gulf; (3) from the Horn of Africa, just across the Red Sea; and (4) from Oman, or from North or South Yemen, at the end of the Arabian peninsula.

Events on all four approaches give the Saudis reason to be nervous.

The Saudis are concerned that any settlement of the Arab-Israeli conflict that does not resolve the Palestinian problem will increase the militancy of the Palestinians. In 1976 the Palestinian Liberation Organization disrupted Lebanon, plunging it into civil war. During my administration they tried twice within three months to assassinate King Hussein of Jordan, they set off a civil war in that country, and they almost succeeded in bringing about the fall of its government. Terrorism is the PLO's stock in trade, and Saudi Arabia is extremely vulnerable to terrorist activities; two thirds of the workers in its oil fields are Palestinians. In addition, anything that strengthens the hand of the Arab radicals—as an unsatisfactory settlement would—weakens the position of the moderate Saudi leadership.

From the direction of the Gulf, the Saudis have multiple concerns. They fear the nearby military power of Iraq. The toppling of the Iranian monarchy makes other crowns in the region, including Saudi Arabia's, sit less securely. Internal problems in the small Gulf sheikhdoms make these, too, potentially unstable. In Kuwait, for example, less than half the population of 1 million are Kuwaitis; more than 250,000 are Palestinians, and another 250,000 are other foreign nationals. In the United Arab Emirates, and also in Qatar, only about one-fourth of the population is indigenous. Strains among the seven tiny sheikhdoms that formed the United Arab Emirates in 1971 could well give rise to exploitable conflicts in the future.

Looking across the Red Sea to the Horn of Africa, the Saudis have seen the Soviet-supported regime in Ethiopia waging a two-front war: to recapture the rebel province of Eritrea—with its Red Sea ports—and, against Somalia, over the Ogaden. The Saudis were partially responsible for weaning Egypt and the Sudan away from their earlier ties to the U.S.S.R., and they have also provided aid to Somalia for the same purpose. They have been deeply disappointed by U.S. unwillingness to provide arms to the Somalis and the Eritreans. Ethiopia has 30 million people—four times as many as Saudi Arabia. Eritrean ports dominate the southern end of the Red Sea, where three quarters of Saudi Arabia's coastline lies.

From the end of the peninsula where Oman and the two Yemens lie, trouble has been more the rule than the exception. South Yemen remains the most pliable Soviet tool in the Arab world. This barren nation is host to Soviet and Cuban advisers and East German police-state experts, who assist the few thousand members of the Communist Party in controlling the nation's 2 million people, while also helping South Yemen make war against its neighbors, North Yemen and Oman.

North Yemen has no oil and little industry, but with 6 million people, its population is almost as great as that of Saudi Arabia. While still pro-Western, North Yemen has recently purchased Soviet arms and shown signs of hedging its bets. If through subversion, conquest, or unification with South Yemen, North Yemen comes under Communist control, the Saudis will be gravely menaced. A million North Yemenis work in Saudi Arabia.

South Yemen—in effect, the Cuba of the Arabian peninsula—also has active designs on its eastern neighbor, Oman. Oman once ruled a far-flung empire of its own. When the United States first established trading relations with Oman in the 1820s, its navy was larger than ours, and at one point its empire included the island of Zanzibar, over 2,000 miles away. It still controls what, in geopolitical terms, is one of the most valuable pieces of real estate in the world: the tip of the Ras Musandan peninsula that forms the southern bank of the Straits of Hormuz, that greatly coveted entrance to the Persian Gulf.

For years the Soviets and South Yemenis backed an insurgency in Oman's Dhofar Province. The Omanis were unable to put this down until the Shah of Iran sent troops to assist them. Key roads were secured, the border with South Yemen was sealed, and by late 1976 the rebellion was ended and Oman was secure—for the moment. When the Shah fell from power in early 1979, however, the crowds had hardly quieted in the streets of Tehran before a spokesman for the Dhofari guerrillas operating out of South Yemen announced that guerrilla efforts would begin again.

Especially ominous, the Soviets have recently equipped the Cuban Army with the latest in armored weaponry, and the Soviet brigade discovered in Cuba in 1979 may well be training Cubans in armored warfare, which requires coordination at the brigade level. At the same time, intelligence reports have indicated that the Soviets are stockpiling in South Yemen precisely the sort of advanced battle tanks, combat carriers, and other arms and equipment that would be needed for an armored strike across the desert. As strategist Edward Luttwak has suggested:

> The pieces are on the chessboard; the operation could unfold at any time. With a revived Dhofar movement providing the political camouflage of an internal revolt, and the chronically aggressive South Yemen government mounting a military attack in the guise of an intra-Arab fight, the Cubans could inject the coup de grace of an armored threat which the small Omani army could not possibly resist. . . . All the oil of Arabia would come under the direct threat of a radical Cuban-supported (and thus Soviet-sponsored) regime, whose mere emergence might well suffice to inspire radical seizures of power in the small Trucial sheikhdoms that have much oil.

It would also bring the Soviets to the Straits of Hormuz.

The Soviet Threat

Wealth and weakness plague the countries of the Persian Gulf. Their riches and their vulnerability combine to make them doubly tempting targets for the Soviet Union.

Watching the Soviet Union crush Afghanistan as the 1970s ended, Egypt's President Anwar Sadat commented: "The battle around the oil stores has already begun." Moscow has struck to within 300 miles of the Straits of Hormuz, the strategic choke point on the West's oil jugular. From bases in southwestern Afghanistan, MiG fighters can reach the Straits, something that was previously beyond them.

From Turkey to Pakistan, the countries of the "northern tier" that once held the Russians in check are either in turmoil or gravely weakened. Sir Robert Thompson has noted that Russia has three fronts: a European or Western front, an eastern front facing China and Japan, and a southern front facing the countries between Turkey and Afghanistan. The third front has now been breached, and Russia is moving southward toward that region in which, as Molotov said, the "center of the aspirations of the Soviet Union" lies.

Since the end of World War II oil from the Middle East has been crucial to Western Europe and Japan. Since 1970, when domestic production peaked, it has become increasingly important to the United States. The Soviet Union now exports 3 million barrels of oil a day; half of its 1978 foreign currency earnings came from oil exports. Forecasts of Soviet oil production suggest that it may peak soon, and decline during the 1980s; the Soviets themselves may well become net oil importers during this period. This is bound to affect their cost-benefit calculations in considering a grab for the riches of the Persian Gulf.

Before their seizure of Afghanistan, the Soviet base closest to the Straits of Hormuz was at Mary, earlier known as Merv, in Soviet Turkmenistan. When the Russians first moved into the Merv oasis in 1884 a great debate occurred in Great Britain over Russian intentions and the threat to the British Empire. Those who were complacent about the tsarist conquests were like our own "so what" school in recent years; they archly accused the hard-liners of "Mervousness." The Russian ambassador in London argued that it was difficult "for a civilized power to stop short in the extension of its territory where uncivilized tribes were its immediate neighbors."

The Russians were halted along the Amu Darya River in the late nineteenth century, and that river formed the border with Afghanistan until Russian troops crashed across it in late 1979. There are no natural barriers separating Afghanistan from the Arabian Sea and the Straits of Hormuz. There is only barren land and, ominously, a zone of instability.

That zone of instability is called Baluchistan. Five million Baluchi tribesmen live in southern Afghanistan, western Pakistan, and southeastern Iran. In recent years the

Baluchis of Pakistan have repeatedly rebelled against the central government. In late 1979 open conflict with the Tehran government erupted in Iranian Baluchistan. Because most Baluchi are Sunni Moslems, Khomeini's theocratic Shiite dictatorship gives them a new grievance. Even before the Soviets openly invaded Afghanistan, there were reports that they were using camps in that country to train, indoctrinate, and supply separatist Baluchi rebels from Pakistan. Baluchistan has 750 miles of strategic shoreline along the Arabian Sea, reaching almost to the Straits of Hormuz. A People's Republic of Baluchistan would give the Soviets a red finger pushing through to the Indian Ocean. This could be a decisive step in the Soviets' northern pincer movement toward the Straits.

The entire industrial economy of the West now depends on oil, and the entire military machine of the West runs on oil. Control over the West's oil lifeline is control over the West's life. Never has the region of the Persian Gulf been so vital to the future of the world. Never have the nations of the Persian Gulf been so vulnerable to an aggressive power that seeks to impose its will on the world.

One after another, nations of the Persian Gulf and the Islamic crescent have fallen to revolutionary forces that, in one way or another, are anti-Western if not actively pro-Soviet. The extreme volatility of Middle Eastern politics has made the region both more tempting to adventurers and more vulnerable to takeover attempts. If the Soviets succeed in taking effective control of the Persian Gulf, Europe and Japan will be at their mercy. And mercy is not one of their most notable virtues.

Needs for the Future

For centuries great forces have collided in the Middle East and the Persian Gulf, great interests have contended, and local quarrels have raged. This will continue to be true in the 1980s. The competition of interests over access to oil from the region at reasonable prices threatens to dwarf all previous conflicts.

Our oil supplies from the Mideast are vulnerable to three major threats—the potentially explosive Arab-Israeli conflict, Soviet adventurism, and local revolutionary forces such as those that overthrew the Shah.

For years Americans thought of Middle Eastern conflicts almost exclusively in terms of the Arab-Israeli contest. But the area has been riven by strife for centuries; for centuries it has been the crossroads of the world, but also a world unto itself. Now its conflicts have intensified as old ways and new collide, sometimes explosively, and as the external restraints that contained local rivalries are removed. The fact is that the West's most important import comes from the world's most volatile region.

There is unrest or the danger of unrest in every country in the Middle East. No border is secure, nor is any state free from worries about internal security. Conflicts rage between Shiite and Sunni, between Iranian and Arab; there are clashes among nationalities, sects, tribes, and classes, as well as the gathering revolt of traditional Islam against modernity, and all of these often erupt into violence. At the end of 1979 former Israeli ambassador to the United States Chaim Herzog summed up part of the record of instability:

> In the past 18 months alone, four Arab presidents were removed, one assassinated in Yemen, one executed by assassins in South Yemen, one removed by a coup in Mauritania and one recently by a coup in Iraq. Thirteen of the current heads of Arab states, over 50 percent of them, have succeeded immediate predecessors who were violently removed from office, in most cases from this life. In the past 15 years there have been 12 fierce bitter wars in which Arabs were pitted against Arabs in bloody internecine strife.

The Soviets are skilled at exploiting trouble, but there would be trouble in the Middle East even without them. The Arab–Israeli conflict is a source of bitter conflict, but there would be conflict without the Arab-Israeli dispute.

Even the "Islamic revolution" defies simple categorization. Among the world's 800 million Moslems there are more non-Arabs than Arabs; Moslems form a majority or a sizable minority in seventy countries. The world's most populous Moslem country is Indonesia. There are more Moslems in India, Nigeria, the Soviet Union, and even China than in most countries of the Middle East.

Modernization—which often means Westernization—has been a wrenching experience for these traditional societies, and the United States has become a convenient whipping boy for those torn between the strict teachings of the past and the lures or demands of the modern world. Conserving the best of traditional Islam while satisfying the needs of the twentieth and twenty-first centuries will challenge the wisest reformers. But it must be done.

With regard to the Arab-Israeli conflict, one premise from which United States policy must proceed is our strong moral commitment to the preservation of the state of Israel. Israel has demonstrated in four wars over the past thirty years that it can more than hold its own against its neighbors. Now that the threat from Egypt has been neutralized, this is even more true. But if the Soviet Union were to stage a full-scale intervention, as it threatened to do in 1973, Israel would go down the tube. Even if Israel has or acquires nuclear weapons, its modest nuclear capability would not be a deterrent against the nuclear might of the Soviet Union. The key to Israel's survival, therefore, is our determination to hold the ring against the Soviets.

Our airlift to Israel and the alert of our forces which I ordered in 1973 with the knowledge that these actions might lead to an Arab oil embargo were a demonstration of how far the United States will go to keep our commitment to Israel's survival and to prevent Soviet intervention in the area.

But that decision was a close call then and it will be even closer in the future as the Soviets gain clear nuclear superiority. The Palestinian time bomb must be defused before we face another Yom Kippur crisis.

It would be presumptuous and foolhardy to suggest that there is some magic formula, some quick fix, for solving the Israeli-Palestinian conflict. There are, however, some basic principles that must form the foundation of any viable policy. First, whatever group does in fact or claims to represent the Palestinians must recognize Israel's right to exist in peace and must reject the use of terrorism or armed action against Israel or Israeli citizens. Second, Israel must comply with the provisions of U.N. Resolution 242 with regard to the return of occupied territories. However, Israel is entitled to secure borders and cannot and should not be expected to agree to setting up a hostile armed state in its gut on the West Bank. Third, occupied territories that are returned should be demilitarized. Finally, Jordan can play a constructive role in resolving the Palestinian issue.

Having in mind these basic conditions, we must recognize that the Palestinian issue is a rallying cry for radical forces throughout the area and is constantly exploited by the Soviet Union. It is in the interests of Israel and every moderate government in the Mideast to make a maximum effort to resolve it. Unless progress is made swiftly, Egypt's President Anwar Sadat, the most effective voice for moderation in the Mideast, will find his position untenable. In the 1956 Suez crisis we learned how destabilizing a radical Egyptian leader can be. Next to the need to keep the Soviets out of the Mideast, the most important thing is for Israel and the moderate Arab governments to do everything possible to defuse the Palestinian issue so that Sadat and other moderate Arab leaders will not be driven from power.

In the long term the problem in this area is the Soviet Union. The Soviets may well need access to Middle East oil themselves during the 1980s. Certainly they want the power to affect the flow of that oil to Europe and Japan. With their nuclear-armed Backfire bombers and SS-20 missiles, their Indian Ocean and Mediterranean naval squadrons, their rapid-deployment airlift forces in the Caucasus, their use of ports in South Yemen and the Horn of Africa, and their new air bases in Afghanistan, the Soviets will be able to project their military power into the area in ways that the United States cannot, and with a speed the United States cannot match. It would take us at least a decade to catch up in this regard. This imbalance casts a long shadow over the politics of the area.

The strategic position of the entire Western alliance hinges on reliable access to crude oil from the Persian Gulf. This, in turn, requires that we successfully block the Soviet drive toward dominant influence in the area.

Since oil is not a convenience for the West, but a necessity, the United States and our allies in Europe and Japan must make it a priority to provide economic and military assistance to governments in the area that are threatened by internal or external aggression. We must be ready and willing to take whatever steps, including a strong military presence and even military action, are required to protect our interests. We must also be able to back up our words. The enunciation of a grandiose "doctrine" that the United States will resist a threat to the region by responding militarily is an empty cannon unless we have the forces in place to give credibility to that pledge. If we make it clear that we are prepared to go this far, and if we show that we can, we will not be forced to do so.

It is essential that the United States have base facilities so located as to enable us to project our power convincingly into the area, and to respond swiftly to sudden threats. We also need to assure access to bases in Western Europe that could be used to facilitate airlift and sealift operations between the United States and the Persian Gulf. And then, when we do project power, we must do so resolutely. Announcing the emergency dispatch of an aircraft carrier to the Gulf only to turn it back to avoid provocation, sending F-15 fighter planes to Saudi Arabia as a show of force but making a point of sending them unarmed—gestures such as these are worse than futile. By inviting contempt, they encourage aggression.

Above all, the leaders of Saudi Arabia, Oman, Kuwait, and other key states must be unequivocally reassured that should they be threatened by revolutionary forces, either internally or externally, the United States will stand strongly with them so that they will not suffer the same fate as the Shah.

It will be necessary not only to be prepared, but to be seen to be prepared. We must not only have the will to use force if required, we must demonstrate that will. We must also have the forces that can be used. We may run risks in defending our interests in the Persian Gulf. We would run far greater risks if we failed to defend those interests.

5

The Vietnam Syndrome

The H-Bomb is more handicap than help to the policy of "containment." To the extent that it reduces the likelihood of all-out war, it *increases* the possibilities of "limited war" pursued by indirect and widespread local aggression.

—*B. H. Liddell Hart*

When it is all over, it [the war in Vietnam] will undoubtedly prove to be one of the decisive wars of this century and, in its influence, more far-reaching than any other war of its type ... and its real effects are still to come.

—*Sir Robert Thompson*

I regard the war in Indochina as the greatest military, political, economic, and moral blunder in our national history.

—*Senator George McGovern*

The final chapters have yet to be written on the war in Vietnam. It was a traumatizing experience for Americans, a brutalizing experience for the Vietnamese, an exploitable opportunity for the Soviets. It was also one of the crucial battles of World War III.

Scores of books have been written on the Vietnam War.

Now Hollywood is drawing on it for dramatic material, and in the process weaving its own interpretations. Each differing view reflects in some measure the author's own particular experience, or lack of experience, with the war.

As Commander-in-Chief during the final five years of the war, my perspective is unique. I believe I understand why we failed in Vietnam. I knew then the stakes we were fighting for. I know now the price we have paid because of our failure, and most importantly, I think I know how we can learn from those mistakes and avoid making them again.

"Revolutionary war"—guerrilla war—has been one of the Soviets' favorite instruments in World War III.

During the period when the European colonial empires were being dismantled, it was relatively simple to co-opt the calls for "liberation"; and new and unstable nations still provide fertile ground for the seeds of revolutionary war. Further, this type of war can be pursued without the consequences, either military or diplomatic, of committing Soviet troops to the battle.

Liddell Hart noted in 1954 that the H-bomb would increase the likelihood of " 'limited war' pursued by indirect and widespread local aggression." Sir Robert Thompson concurred, and has written that "the invention of atomic weapons and the rise of nationalism" have had an enormous influence on the development of Soviet foreign policy since World War II. He observes: "The great advantage of revolutionary war as an instrument of policy in the nuclear age was to be that it avoided direct confrontation. . . . For the communist powers, therefore, revolutionary war was a low-risk war," a vital consideration in the nuclear era. The other great advantage of revolutionary war was that it took advantage of Third World nationalism, a force that swept the world soon after World War II and continues strong today. Communism's "anti-imperialist" message was a clever front for totalitarian parties, and many genuine nationalists were hoodwinked by this seemingly legitimate patriotic response to European colonialism. The first testing ground for this new Soviet weapon was East Asia.

•   •   •

After World War II a vacuum of power was left in East Asia. Among the noncommunist nations only the United States had the capability of filling it. The defeat and demilitarization of Japan, the consolidation of power by Mao Zedong in China, and the availability of Soviet and Chinese arms to any guerrilla force, whether communist or nationalist, that would launch internal or external aggression against noncommunist governments combined to create an extremely dangerous situation throughout the area. Only American aid and even armed intervention could prevent a communist conquest of all of East Asia.

The first test came in Northeast Asia, in Korea. U.N. forces held the line there against North Korean communists armed with Soviet weapons and aided in the later stages of the war by Chinese communist troops. Those U.N. forces were predominantly American.

In Southeast Asia the Japanese conquests in World War II—in which Asians had routed the previously invincible Europeans—sparked a new spirit of independence after World War II. When the Europeans tried to reclaim their colonies, they found they were no longer held in awe; their former subjects would no longer tolerate colonial rule. As a result, they either got out voluntarily or were driven out. Indonesia gained independence from the Netherlands in 1949. The British, weakened by the enormous exertions of World War II, began the long process of withdrawing from "East of Suez." To their great credit, they played an outstanding role in helping the Malaysians develop an effective program for liquidating that country's communist guerrilla forces. Unfortunately, in Vietnam neither the French nor the Americans who followed them learned adequately from the British experience.

The Philippines and Thailand managed to handle their own guerrilla insurrections without the assistance of American personnel, but with generous provision of American military and economic aid.

Indochina—Vietnam, Cambodia, and Laos—was totally within the French sphere of influence. Because the

French would not make adequate guarantees of independence, many Vietnamese who would not otherwise have done so joined the openly communist forces of Ho Chi Minh, a charismatic leader with impressive nationalist credentials gained by fighting against the French.

The French suffered 150,000 casualties from 1946 until 1954 in their attempt to hold on to Indochina. In March 1954 10,000 French soldiers were trapped in a fortress at Dien Bien Phu. Though they were only 5 percent of the French forces in Vietnam, their fate sealed the fate of France in Vietnam. They fought bravely for fifty-five days but eventually surrendered. It has been estimated that a limited commitment of conventional American air power might have turned the tide of battle. President Eisenhower considered it but insisted that the United States not act alone. Winston Churchill refused to commit British forces, commenting that if the British would not fight to stay in India, he saw no reason why they should fight to help the French stay in Indochina. Even if the strike had taken place, it is probable that the French would have lost in Indochina eventually because of their stubborn refusal to provide adequate guarantees of eventual independence.

Vietnam was destined to be independent after World War II. The real question was who would control it. The best course for France to have followed would have been to promise Vietnam independence, and then to help the noncommunist Vietnamese prevail over the communist Vietnamese. Even without the actual promise of independence, it still would have been far better for the Vietnamese, as well as for the West, if France had won its war against the Ho Chi Minh forces. Then, when independence came—as it inevitably would have come—Vietnam could have emerged as a free, noncommunist nation. Having taken on itself the responsibility for winning the war, however, France then lost it—not in Vietnam but in Paris. After Dien Bien Phu the French no longer had the will to carry on, and the French government welcomed the opportunity to withdraw from Indochina.

*   *   *

Vietnam was partitioned in 1954, with a communist government in the North under Ho Chi Minh and a non-communist government in the South with its capital in Saigon. Between the two was a demilitarized buffer zone—the DMZ. Soon Ho's government in Hanoi was infiltrating large numbers of agents into the South, where they worked with guerrilla forces to set up networks of subversion and terrorism designed to undermine the Saigon government.

The interim premier of South Vietnam, Ngo Dinh Diem, became its first president in 1955. He proved to be a strong and effective leader, particularly in containing the communist guerrilla forces that were directly supported by the North in violation of the 1954 Partition Agreement. The Eisenhower administration provided generous economic assistance and some military aid and technical advisers, but Eisenhower rejected proposals to commit American combat forces.

Large-scale infiltration from the North began in 1959, and by 1961 the communists had made substantial gains. Sir Robert Thompson arrived in Vietnam that year to head the British Advisory Mission. Thompson had been Secretary of Defense of the Malayan Federation when the communist insurgency had been defeated there. He and the CIA people on the scene understood the importance of local political realities in guerrilla war. In putting down the rebellion in Malaya over the course of twelve years, from 1948 to 1960, the British had learned that local, low-level aggression was best countered by local, low-level defense. Britain had used only 30,000 troops in Malaya, but had also employed 60,000 police and 250,000 in a home guard.

With the excellent advice he was getting, Diem was able to reverse the momentum of the war and put the communists on the defensive. Just as the war in Malaya had been won, the war in Vietnam was being won in the early 1960s. But then three critical events occurred that eventually turned the promise of victory into the fact of defeat.

The first took place far from Vietnam, in Cuba, in 1961: the Bay of Pigs invasion. That disastrous failure prompted President John F. Kennedy to order a postmortem, and General Maxwell Taylor was chosen to conduct it. He concluded that the CIA was not equipped to handle large-scale paramilitary operations and decided that the American effort in Vietnam fit into this category. He therefore recommended that control of it be handed over to the Pentagon, a decision that proved to have enormous consequences. The political sophistication and on-the-spot "feel" for local conditions that the CIA possessed went out the window, as people who saw the world through technological lenses took over the main operational responsibility for the war.

Another key turning point came the next year, in 1962, in Laos. At a press conference two months after his inauguration Kennedy had correctly declared that a communist attempt to take over Laos "quite obviously affects the security of the United States." He also said, "We will not be provoked, trapped, or drawn into this or any other situation; but I know that every American will want his country to honor its obligations." At the Geneva Conference in July 1962 fifteen countries signed an agreement in which those with military forces in Laos pledged to withdraw them and all agreed to stop any paramilitary assistance. All the countries complied except one: North Vietnam. North Vietnam never took any serious steps to remove its 7,000-man contingent from Laos—only 40 men were recorded as leaving—and the United States was therefore eventually forced to resume covert aid to Laos to prevent the North Vietnamese from taking over the country.

North Vietnam's obstinacy in keeping its forces in Laos—which had increased to 70,000 by 1972—created an extremely difficult situation for the South Vietnamese. The communists used the sparsely inhabited highlands of eastern Laos, and also of Cambodia, as a route for supplying their forces in South Vietnam. These areas also gave them a privileged sanctuary from which to strike, enabling them to concentrate overwhelmingly superior forces against a single local target and then slip back across the border before reinforcements could be brought in. The "Ho Chi Minh Trail" through Laos enabled the communists to do an end run around the demilitarized zone between North and South and to strike where the defenders were least prepared.

If South Vietnam had only had to contend with invasion and infiltration from the North across the forty-mile-long DMZ, it could have done so without the assistance of American forces. In the Korean War the enemy had had to attack directly across the border; North Korea could hardly use the ocean on either side of South Korea as a "privileged sanctuary" from which to launch attacks. But Hanoi was able to use sanctuaries in Laos and Cambodia as staging grounds for its assault on South Vietnam. In addition to making hit-and-run tactics possible, these lengthened the border the South had to defend from 40 to 640 miles, not counting indentations. Along these 640 miles there were few natural boundaries. The North Vietnamese were free to pick and choose their points of attack, always waiting until they had an overwhelming local advantage, in accordance with the strategy of guerrilla warfare. Our failure to prevent North Vietnam from establishing the Ho Chi Minh Trail along Laos' eastern border in 1962 had an enormous effect on the subsequent events in the war.

The third key event that set the course of the war was the assassination of Diem. Diem was a strong leader whose nationalist credentials were as solid as Ho Chi Minh's. He faced the difficult task of forging a nation while waging a war. In the manner of postcolonial leaders he ran a regime that drew its inspiration partly from European parliamentary models, partly from traditional Asian models, and partly from necessity. It worked for Vietnam, but it offended American purists, those who inspect the world with white gloves and disdain association with any but the spotless. Unfortunately for Diem, the American press corps in Vietnam wore white gloves, and although the North was not open to their inspection, the South was. Diem himself had premonitions of the fatal difference this might make when he told Sir Robert Thompson in 1962, "Only the American press can lose this war."

South Vietnam under Diem was substantially free, but, by American standards, not completely free. Responsible reporting seeks to keep events in proportion. The mark of irresponsible reporting is that it blows them out of proportion. It achieves drama by exaggeration, and its purpose is not truth but drama. The shortcomings of Diem's regime, like other aspects of the war, were blown grossly out of proportion.

"The camera," it has been pointed out, "has a more limited view even than the cameraman and argues always from the particular to the general." On June 11, 1963, the camera provided a very narrow view for the television audience in the United States. On that day, in a ritual carefully arranged for the camera, a Buddhist monk in South Vietnam doused himself with gasoline and set himself on fire. That picture, selectively chosen, seared a single word into the minds of many Americans: repression. The camera's focus on this one monk's act of self-immolation did not reveal the larger reality of South Vietnam; it obscured it. Even more thoroughly obscured from the television audience's view were the conditions inside North Vietnam, where unfriendly newsmen were not allowed.

Recently, in the Soviet Union, a Crimean Tartar set himself on fire to protest the thirty-five-year exile of his people from their ancestral homeland. A picture of this did not make the network news; it did not even make the front pages; I saw a story about it, with no pictures, buried on page twenty-one of the Los Angeles *Times*.

Communist regimes bury their mistakes; we advertise ours. During the war in Vietnam a lot of well-intentioned Americans got taken in by our well-advertised mistakes.

Some Buddhist temples in Vietnam were, in effect, headquarters of political opposition, and some Buddhist sects were more political than religious. The fact that Diem was a devout Catholic made him an ideal candidate to be painted as a repressor of Buddhists. They also played very skillful political theater; the "burning Buddhist" incident was an especially grisly form. But the press played up the Buddhists as oppressed holy people, and the world placed the blame on their target, Diem. The press has a way of focusing on one aspect of a complex situation as "the" story; in Vietnam in 1963 "the" story was "repression."

President Kennedy grew increasingly unhappy at being allied with what was being portrayed as a brutal, oppressive government. Apparently without seriously considering the long-term consequences, the United States began putting some distance between itself and Diem.

On November 1, 1963, Diem was overthrown in a coup and assassinated. Charges that the U.S. government was directly involved may be untrue and unfair. However, the most charitable interpretation of the Kennedy administration's part in this affair is that it greased the skids for Diem's downfall and did nothing to prevent his murder. It was a sordid episode in American foreign policy. Diem's fall was followed by political instability and chaos in South Vietnam, and the event had repercussions all over Asia as well. President Ayub Khan of Pakistan told me a few months later, "Diem's murder meant three things to many Asian leaders: that it is dangerous to be a friend of the United States; that it pays to be neutral; and that sometimes it helps to be an enemy."

The months of pressure and intrigue preceding the coup had paralyzed the Diem administration and allowed the communists to gain the initiative in the war. Once Diem was disposed of, the gates of the Presidential Palace became a revolving door. Whatever his faults, Diem had represented "legitimacy." With the symbol of legitimacy gone, power in South Vietnam was up for grabs. Coup followed coup for the next two years until Nguyen Van Thieu and Nguyen Cao Ky took over in 1965. The guerrilla forces had taken advantage of this chaotic situation and gained a great deal of strength in the interim.

President Kennedy had sent 16,000 American troops to Vietnam to serve as combat "advisers" to the regular South Vietnam units, but after Diem's assassination the situation continued to deteriorate. In 1964 Hanoi sent in troops in order to be in a position to take over power when the government of South Vietnam fell. By 1965 South Vietnam was on the verge of collapse. In order to prevent the conquest by the North President Johnson in February started bombing of the North, and in March the first independent American combat units landed in Danang. As our involvement deepened, reaching a level of 550,000 troops by the time Johnson left office, fatal flaws in the American approach became manifest.

In World War II we won basically by outproducing the other side. We built more and better weapons, and we were able to bombard the enemy with so many of them that he was forced to give up. Overwhelming firepower, unparalleled logistical capabilities, and the massive military operations that our talent for organization made possible were the keys to our success. But in World War II we were fighting a conventional war against a conventional enemy. We also were fighting a total war, and therefore, like the enemy, we had no qualms about the carnage we caused. Even before Hiroshima an estimated 35,000 people were killed in the Allied firebombing of Dresden; more than 80,000 perished in the two-day incendiary bombing of Tokyo a month later.

Vietnam, like Korea, was a limited war. The United States plunged in too impulsively in the 1960s, and then behaved too indecisively. We tried to wage a conventional war against an enemy who was fighting an unconventional war. We tried to mold the South Vietnamese Army into a large-scale conventional force while the principal threat was still from guerrilla forces, which called for the sort of smaller-unit, local-force response that had proved so successful in Malaya. American military policy-makers tended to downplay the subtler political and psychological aspects of guerrilla war, trying instead to win by throwing massive quantities of men and arms at the objective. And then, the impact even of this was diluted by increasing American pressure gradually rather than suddenly, thus giving the enemy time to adapt. Eisenhower, who refrained from publicly criticizing the conduct of the war, privately fumed about this gradualism. He once commented to me: "If the enemy holds a hill with a battalion, give me two battalions and I'll take it, but at great cost in casualties. Give me a division and I'll take it without a fight."

In Vietnam during that period we were not subtle enough in waging the guerrilla war; we were too subtle in waging the conventional war. We were too patronizing, even contemptuous, toward our ally, and too solicitous of our enemy. Vietnamese morale was sapped by "Americanization" of the war; American morale was sapped by perpetuation of the war.

Democracies are not well equipped to fight prolonged wars. A democracy fights well after its morale is galvanized by an enemy attack and it gears up its war production. A totalitarian power can coerce its population into fighting indefinitely. But a democracy fights well only as long as public opinion supports the war, and public opinion will not continue to support a war that drags on without tangible signs of progress. This is doubly true when the war is being fought half a world away. Twenty-five hundred years ago the ancient Chinese strategist Sun Tzu wrote, "There has never been a protracted war from which a country has benefited . . . . What is essential in war," he went on, "is victory, not prolonged operations." Victory was what the American people were not getting.

We Americans are a do-it-yourself people. During that period we failed to understand that we could not win the war for the South Vietnamese: that, in the final analysis, the South Vietnamese would have to win it for themselves. The United States bulled its way into Vietnam and tried to run the war our way instead of recognizing that our mission should have been to help the South Vietnamese build up their forces so that they could win the war.

When I was talking with an Asian leader before I became President, he graphically pointed out the weakness in what was then the American policy toward South Vietnam: "When you are trying to assist another nation in defending its freedom, U.S. policy should be to help them fight the war but not to fight it for them." This was exactly where we had been going wrong in Vietnam. As South Vietnam's Vice President Ky later said, "You captured *our* war."

When I took office in 1969 it was obvious the American strategy in Vietnam needed drastic revision. My administration was committed to formulating a strategy that would end American involvement in the war and enable South Vietnam to win.

Our goals were to:
— Reverse the "Americanization" of the war that had occurred from 1965 to 1968 and concentrate instead on Vietnamization.

— Give more priority to pacification so that the South Vietnamese could be better able to extend their control over the countryside.

— Reduce the invasion threat by destroying enemy sanctuaries and supply lines in Cambodia and Laos.

— Withdraw the half million American troops from Vietnam in a way that would not bring about a collapse in the South.

— Negotiate a cease-fire and a peace treaty.

— Demonstrate our willingness and determination to stand by our ally if the peace agreement was violated by Hanoi, and assure South Vietnam that it would continue to receive our military aid as Hanoi did from its allies, the Soviet Union and, to a lesser extent, China.

En route to Vietnam for my first visit as President, I held a press conference in Guam on July 25, 1969, at which I enunciated what has become known as the Nixon Doctrine. At the heart of the Nixon Doctrine is the premise that countries threatened by communist aggression must take the primary responsibility for their own defense. This does not mean that U.S. forces have no military role; what it does mean is that threatened countries have to be willing to bear the primary burden of supplying the manpower. We were already putting the Nixon Doctrine into effect in Vietnam by concentrating on Vietnamization. This meant, as Secretary of Defense Melvin Laird put it, helping South Vietnam develop "a stronger administration, a stronger economy, stronger military forces and stronger police for internal security."

The most important aspect of Vietnamization was the development of South Vietnam's army into a strong, independent fighting force capable of holding its own against the communists—both the guerrilla forces and the main-force units from the north that were then waging conventional war.

In October 1969 I sent Sir Robert Thompson to Vietnam as my special adviser, with instructions to give me a candid, first-hand, independent evaluation of the situation. He reported that he was able to walk safely through many villages that had been under Vietcong control for years. He was so impressed with the progress that had been made that he thought we were in "a winning position" to conclude a just peace if we were willing to follow through with the efforts we were making.

After giving sharply increased emphasis to Vietnamization and pacification, the first order of military business was to hit at the enemy sanctuaries and supply lines in Laos and Cambodia.

Cambodia

After the 1962 Laos agreement, which in effect allowed North Vietnam continued use of sanctuaries in Laos, Cambodia's Prince Sihanouk maneuvered to appease the North Vietnamese, who appeared to him to represent the side with the best chance of winning. In 1965 he broke relations with the United States and acquiesced in the establishment of North Vietnamese base areas in eastern Cambodia, from which over 100,000 North Vietnamese and Vietcong troops launched attacks on South Vietnamese and American troops for four years before I took office.

By January 1968 Sihanouk had grown deeply concerned about the number of Vietnamese in Cambodia, and he told presidential emissary Chester Bowles, "We don't want any Vietnamese in Cambodia. . . . We will be very glad if you solve our problem. . . . I want you to force the Vietcong to leave Cambodia."

In March 1969, in response to a major new offensive that the North Vietnamese had launched against our forces in South Vietnam, I ordered the bombing of enemy-occupied base areas in Cambodia. The bombing was not publicly announced because of our concern that if it were, Sihanouk would be forced to object to it. However, even after it was disclosed by leaks to the New York *Times* in April, Sihanouk did not object. On the contrary, in May 1969, two months after the bombing had started, he said, "Cambodia only protests against the destruction of the property and lives of Cambodians. . . . If there is a buffalo or any Cambodian killed, I will be informed immediately . . . (and) I will protest."

In June 1969 Sihanouk said at a press conference that one of Cambodia's northeast provinces was "practically North Vietnamese territory," and the next month he invited me to visit Cambodia to mark the improvement of relations between our two countries. But Sihanouk's tilt toward the United States did not satisfy Cambodian public opinion. The Cambodians strongly objected to North Vietnam's violation of their sovereignty. In a series of rapidly moving events in March 1970 demonstrations against North Vietnamese occupation of Cambodian territory led to the sacking of the North Vietnamese and Vietcong embassies in Phnom Penh. Within a matter of days the North Vietnamese were given forty-eight-hours' notice to vacate the country. Tiring of Sihanouk's careful balancing act, the Cambodian Parliament voted unanimously to depose him.

This was a brave move but a dangerous one. The North Vietnamese did not pack their bags and move out of Cambodia; instead they moved in—toward Phnom Penh. In 1978 the communist regime in Cambodia put out an official report that estimated that there were about 250,000 Vietnamese and communist forces in northeastern Cambodia when I ordered the move into that country, a number far greater than our own substantial estimates.

In early April the Vietnamese communist forces began their offensive, steadily expanding their base areas until by the end of that month they threatened to convert all of eastern Cambodia into one huge base area from which they could strike at both Phnom Penh and South Vietnam at will. To have acquiesced in this development would have been to sign a death warrant not only for the Cambodians but for the South Vietnamese as well. A communist-dominated Cambodia would have placed South Vietnam in an untenable military situation and would also have endangered the lives of thousands of U.S. servicemen.

Throughout April we showed restraint while the Vietnamese communist forces ran rampant through Cambodia. Our total military aid delivered to Cambodia consisted of 3,000 rifles provided covertly. The communists did not show similar restraint; they made it clear that their sole objective was domination of Cambodia.

Finally, on April 30 I announced our decision to counter the communist offensive by attacking North Vietnamese-occupied base areas in Cambodia bordering on South Vietnam. Our principal purpose was to undercut the North Vietnamese invasion of that country so that Vietnamization and plans for the withdrawal of American troops could continue in South Vietnam. A secondary purpose was to relieve the military pressure exerted on Cambodia by the North Vietnamese forces that were rapidly overrunning it. The North Vietnamese had been occupying parts of eastern Cambodia for over five years and returned there after we left; in contrast we limited our stay to two months and advanced only to a depth of twenty-one miles. It is obvious to any unbiased observer who the aggressor was. To contend, as many still do, that the United States and the South Vietnamese "invaded" Cambodia—in the sense of committing an aggressive act—is as absurd as it would be to charge that Eisenhower was committing aggression against France

when he ordered the Normandy landings. As New York
Times columnist William Safire observed in 1979:

> The United States did not invade Cambodia in 1970;
> on the contrary, we know now that the Vietnamese in-
> vaded Cambodia and we struck their positions with some
> success. The U.S. did not brutalize Cambodia with our
> bombing; on the contrary, we now know that we bombed
> an aggressor—which, now that we are gone, today over-
> runs that country.

In a letter to the New York *Times* recently a man
whose only son was killed in Vietnam wrote:

> Had the fathers of these young men known that this
> nation would countenance a sanctuary a scant 50 miles
> from Saigon, we would have counseled them against in-
> duction. That we did not is a burden we will always bear.
> A great percentage of our ground dead from 1965 to 1970
> came from an enemy who with impunity was staged,
> trained and equipped in the Parrot's Beak of Cambodia.
>
> The perfidy . . . is anything but the U.S. bombing of
> the sanctuary itself. The perfidy lies in the fact that for
> more than four years the United States of America, with-
> out serious recorded concern, allowed her fighting men
> to be attacked, maimed and killed from a position which
> was itself privileged from either ground or air retaliation.

The joint operations by the U.S. Army and ARVN
wiped out huge stores of North Vietnamese equipment—1
million rounds of ammunition (a full year's supply), 14 million pounds of rice (four months' supply), 23,000 weapons
(enough for seventy-four full-strength North Vietnamese
battalions), and much more.

Thanks to this and the following year's Lam Son operation in Laos by the South Vietnamese forces, Hanoi was
unable to stockpile enough supplies for a full-scale attack on
South Vietnam until two years later—in 1972. Valuable
time had been won with which to complete the task of Vietnamization. And even when the 1972 offensive came, it was
weakest and easiest to contain from the direction of the
sanctuaries in Cambodia, a testimony to the effectiveness of
our measures.

•   •   •

Militarily, the operation in Cambodia was a huge success. At the time, however, we were mercilessly attacked at home for our efforts to help South Vietnam and Cambodia survive. Many people perceived the joint operations as an American expansion of the war, ignoring the North Vietnamese invasion that had preceded it and forced us to respond. Now that Cambodia has been overrun by two separate communist armies, with its population driven out of the cities on death marches and then systematically starved as a matter of policy, voices echoing those of ten years ago say that it is our fault, that the United States is to blame. Perhaps it is guilt that causes these people to ignore the obvious and blame the genocide the Cambodian and Vietnamese communists have indulged in on the limited military moves the American government made a decade ago.

In fact, if the U.S. had not attacked the North Vietnamese sanctuaries, the communists would have overrun Cambodia in 1970 rather than five years later, when the Congress refused to provide military aid to the anticommunist Lon Nol government. As Henry Kissinger has pointed out:

> The genocidal horrors perpetrated by the Khmer Rouge in Cambodia in 1975 (even before the boat people dramatized the brutality of Communist Vietnam) have obviously been profoundly disquieting to antiwar critics who for so long advocated that we abandon Indochina to its fate. But those whose pressures rigidly restricted American assistance to Cambodia, who cut off all American military action to help resist the Khmer Rouge, and who finally succeeded in throttling all aid to a still resisting country in 1975, cannot escape their responsibility by rewriting history.

American military actions taken in defense against totalitarian aggressors did not cause those aggressors to become totalitarian. If war had anything to do with the brutalization of the Khmer Rouge, it was war instigated and relentlessly pursued by the North Vietnamese.

The 1972 Invasion

The American and South Vietnamese operations in Cambodia and Laos in 1970 and 1971 successfully prevented major North Vietnamese and Vietcong offensives in South Vietnam during those years and made it possible for the United States to continue to withdraw its forces on schedule.

By the spring of 1972 Hanoi recognized that it could not conquer South Vietnam through guerrilla war tactics, even with the help of conventional units, and that it could not win the support of the South Vietnamese people. There was no credible way for Hanoi to claim any longer that the war in the South was a civil war between the Saigon government and the Vietcong, so North Vietnam dropped the façade of "civil war" and launched a full-scale conventional invasion of the South. Fourteen divisions and twenty-six independent regiments invaded the South. This left only one division and four independent regiments in Laos and no regular ground forces at all in North Vietnam.

As Sir Robert Thompson put it, "It was a sign of the times that this Korean-type communist invasion, which twenty years before would have prompted united Western action and ten years before a Kennedy crusade, immediately put in doubt American resolve and probably won the Wisconsin primary for Senator George McGovern."

U.S. mining of Haiphong Harbor and the use of our airpower against targets in North Vietnam helped save the day, but the fighting on the ground was done exclusively by South Vietnamese forces. North Vietnam lost an estimated 130,000 killed and disabled. The invasion was a failure.

When I ordered the mining of Haiphong Harbor and the intensified bombing of North Vietnam on May 8, 1972 there was a great deal of speculation that this would lead to Soviet cancellation of the summit meeting scheduled for June. It did not. Brezhnev and his colleagues came to the support of their ally with words; they objected to our action strenuously in public. But they went forward with the sum mit because they wanted and needed better relations with us, particularly in view of our Chinese initiative. Also, our actions in Vietnam had demonstrated not only that we had the power but also that we had the will to use it when our interests were threatened, and that fact made us worth talking to. We were able to go to the summit in a position of strength. If we had failed to take these actions, and as a result had gone to Moscow while Soviet-made tanks were rumbling through the streets of Hué and Saigon, we would have been in an intolerable position of weakness. The Soviet leaders would have assumed that if we could be pushed around in Vietnam, we could also be pushed around in Moscow.

The Chinese also publicly condemned our May 8 action. From an ideological standpoint they had no other choice. From the standpoint of their survival, however, they desperately needed a relationship with an America that was not only strong, but also determined and reliable.

In sum, our actions in 1972 strengthened rather than weakened our new relationship with the Soviets and the Chinese. They both could see that we had power, the will to use it, and the skill to use it effectively. This meant that we were worth talking to. We could be a reliable friend or a dangerous enemy. This did not mean that they could publicly abandon their communist allies in Hanoi. However, their support for Hanoi noticeably cooled, which increased the incentive for Hanoi's leaders to make a peace agreement.

As a result of their decisive defeat in the 1972 offensive and their growing concern about the reliability of their Soviet and Chinese allies, the North Vietnamese finally began to negotiate seriously. But they were as stubborn at the conference table as they were on the battlefield. They wanted victory more than they wanted peace. Despite the overwhelming defeat of the peace-at-any-price candidate in the U.S. November elections, they continued to balk at our minimum terms.

On December 14 I made the decision to renew and increase the bombing of military targets in North Vietnam.

The bombing began on December 18. It was a necessary step, and it proved to be the right decision. Although it was a very difficult choice, the realities of war, and not the wishful thinking of the ill-informed, demanded this action. The bombing broke the deadlock in negotiations. The North Vietnamese returned to the negotiating table, and on January 23, 1973, the long-awaited peace agreement was finally achieved.

After their decisive defeat on the ground by South Vietnamese forces in the spring offensive and the destruction of their war-making capabilities by the December bombing, the North Vietnamese knew that militarily they were up against almost impossible odds. As the South Vietnamese economy continued to prosper far more than that of the North, Hanoi's communist ideology had less and less appeal. Thieu's Land to the Tiller program, for example, had reduced tenancy from 60 to 7 percent by 1973, a truly revolutionary development that undercut the communists' argument that the government allied itself with the rich and oppressed the people. Also, the North Vietnamese knew that both the Soviets and the Chinese had a stake in their new relationship with us and might not be willing to endanger that relationship by providing military supplies in excess of those allowed by the Paris peace agreement of January 1973.

From Victory to Defeat

We had won the war militarily and politically in Vietnam. But defeat was snatched from the jaws of victory because we lost the war politically in the United States. The peace that was finally won in January 1973 could have been enforced and South Vietnam could be a free nation today. But in a spasm of shortsightedness and spite, the United States threw away what it had gained at such enormous cost.

After the disillusionment of the mid-1960s many Americans refused to believe that we could win in Vietnam

After years of fighting the war the wrong way and losing, many believed we could not fight it the right way and win. Egged on by the media and often by conscience-stricken "dissenters" who had been responsible for policy errors in the first place, American public opinion was poisoned. In the mid-sixties the "best and the brightest" told us that we could win in Vietnam overnight; that we could win the war on an assembly-line basis, as if entire nations operated like a Ford plant. Now the "best and the brightest" told us that there was no way we could win the war and that we should get out as soon as we could, abandoning South Vietnam to its fate. What they really meant was that since *they* could not win in Vietnam, they automatically assumed that nobody could. Arrogant even in defeat, with their guilt-ridden carping they poisoned an already disillusioned American public and frustrated all the military and political efforts we made in Vietnam to win the war. Now, shocked by the bloodbath in Cambodia and the tragic plight of the boat people fleeing from "liberated" South Vietnam, they frantically thrash about trying to find someone to blame. All they have to do is to look in the mirror.

In retrospect it is remarkable that the public continued to support our efforts in Vietnam to the extent that it did for as long as it did. As *Newsweek* columnist Kenneth Crawford observed, this was the first war in our history during which our media were more friendly to our enemies than to our allies. American and South Vietnamese victories, such as the smashing of the Tet offensive in 1968, were portrayed as defeats. The United States, whose only intent was to help South Vietnam defend itself, was condemned as an aggressor. The Soviet-supported North Vietnamese were hailed as liberators.

The My Lai atrocities against 200 Vietnamese were justifiably deplored, and Captain William Calley was prosecuted and convicted for his role in them, but brutal murders of tens of thousands of civilians by the North Vietnamese were virtually ignored. During February of 1968 a Vietcong-North Vietnamese force occupied Hué and 5,800 civilians were executed or kidnapped. Following the city's recapture, at least 2,800 were found in mass graves—many of them apparently buried alive.

Hanoi's totally false and cynical charge that the United States had a policy of bombing dikes in the North and causing thousands to drown were given enormous coverage, and as a result of that coverage the charge was widely accepted as true. The truth—that there was no such policy and that no one was drowned—received scarcely any attention.

The South Vietnamese were loudly condemned for their treatment of prisoners. When actress Jane Fonda and former Attorney General Ramsey Clark traveled to Hanoi, they received massive, largely positive American media coverage of their statements praising the treatment of the American prisoners of war, who in fact were being subjected to the most barbaric and brutal torture by their North Vietnamese captors.

The dishonest, double-standard coverage of the Vietnam War was not one of the American media's finer hours. It powerfully distorted public perceptions, and these were reflected in Congress.

On January 2, 1973, the House Democratic Caucus voted 154–75 to cut off all funds for Indochina military operations as soon as arrangements were made for the safe withdrawal of U.S. troops and the return of our prisoners of war. Two days later a similar resolution was passed by the Senate Democratic Caucus, 36–12. This, it should be noted, was before Watergate began to weaken my own position as President, and only three months before withdrawal of American forces was completed, and the last of the 550,000 American troops that were in Vietnam when I took office in 1969 were brought back.

Thompson has observed:

> The point was that President Nixon, having gained a dominant bargaining position when the bombing halted on 29 December, 1972, could not press his advantage because antagonism to the bombing itself, and the very fact of his strong bargaining position, brought him under increased pressure in Congress and in the United States to

accept a ceasefire on any superficially acceptable terms which would immediately end direct American involvement. . . .

President Nixon was therefore compelled to accept terms because they coincided, at least on paper, with the terms previously laid down as representing "peace with honor." Even so, if these terms had been meticulously kept or had been enforceable, there would have been an end to the war and "peace with honor."

If the peace agreement was to have any chance to be effective, it was essential that Hanoi be deterred from breaking it. In a private letter to Thieu I had stated that "if Hanoi fails to abide by the terms of this agreement, it is my intention to take swift and severe retaliatory action." At a news conference on March 15, with regard to North Vietnamese infiltration into South Vietnam and violation of the agreement, I stated, "I would only suggest that based on my actions over the past four years, the North Vietnamese should not lightly disregard such expressions of concern, when they are made with regard to a violation."

In April, May, and June of 1973, with my authority weakened by the Watergate crisis, retaliatory action was threatened but not taken. Then Congress passed a bill setting August 15 as the date for termination of U.S. bombing in Cambodia and requiring congressional approval for the funding of U.S. military action in any part of Indochina. The effect of this bill was to deny the President the means to enforce the Vietnam peace agreement by retaliating against Hanoi for violations.

Once Congress had removed the possibility of military action against breaches of the peace agreement, I knew I had only words with which to threaten. The communists knew it too. By means of the bombing cutoff and the War Powers resolution passed in November 1973, Congress denied to me and to my successor, President Ford, the means with which to enforce the Paris agreement at a time when the North Vietnamese were openly and flagrantly violating it. It is truly remarkable that, for two years after the signing of the peace agreement in January 1973, the South Vietnamese held their own against the well-supplied North, without American personnel support either in the air or on the ground and with dwindling supplies.

Throughout 1974 the Russians poured huge amounts of ammunition, weaponry, and military supplies into North Vietnam, and the North in turn poured them into the South. In March 1974 Hanoi was estimated to have 185,000 men, 500 to 700 tanks, and 24 regiments of antiaircraft troops in the South. With the threat of American air power gone, the North Vietnamese built new roads and pipelines to move their armies and supplies about. At the same time that the Soviet Union was arming Hanoi for the final assault, the United States Congress was sharply curtailing the flow of aid to South Vietnam. U.S. aid to South Vietnam was halved in 1974 and cut by another third in 1975. The United States ambassador to South Vietnam, Graham Martin, warned the Senate Foreign Relations Committee that such cuts in military aid would "seriously tempt the North to gamble on an all-out military offensive." His warning was tragically prophetic.

The original plan of the North Vietnamese was to launch their final offensive in 1976. But then they stepped up their timetable. At the start of 1975 Phuoc Long province fell to the communists, the first province South Vietnam had lost completely since 1954. There was relatively little reaction in the United States. Hanoi decided to make larger attacks in 1975 in preparation for the final offensive in 1976. On March 11 Ban Me Thout fell, and on the same day the U.S. House of Representatives refused to fund a $300 million supplemental military aid package that President Ford had proposed. Together with the earlier cutback of aid, this had a devastating effect on the morale of the South Vietnamese, as well as denying them the means with which to defend themselves; they were desperately short of military supplies and dependent for them on the United States. It also gave a tremendous psychological boost to the North. The North threw all of its remaining troops into the battle. Thieu tried to regroup his undersupplied forces in more defensible perimeters, and the hastily executed maneuver turned into a rout. By the end of April it was all over. Saigon became Ho Chi Minh City.

Hanoi had suffered an overwhelming defeat when it launched a conventional attack on the South in 1972. Then the North Vietnamese had been stopped on the ground by the South Vietnamese, while bombing by our air force and mining by our navy crippled their efforts to resupply their forces in the South. B-52 strikes could have had a devastating effect on the large troop concentrations that Hanoi used in its final offensive, but in 1975 Hanoi did not have to reckon with our air and naval forces, and thanks to ample Soviet military aid they had overwhelming advantages in tanks and artillery over South Vietnam's ground forces. After North Vietnam's victory, General Dung, Hanoi's field commander in charge of the final offensive, remarked that "The reduction of U.S. aid made it impossible for the puppet troops to carry out their combat plans and build up their forces. . . . Thieu was then forced to fight a poor man's war. Enemy firepower had decreased by nearly 60 percent because of bomb and ammunition shortages. Its mobility was also reduced by half due to lack of aircraft, vehicles and fuel."

Our defeat in Vietnam can be blamed in part on the Soviets because they provided arms to Hanoi in violation of the peace agreement, giving the North an enormous advantage over the South in the final offensive in the spring of 1975. It can be blamed in part on the tactical and strategic mistakes made by President Thieu and his generals. It is grossly unfair to put the blame on South Vietnam's fighting men, the great majority of whom fought bravely and well against overwhelming odds. A major part of the blame must fall on the shoulders of those members of the Congress who were responsible for denying to the President, first me and then President Ford, the power to enforce the peace agreements, and for refusing to provide the military aid that the South Vietnamese needed in order to meet the North Vietnamese offensive on equal terms.

But Congress was in part the prisoner of events. The

leaders of the United States in the crucial years of the early
and mid-1960s failed to come up with a strategy that would
produce victory. Instead, first they undermined a strong regime, and then simply poured more and more U.S. troops
and matériel into South Vietnam in an ineffective effort to
shore up the weaker regimes that followed. They misled the
public by insisting we were winning the war and thereby
prepared the way for defeatism and demagoguery later on.
The American people could not be expected to continue indefinitely to support a war in which they were told victory
was around the corner, but which required greater and
greater effort without any obvious signs of improvement.

By following the strategy I initiated in 1969, we and the
South Vietnamese were able to win the war militarily by the
time of the Paris accords of January 27, 1973. The 550,000
American troops that were in Vietnam when I came into office in 1969 had been withdrawn and South Vietnam was
able to defend itself—if we supplied the arms the Paris accords allowed.

But the public had been so misinformed and misled by
unwise government actions and the shallow, inflammatory
treatment of events by the media that morale within the
United States collapsed just when the North was overwhelmingly defeated on the battlefield. We won a victory
after a long hard struggle, but then we threw it away. The
communists had grasped what strategic analyst Brian Crozier said is the central point of revolutionary war: "that it
is won or lost on the home front." The war-making capacity
of North Vietnam had been virtually destroyed by the
bombings in December of 1972, and we had the means to
make and enforce a just peace, a peace with honor. But we
were denied these means when Congress prohibited military
operations in or over Indochina and cut back drastically on
the aid South Vietnam needed to defend itself. In the final
analysis, a major part of the blame must be borne by those
who encouraged or participated in the fateful decisions that
got us into the war in the 1960s, and who then by their later

actions sabotaged our efforts to get us out in an acceptable way in the 1970s.

By inaction at the crucial moment, the United States undermined an ally and abandoned him to his fate. The effect on the millions of Cambodians, Laotians, and South Vietnamese who relied on us and have now paid the price of communist reprisals is bad enough. But the cost in terms of raising doubts among our allies as to America's reliability, and in terms of the encouragement it gives to our potential enemies to engage in aggression against our friends in other parts of the world, will be devastating for U.S. policy for decades to come.

The signals it sent around the world were pithily summed up by an Indonesian cabinet minister who has a Ph.D. from an American university. International analyst Pierre Rinfret reports that the minister told him just after the fall of Vietnam, "You Americans have lost your guts. You had the hell kicked out of you in Vietnam. You won't solve your energy problem. We'll make you pay and pay for oil, and you'll pay. You've lost your guts. Vietnam was your Waterloo." And for the Soviets, it meant that in Afghanistan, Ethiopia, and Angola détente became a one-way street.

In essence, the final climactic battle at the end of a struggle that had been going on for twenty-five years was decided in favor of the communists because when the chips were down, the Soviet Union stood by its allies and the United States failed to do so. As I stated in 1972, "All the power in the world lodged in the United States means nothing ... unless there is some assurance, some confidence, some trust that the United States will be credible, will be dependable."

One of the hidden costs of our abandonment of South Vietnam may well be the proliferation of nuclear weapons to the small nations faced with overwhelming hostile forces who used to trust the U.S. guarantee and no longer do. Those who protested against Vietnam to avoid a nuclear war may have helped to bring one closer.

In Indochina the consequences of the American defeat have been tragic and profound. The United States got out of the war, but the killing did not stop. In Cambodia, it accelerated massively when the Pol Pot regime launched the most brutal bloodbath in recent history.

Estimates of deaths have been staggering; so too has been the brutalization of the populace. Refugees reported that for "serious mistakes, such as stealing a banana . . . , you would be executed immediately." Other reports indicated that the Khmer Rouge had set aside a period of two days, once or twice a year, as the "mating period." It was only during this time that men and women were allowed to talk to each other, "except for talk about developing the country." As for those who violated this statute, a refugee reports, "I knew of about twenty young men and women caught flirting, who were executed." Complaining about food also became a capital crime in the brave new world the Khmer Rouge was building, one in which they boasted, "Our Communism will be better than in Russia or China, where there are still classes. . . ." So did joking; one refugee told of a person who was executed because he was "too jovial." At one point it was announced that holding hands was henceforth a capital crime.

In 1979 a new wave of disaster overcame Cambodia as Pol Pot's scorched-earth tactics and North Vietnam's starvation policy caught the Cambodian people in a vise of horror. The world watched aghast as the communist factions tore the remnants of the country to shreds. Some estimate that half of Cambodia's population may have perished already.

In South Vietnam the communists were more subtle in their methods, but they moved just as relentlessly to uproot the old order and replace it with their own. The thousands of boat people have served to remind us starkly of the terrors of life under that new order, especially since one fourth or more of the refugees, it is estimated, drowned before reaching shore.

In June 1979 U.N. Ambassador Andrew Young, speaking in Bonn, West Germany, stated that "There is no sense in trying to cast blame or condemn anyone" for the atrocities practiced by the new communist governments of Southeast Asia. He went on to suggest that these atrocities "automatically" could be traced to America's involvement in Vietnam. This is malevolent nonsense. Worse, it is self-serving nonsense. Many of those who wish to close their eyes to today's horrors in Southeast Asia also wish to close everyone else's eyes to their own sabotage of the American effort there, and the ghastly effects that sabotage has brought about. But like the blood on Lady Macbeth's hand, it is a permanent stain.

The U.S. failure to keep its commitments to South Vietnam led to national tragedies as the countries of Indochina were engulfed in a modern-day holocaust. But the effects on the leadership class of the United States may make the loss of the war in Vietnam an even greater international tragedy. Some think the "lessons" of Vietnam are: it is dangerous for the United States to have power because we may use it wrongly; we should avoid more Vietnams in the future by not getting involved when small nations, even those that are friends and allies, are threatened by communist aggression; the United States is on the "wrong side" of history in opposing communist revolutionary forces in Asia and Africa and Latin America; it is impossible to win wars against communist-supported guerrillas; we should look after ourselves and leave the responsibility for leadership of the free world to others.

These are the wrong lessons, and if our leadership class follows them, our country and the West will go down the road to destruction. These lessons confuse the abuse of power with its intelligent application.

Since our failure in Vietnam, Americans have been unduly gun-shy about using force, an inhibition the Soviets and their proxies have not shared. We have stood aside and let the Soviets go unopposed into Angola, Ethiopia, Afghanistan, and the Persian Gulf. They have not become stuck in a quagmire; unfortunately for us, they are expert practitioners in the arts of war and have used their power skillfully. Unless the United States shakes the false lessons of Vietnam and puts the "Vietnam syndrome" behind it, we will forfeit the security of our allies and eventually our own. This is the real lesson of Vietnam—not that we should abandon power, but that unless we learn to use it effectively to defend our interests, the tables of history will be turned against us and all we believe in.

More nuclear power in our arsenal would not have saved Vietnam. More U.S. conventional forces would not have saved Vietnam. Vietnam was lost, not because of a lack of power, but because of a failure of skill and determination at using power. These failures caused a breach in public trust and led to a collapse of our national will. Finally, the presidency was weakened by the restrictions Congress placed on the President's war-making powers and by the debilitating effects of the Watergate crisis. The South Vietnamese demonstrated in 1972 that they could effectively stop an invasion on the ground if they were adequately armed and provided with air support. Revolutionary wars cannot be fought and won by outside armies. But if those within a nation threatened by guerrillas are adequately armed, trained, and supplied, they can meet and defeat a guerrilla attack, provided they are fighting for their own independence and freedom. Under the Nixon Doctrine we should certainly do as much for those who are fighting to defend their independence as the Soviet Union does for those who are attempting to destroy it.

Vietnam did *not* prove that guerrilla wars are unwinnable or that "revolutionary" forces are invincible. Quite the contrary: our side won the guerrilla war, and it was winning the conventional war—until the United States pulled the rug out from under its ally by drastically cutting back supplies while the Soviets poured huge quantities of arms and ammunition into the arsenals of their ally. When that happened, Vietnam finally fell to the same kind of large-scale conventional assault we successfully repelled in Korea.

•   •   •

As William Colby has pointed out, "In an ironic asymmetry, the Communists initiated the war against Diem in the late 1950s as a people's war and the Americans and the Vietnamese initially responded to it as a conventional military one; in the end the Thieu government was fighting a successful people's war, but lost to a military assault. The Presidential Palace in Saigon was not entered by a barefoot guerrilla but by a North Vietnamese tank with an enormous cannon."

Revolutionary war will remain in the Soviets' repertoire, but now—partly as a result of Vietnam—they have been emboldened to a greater use of more direct means as well.

The Soviets started out in Vietnam by giving matériel to the communist guerrillas; they later graduated to supplying massive arms for North Vietnam's conventional invasion of the South. Then in 1975, having succeeded in Southeast Asia, they stepped aggression up a notch by shipping Cuban proxy troops across the Atlantic to achieve the conquest of Angola. On Christmas Eve in 1979 they escalated to a new level, sending the Red Army itself into Afghanistan, the "hinge of Asia's fate," to crush a rebellion against a communist government imposed by coup less than two years earlier. The next logical Soviet step is use of the Red Army against a friend or ally of the West.

Hanoi seems as determined as ever to fulfill its long-proclaimed ambition to conquer not only South Vietnam but all of Indochina. In Cambodia the Vietnamese are pressing what may be the final offensive against the Cambodians opposing them. In Laos they have dropped poison gas on hill tribesmen who oppose their rule. Thailand is feeling the heat of Vietnamese ambitions; its armed forces of 216,000 are outnumbered 5:1 by the North Vietnamese war machine. Vietnam's armed forces now approach the size of India's—the second most populous country in the world. This medium-sized country now has the fifth largest armed forces in the world, half the size of the American forces. If they complete the conquest of Indochina and then decide to move on to the rest of Southeast Asia, it will take an enormous effort to stop them.

Had the United States stayed the course and taken the action necessary to ensure adherence to the peace agreement of January 23, 1973, the Soviet leaders would have been less tempted to engage in their aggressive probes in other parts of the world. Our friends and allies would have less doubt about the reliability of American will as well as the effectiveness of American power. And most important, the American people could look back on ten years of sacrifice of men and money in Vietnam with pride rather than with apology and frustration, which lead so many to say, even where America's vital interests may be involved, "Do nothing—no more Vietnams."

6
The Awakening Giant

China? There lies a sleeping giant. Let him sleep! For when he wakes he will move the world.

—Napoleon

Seek truth from facts.

—Deng Xiaoping

China now is awakening, and it may soon move the world.

Exotic, mysterious, fascinating—China from time immemorial has tantalized the imagination of Western man. However, even the prescient Tocqueville, who predicted 150 years ago that the United States and Russia would emerge as two great contending world powers, could not have foreseen that the nation that potentially could decide the world balance of power in the last decades of the twentieth century, and that could become the most powerful nation on earth during the twenty-first century, would be China.

China is a nation of almost limitless possibilities that is only beginning to realize those possibilities. The seventeenth, eighteenth, nineteenth, and twentieth centuries all exist side by side in China. Peasants still stoop over the rice fields as they have for centuries, planting the shoots individually by hand. They walk barefoot along dusty paths with long wooden poles over their shoulders, baskets of produce slung from the poles. Many live in mud huts. In the central cities cars and trucks share crowded streets with rustic horse-drawn carriages, tractor carts, and bicycle carts, as well as with masses of pedestrians and swarms of bicycles. For all its huge population, China still has only limited military strength, primitive agriculture, and a largely preindustrial economy. But it has enormous natural resources, and some of the ablest people in the world—a fourth of all the people alive today. It could emerge during the twenty-first century as the strongest power on earth, and also one of the more advanced economically—if it successfully completes its transition to the modern world, and if it continues to move away from doctrinaire communist economic theories.

Which of its possible courses China takes might eventually determine whether the West survives.

Getting to know China is more than the work of a lifetime. The most a person can hope for is some understanding of some parts of the Chinese experience, and the more deeply one probes into that experience, the clearer it becomes that the mysteries are infinite. Teilhard de Chardin once advised, "Write about China before you have been there too long; later you would break your pen."

But if we can never know everything about China, we can learn something about it—particularly what we might reasonably expect in the way of Chinese behavior. China's present leaders are statesmen with a keen sense of the world who think in global terms. They also are communists. They also are Chinese. Since Mao's death they have seemed to grow less communist and more Chinese, less the prisoners of ideology and more pragmatic, less revolutionary and more traditional.

I have visited China three times, in 1972, 1976, and 1979. The first time, in 1972, Mao Zedong and Zhou Enlai were in power. The second time, in 1976, Zhou was dead; Mao and Hua Guofeng were in power. The third time, in 1979, Mao also was dead, and power was shared between Hua and Deng Xiaoping.

In China, as the leaders have changed, so also have the policies—whether temporarily or permanently remains to be seen. It could even be said that for China watchers today the key word is *change.* China is changing, and the changes in China, if they continue, may profoundly change the world.

As with Russia, we can only hope to understand present-day China if we know something about its past. Even the changes now taking place have roots in the past, and in some respects are a return to tradition. More than most countries, China is a product of its past, and its history is unique. Other nations come and go, other empires rise and fall, but China endures; China is forever.

China's civilization stretches back four thousand years—the oldest continuous civilization in the world. While Greek and Roman civilizations rose and fell, China's continued. While Europe was plunged into the Dark Ages, Chinese learning, science and philosophy flourished uninterrupted. China is the only large region of the world that has never been under Western rule. Even Japan, which never lost its independence, was run by General MacArthur in the years after World War II. China has repeatedly been invaded, but each time it has absorbed the invaders and eventually converted them. Over the centuries this has produced a sort of stoicism; in 1976 Hua Guofeng commented to me, "Let the Russians come in. They may get in a long way, but they will never get out."

China's past is distinguished by more than longevity, resiliency, and culture. Historically, the Chinese saw China as "the Middle Kingdom"—as the center of the world, the celestial empire, "all under Heaven." Other nations existed, but they were barbarian, of no consequence. The Chinese became aware of other civilizations, but these were too remote to be viewed as either threats or alternatives. To the Chinese, theirs was not *a* civilization, but *the* civilization. In 1793 the emperor Qian Long rebuffed a British trade mission by writing to King George III: "The Celestial Empire, ruling all within the four seas . . . does not value rare and precious things. . . . We have never valued ingenious articles, nor do we have the slightest need of your country's manufactures." As late as the nineteenth century, Chinese maps still showed a vast China at the center of the world, with a scattering of tiny islands—with names such as France, England, America—in the sea around it.

The Chinese empire lasted more than two thousand years, from its founding in 221 B.C. until its overthrow early in the twentieth century. At times, it was the largest empire in the world. Yet it never extended beyond China, except into border regions. There were no overseas outposts of empire. Greeks, Romans, and other architects of empire in the West set out in search of worlds to conquer; the emperors of China already ruled the "world," and their chief aim was to keep the barbarians out. In our own time, the Russians built the Berlin Wall to keep their subjects in; for more than two thousand years the Chinese maintained the Great Wall to keep invaders out. Beyond the Great Wall there is not enough rainfall to support agriculture; below it there is. To the north, nomadic tribes have always roamed, developing skills of horsemanship, raiding, and warfare. To the south, sedentary cities and civilizations with all their riches evolved. For all but the last 150 years of China's history the threat to Chinese civilization has always come from the north, from the nomadic barbarians who periodically swept in to conquer and plunder. As the Chinese look today at the new "barbarians" again threatening from the north, the specter invokes national memories so deeply rooted as to be almost instinctive.

For China, the nineteenth and twentieth centuries have been a time of shattering collision with the outside world, and of shattering change within China itself.

From China's standpoint, its early contacts with the West—and many of its later contacts as well—were both humiliating and disastrous, and served only to solidify hostility toward the "foreign devils," while intensifying a sense of cultural superiority. Some Westerners came to colonize; others came to convert; most came to exploit. The most demoralizing impact, however, was not economic or political, but was rather the affront to the dignity of the Chinese people. On my first visit to Hong Kong in 1953 I asked a very successful pro-British Chinese businessman how the people of Hong Kong would vote if they had a choice between independence and remaining a British colony. He replied that in spite of the fact that the Chinese living in Hong Kong were better off economically than those living under independent governments elsewhere in non-communist Asia, 95 percent would probably vote for independence. I asked why. He said that the British were certainly the most respected and most progressive of European colonizers, but that there was a common saying among Chinese throughout Asia that when the British set up a colony, they built three institutions in this order: first, a church; then a racetrack; then a club to which Orientals could not belong. In 1972, while escorting me to the airport, the hard-line Communist Party chairman of Shanghai pointed proudly to an immaculate children's playground. He said quietly that it had formerly been a golf course, and that the sign at the entrance read, "No dogs or Chinese allowed." Nothing more was said, or needed to be. On my last trip, in 1979, my host in China's third largest city repeatedly pointed out hospitals, schools, and other buildings that had once been part of a British, German, French, Dutch, or other European "concession," that Chinese had been allowed to enter only when invited by Europeans. To the Chinese, with their enormous pride, these slights were unforgivable.

Readers of American fiction associate China with "opium dens," and many probably imagine that the drugs that later ravaged so many young Americans were insidiously introduced from there. Hearing that Britain and China fought two "Opium Wars" in the mid-nineteenth century, an American today might suppose that these were righteous British efforts to stamp out the opium trade. In fact, opium was pressed on China, over vigorous Chinese objections, by British merchants; the Chinese tried to prohibit both its importation and its use. Britain went to war against China in part to compel the Chinese to accept the continued sale of opium. The Opium Wars were also pretexts to force China open to foreign trade and exploitation, and to wrest special

commercial and other privileges from China. Britain took
Hong Kong in the first Opium War, secured the designation
of five "treaty ports," and won rights of extraterritoriality
for its citizens in China; in the second Opium War, Britain
and France together forced more of China open to foreign
trade, and won more special privileges for Western nationals. These humiliations were followed by more territorial
grabs and establishments of foreign "spheres of influence" in
China, with Russia and Japan joining the Western nations
in the scramble.

The Chinese themselves were bitterly divided over how
to respond to the Western inroads, whether to reach back
to Chinese isolation or reach out to Western technology in
the hope of gaining sufficient strength to repel the foreigners. But even those who argued for adoption of Western
technology saw Western ways as a corrupting, unwelcome
influence. The fact that the Westerners came with greater
firepower, and therefore were able to impose their will on
China, hardly lessened the Chinese tendency to view them
as barbarians and devils. A Cantonese denunciation of the
British in 1841 read: "We note that you English barbarians
have formed the habits and developed the nature of wolves,
plundering and seizing things by force. . . . Except for your
ships being solid, your gunfire fierce, and your rockets powerful, what other abilities have you?"

Hatred of the foreigner exploded dramatically at the
turn of the century in the Boxer Rebellion. The "Boxers"
were a group who called themselves the "Fists of Righteous
Harmony," and who bitterly resented Western interference
with traditional Chinese ways. They saw the foreigners as
desecrators of holy places, and many believed that tall buildings had been put up by the "foreign devils" so that low-fly-
ing good spirits would be killed as they crashed into them;
they were sure that the rusty water that fell from railroad
tracks and telegraph lines when it rained was the blood of
good spirits who died on them. Religious fervor combined
with xenophobia. Roving bands of Boxers not only burned
and pillaged, but also killed Chinese converts to Christianity. In 1900 they swept into Peking, murdered the German

and Japanese ministers, and besieged the foreign legations. The Western powers moved in with overwhelming force, smashed the rebellion, and exacted even more concessions—as well as reparations—from the Chinese as punishment.

China was ripe for revolution in 1911 because it needed a revolution. It had been plagued too long by governments that could neither control the marauding brutalities of local warlords nor resist the encroachment and exploitation by foreigners. After years of struggle, the revolutionary forces led by Dr. Sun Yat-sen—a physician who received his early education in Hawaii—finally triumphed, and the empire that had lasted more than two thousand years was overthrown. But the victory of the revolution only ushered in a new time of turmoil.

Throughout the twentieth century China has been in upheaval. The revolutionaries of 1911 themselves had divergent aims. The new government was torn by rivalries, and was unable to establish its authority throughout China. After Sun Yat-sen's death in 1925 the faction led by Chiang Kai-shek and the one that eventually was led by Mao Zedong battled each other until Mao won final control of the mainland in 1949. Meanwhile, China fought a grueling war with Japan and suffered brutally under the Japanese invasion. Since 1949 China also has fought the United States in Korea, it has fought India, it has engaged in border warfare with the Soviet Union, and more recently it has fought its former client state of Vietnam. But more fundamentally, during much of the century China fought China. The long civil war was followed by one upheaval after another, as Mao purged first one faction and then another, launching his Great Leap Forward and his Cultural Revolution, "purifying" the party by eliminating first one group and then another—with millions dying in the process of that purification.

The rape of China by the Western powers in the nineteenth century left an indelible imprint, but so too did the struggles of the twentieth century.

Like family quarrels, civil wars are often the most bit-

terly fought of all. Yet again like family quarrels, they also
produce a certain ambivalence. Chinese on both sides of the
long struggle were still Chinese, with the same pride in China, the same feelings of Chinese nationalism, the same
shared heritage. Chiang and Mao both served under Sun
Yat-sen; Madame Chiang is the sister of Madame Sun, who
remained on the mainland and continues to be a revered figure in China. In the 1920s, Chiang was commander and
Zhou the political director of the Chinese military academy
at Whampoa. In my talks with the Chinese leaders, I found
that they had curiously mixed feelings toward Chiang. As
communists they hated him, but as Chinese they respected
and, grudgingly, even admired him. At my first meeting
with Mao in 1972, he made a sweeping gesture with his
hand and said, "Our common old friend Generalissimo
Chiang Kai-shek doesn't approve of this," adding: "He calls
us communist bandits." I asked Mao what he called Chiang
Kai-shek. Mao laughed; Zhou replied, "Generally speaking,
we call them 'Chiang Kai-shek's clique.' In the newspapers
sometimes we call him a bandit; he calls us bandits in turn.
Anyway, we abuse each other." Mao added, "Actually, the
history of our friendship with him is much longer than the
history of your friendship with him."

The leaders of China's communist revolution were
toughened by hardship, and driven by a zeal that often
verged on fanaticism. This should not be surprising. Setting
value judgments aside, the sheer magnitude of the task they
set for themselves required both toughness and zeal. Mao
sometimes identified himself with the first Emperor of Qin,
Qin Shihuang-di, who unified the warring states of China
into a single empire in 221 B.C. Even by the standards of
China's history, which, as the scholar O. Edmund Clubb has
put it, "yields to none in bloodshed," the brutality of the
Qin is legendary. Once, when an army of 400,000 surrendered to them, the entire 400,000 were massacred; to discipline the intellectuals of his day, Qin Shihuang-di ordered
460 scholars executed and buried in a mass grave. Mao himself, when China's population was smaller than it is now,
once dismissed the threat of nuclear war by commenting

that even if 300 million Chinese were killed, there would still be 300 million left.

When I first met Mao in 1972, he was enfeebled by age and ill health. But his mind was sharp, and there was no question that he was in command on the Chinese side. He spoke in broad terms of philosophy, of history, of the sweep of events; and yet also in peculiarly humble terms he spoke of his own limits. Once when I commented to him that his writings had "moved a nation and have changed the world," he replied self-deprecatingly, "I haven't been able to change it. I've only been able to change a few places in the vicinity of Peking." Before my visit André Malraux, who had known Mao for many years, commented to me that in Mao's view "the great leaders—Churchill, Gandhi, de Gaulle—were created by the kind of traumatic historical events that will not occur in the world anymore. In that sense he feels that he has no successors. I once asked him if he did not think of himself as the heir of the last great Chinese emperors of the sixteenth century. Mao said, 'But of course I am their heir.' Mr. President, you operate within a rational framework, but Mao does not. There is something of the sorcerer in him. He is a man inhabited by a vision, possessed by it."

The vision that possessed Mao convulsed China.

During the decades that followed Mao's victory on the mainland, three lines of thought were in more or less constant contention among the Chinese leadership. One, identified with Liu Shaoqi, was the classic, doctrinaire Marxist-Lennist-Stalinist line that looked to Moscow for leadership, example, and assistance. This was in the ascendancy in the early years. Another, identified today with Vice-Premier Deng Xiaoping, was essentially pragmatic, concerned with economic development and willing to compromise ideology and deal with the West. This is in the ascendancy now. The third, Mao's own, was rooted in the experience of the Long March and devoted to the ideal of constant struggle: revolution was an end in itself; whenever any group, including the Communist Party bureaucracy, got too entrenched or too comfortable, it was time to turn the country upside down. The people's communes, the Great Leap Forward, the Cultural Revolution, all were examples of Mao's determination to maintain the spirit of struggle and purify through purge, chaos, and dislocation; millions died in his drive to keep the "revolution" revolutionary.

The Sino-Soviet Split

The communist victory in China came only four years after the end of World War II, and it was aided by the Soviet Union. At first the new regime was firmly allied with the Soviet Union. But strains soon developed. The Soviets turned out to be unreliable allies; the Chinese government, being Chinese, was not long willing to concede Moscow unchallenged supremacy as leader of the communist world.

The Chinese-American rapprochement of 1972 may have been the most dramatic geopolitical event since World War II, but the most significant geopolitical event was the Sino-Soviet split that preceded it. This split made the later rapprochement with the United States possible. Together with continuing Soviet belligerence, it also made the rapprochement indispensable from both the Chinese and the American viewpoints.

Perhaps the split was inevitable, given the respective backgrounds of the two countries, their history of conflict, and their differing interests. But its inevitability was not apparent to most Americans, including myself, during the first decade of communist rule in China. The specter that haunted the world then was that of an aggressive, monolithic Sino-Soviet bloc, a new and menacing force on the world scene. The Chinese at that stage were even more implacably hostile toward the West than were the Soviets. Both Peking and Moscow supported North Korea's invasion of South Korea in 1950. But the Soviet Union provided only arms; thousands of Chinese were killed in action, including one of Mao's sons. As competition between the two communist giants developed, it was increasingly directed toward leadership of the communist world, with each accusing the other of deviation from "true" communist orthodoxy. Ultimately, one of the key forces that drove them apart was precisely the one—communism—that many of us had thought would hold them together. They could not both be number one, and neither was willing to be number two; in the rigidly hierarchical structure of world communism there was room for only one supreme authority. Russia was accustomed to being supreme in the communist world; China was accustomed to being supreme in its own world.

Exacerbating this conflict was a deep-rooted distrust and dislike between the two peoples themselves. Historically, the Chinese have despised the Russians, just as they have had contempt for the Indians. The Soviet leaders constantly denigrated the Chinese. Russian leaders as far back as Khrushchev privately warned their American counterparts against the Chinese disregard for human life—which, given the Soviet record, invites its own wry commentary. At our U.S.-Soviet summit meetings. Brezhnev repeatedly warned me against the Chinese threat, and described the Chinese leaders as brutal and barbaric in their treatment of their own people; he urged that "we Europeans" should unite, to contain the potential great threat from China. The Chinese, for their part, make clear in their private conversations that they consider the Russians crude, ruthless barbarians. On neither side are these sentiments the stuff of which lasting friendships are made.

Hua Guofeng told me of a conversation between Mao and Soviet Premier Kosygin in 1965, in which Mao told Kosygin that the debate between China and the Soviet Union would go on for ten thousand years. Kosygin protested, and as their conversation ended he asked Mao whether he had finally convinced him that ten thousand years was too long an estimate. Mao replied that Kosygin had indeed been persuasive, and that because of this he would knock off a thousand years—but that the debate would go on for at least nine thousand years.

The Sino-Soviet split developed in the late 1950s and early 1960s, barely a decade after Mao took power; by 1961 it was virtually complete. Among the contributing factors were Chinese disappointment at not getting more Soviet assistance in developing their nuclear capacity, and the abrupt withdrawal in 1960 of Soviet technicians from China, leaving many development projects uncompleted. Following this break, the ideological warfare between the two communist giants grew more intense, as did their rivalry on the international scene. China then was more hard-line than Russia in its confrontation with the West, and was vigorous in its support of "wars of national liberation." Still in the first flush of its communist power, China sought to expand communist power—Chinese style—everywhere that it could, and in doing so it followed Mao's dictum: "Every communist must grasp the truth: Political power grows out of the barrel of a gun."

At that point, the Sino-Soviet split made the Sino-Soviet bloc less menacing to the world, but it did not make China less menacing. That came later, as China began to change.

The U.S. and China

When *Air Force One*—or *The Spirit of '76*, as we then called it—landed at Peking's airport on February 21, 1972, I was keenly aware that the world would never again be the same. How it would change would depend heavily on the nature of our talks during the following week. But profound change was inevitable. The trip itself, and the calculated decisions on both sides to proceed with it, had already set that change in motion.

At the head of the waiting delegation was Zhou Enlai, his frail frame covered by a heavy overcoat. Years earlier, at the Geneva Conference in 1954, Zhou had been deeply offended when he extended his hand to John Foster Dulles at a public gathering and Dulles refused to shake it. This had been one of those small ceremonial slights that may seem justified, even necessary, at the time, but that can rankle for years afterward and even have substantial diplomatic consequences. I was determined that my first act on arriving in

China would be to undo the act of omission. As I came down the ramp, Zhou began to applaud. I returned the gesture, and then, as I reached the bottom step, I stretched out my hand to Zhou. When he took it, it was more than a handshake. We both knew that it marked a turning point in history.

Nearly five years earlier, in a 1967 article in the quarterly *Foreign Affairs,* I had written that "taking the long view, we simply cannot afford to leave China forever outside the family of nations, there to nurture its fantasies, cherish its hates and threaten its neighbors. There is no place on this small planet for a billion of its potentially most able people to live in angry isolation." But I also argued that for the short run we needed "a policy of firm restraint, of no reward, of a creative counterpressure designed to persuade Peking that its interests can be served only by accepting the basic rules of international civility," so that China could finally be pulled "back into the world community—but as a great and progressing nation, not as the epicenter of world revolution." The time when "the dialogue with mainland China can begin," I wrote, would be when the leaders in Peking were persuaded "to turn their energies inward rather than outward." One of my first acts as President was to direct that we explore privately the possibilities of a rapprochement wth China. This proceeded at first as a sort of slow ritual dance, but the steps rapidly gained momentum in 1971 until, on July 15, I made the surprise announcement that I would visit China in early 1972.

This opening to China represented a wrenching change for the United States, not to mention for me personally. We had supported the government in Taiwan for more than twenty years. They were staunch allies, and in a world where too many governments behaved irresponsibly, they had always played a constructive international role and conducted themselves with a high degree of responsibility. They were one of our major trading partners; beyond this, they were our friends. Taiwan's leaders, including Chiang, were also my personal friends. In our negotiations with China we refused to renounce our treaty commitment to Taiwan, and we stated clearly in the communiqué our firm position that the Taiwan question should be settled peacefully. But we knew that the entire shift in American policy was intensely painful to Taiwan, and this in turn was painful to us.

The opening to the United States also represented a wrenching change for China. For years the United States had been the number one enemy, the target of China's most vitriolic propaganda. The Chinese made this change because it was in their interest; because at that point they needed the United States, just as the United States needed China.

Both we and the Chinese approached that first opening toward each other with caution, uncertainty, even trepidation. Neither of us knew just what to expect, and both of us had been conditioned by years of hostility. Under Chiang's Nationalist rule, China was our ally in World War II, but Mao and Chiang had long been enemies. China then became our own bitter enemy after the communist conquest of the mainland in 1949. In the Korean War U.S. troops fought Chinese troops; in Vietnam China supplied and aided our North Vietnamese enemy.

For generations, American attitudes toward China had alternated between romantic attachment and dread. It used to be common for Americans to refer to the Chinese as "the yellow peril." Theodore Roosevelt used the term, as did Albert Beveridge; in our own time, Americans as distinguished as Herbert Hoover and Douglas MacArthur referred to the Chinese that way in conversations with me. So too, for that matter, did Leonid Brezhnev. Hoover, who spent years in China as a mining engineer, spoke of the Chinese to me in the mid-1960s as being "bloodthirsty" not only toward foreigners, but also toward their own people. To many, the sheer numbers of China's people were menacing, and exclusionary immigration laws were enacted to keep them out.

In part, this reflected the fact that China was distant, mysterious, *different,* and that even in our own cities the "Chinatowns" were exotic enclaves. In part, it reflected racist condescension. In part, it reflected the reality that even as Chinese civilization flourished, for most of the Chinese people life was harsh and cruel, and had been for centuries—so that in China, where people were plentiful, and where famine or flood often took those that the warlords did not, it appeared to Western eyes that life was cheap.

Yet Americans and Chinese, when they get to know one another, usually do get along extraordinarily well. The U.S. record with regard to China in the pre-Mao period, while mixed, is better than that of most Western powers. Though the United States did to some extent exploit the advantages that European countries seized in China, the United States never established concessions of its own. American missionaries in China were sometimes resented, but many did fine humanitarian work. Large numbers of Chinese studied in the United States. The hostilities that existed between China and the United States in the 1949–1972 period were the result of politics, not of personality; they stemmed from a clash of national interests, not a clash of national cultures. Therefore, as policies changed and interests shifted, hostility could more readily be replaced by respect, cordiality, even friendship.

To a considerable extent, this happened in my own dealings with China's leaders. We began our talks with no illusions about our philosophical differences, and with no effort to conceal or paper them over. But we were cordial. We were respectful. And, in exploring together both our common interests and our divergent interests, we developed a high degree of trust and a considerable personal rapport. When I returned to China in 1976 and 1979 as a private citizen—though as a guest of the Chinese government—I found myself genuinely looking forward to renewing old acquaintances among the Chinese leaders, as well as to making new ones; for their part, my Chinese hosts were unfailingly gracious and warmly hospitable. In cementing a new relationship these things are important. Great nations act on the basis of interest, not sentiment, but good personal relationships can do a great deal toward making differences manageable and ties stronger.

• • •

China turned toward the United States because it saw itself surrounded by potentially hostile forces. To the north—the direction from which, historically, the "barbarian" invasions had come—stood the Soviet Union, no longer comradely, with huge concentrations of troops stationed menacingly along its border with China. To the south was India. China had had a border clash with India in 1962 and more recently had seen the ease with which, with Soviet aid, India dismembered China's ally, Pakistan. Despite the contempt that the Chinese felt toward the Indians, with India on the way toward adding a nuclear capability to its Soviet-supplied arsenal, India's potential had to give China pause.

To the northeast, China saw Japan. Japan was already the third largest economic power in the world, and though it did not have nuclear weapons, it had the industrial base to develop them if it ever chose to do so. Within recent memory Japan had invaded and occupied China. Though the Chinese did not now fear Japan, they had enormous respect for its potential. As for the United States, the Chinese knew that we had no territorial designs on them—which they could not say about the Soviets. Though our system was opposed to theirs, our interests were opposed to those of the Soviet Union, the neighbor that posed the most serious and most immediate threat to China itself. So the Chinese had reason to want better relations with us.

What we had to show the Chinese was that we could be counted on: that we had a clear enough view of our own interests, and a sufficient will to defend those interests, to be a reliable friend. Further, the Chinese had to be persuaded that as a society, the United States had the strength and the stamina to be reliable over the long term.

For China, the new relationship with the United States represented a "great leap forward" into the world of independent great-power politics. It meant accommodating positions that cut directly against the grain of revolutionary communist ideology. For a regime as dogmatic as Mao's had been, this was a tremendous change. Revolutionary

Chinese ideology told China to oppose the U.S.-Japanese defense treaty, and to oppose the U.S. presence in Asia. Yet China's interests dictated otherwise, and China's leaders recognized this—privately if not publicly. When it came to the choice, interests prevailed. Even on the intensely emotional issue of Taiwan, China, while not retreating from its own position, had to accept the fact that we would not accede to the demand that we abandon our commitment to Taiwan.

In my conversations with Hua in 1976 I stressed that there are times when a great nation must choose between ideology and survival. This, essentially, is what China did in responding to our initiatives and embarking on the new relationship.

Less than a decade has passed since that opening to China in 1972 and already our relations have been transformed—and so has China's approach to the world. Mao had the authority to make the turn toward the United States; his successors have had the wisdom to make use of it, and to change Mao's policies so that the opportunities it created can be used.

China's Future

Singapore's Prime Minister Lee Kuan Yew commented to me in 1967 that "Mao is painting on a mosaic. Once Mao dies and the rains come, what he has painted will wash away."

Now Mao has died, and the rains are coming. How much of what he painted will be washed away is not yet clear. When I was in Peking in 1979 heroic pictures of Mao still dominated the cityscape, but the huge official posters carrying his revolutionary slogans were being quietly taken down.

Certainly Mao's revolutionary ideas have made a massive impression. The Communist Party remains China's organizing force. Premier Hua still prefaces many of his comments with, "As Chairman Mao said. . ." Mao remains a god. But China is changing, and the more it changes, the more the ancient mosaic of China itself emerges.

Mao had a strong sense of history, and also a strong sense of his own mortality. When we first met in 1972 it was clear that he could see the end of his own life approaching. He wanted to be sure that the directions he had set China on would last, and he also wanted China to be secure enough so that they could last; so he took the revolutionary step of reaching out to the United States and fundamentally altering the balance of power in the world. One of the ironies of history is that this daring move has, since Mao's death, both enhanced China's security and accelerated its turn away from Mao's own internal policies.

Mao made a revolution. He successfully won and consolidated power over the most populous nation on earth, and he used that power to bring about a series of social upheavals that cost millions of lives and transformed one of the world's oldest civilizations. But China was not totally transformed. One thing that must powerfully impress any visitor today, in fact, is the extent to which it is still China. Mao did "change a few places in the vicinity of Peking," and he did change much else. But millions of peasants still till the land much as they have for centuries, and the educated Chinese mind remains the same subtle, sophisticated instrument it has been for centuries. Just as China absorbed invading barbarians until they became Chinese, so there is good reason to believe that the communist revolution, too, will be absorbed into the body of China. In fact, the process has already begun. The question is how far and how fast it will go, and how many reversals there will be along the way.

Among the great questions of the last decades of the twentieth century and most of the twenty-first will be how long the Sino-Soviet split lasts, how permanent the new U.S.-China relationship will be, how far along the paths of pragmatism the Chinese will go in order to develop their immense economic potential, what sort of world view the Chinese leaders will hold and what sort of world role they will play. Related to these is the question of how long they will continue to go along with the existence of an independent Taiwan. The answers to these will depend as much on Washington as on Peking.

The Chinese know that we have no territorial designs on them. They respect and want our technological and financial assistance. They realize that we are the only power capable of checking the designs of the Soviet Union. Some argue that economic interdependence is enough to hold us together. This is not true. Above all, the Chinese leaders want China to survive. To them, this means maintaining an effective counter to the Soviet threat. If, with our assistance, they become stronger economically, this will help them to develop on their own the military strength to defend their interests. But this is a long-term prospect. In the next twenty years they will not have that capability, and they are going to look closely at the United States to see whether we have the power and leadership with the will to use it, not just in our own defense but also in defense of our friends and allies in the event that they become targets of Soviet aggression.

If the Chinese lose confidence in the United States in this respect, no amount of trade or financial aid will keep the U.S.-Chinese relationship viable. China then will have to revert to its historical pattern of accommodating its enemies and hoping to absorb them.

Economically, China today is in a rush to catch up. The task is one to stagger the imagination. Western experience has no parallel: a billion people, most of them living almost as their ancestors did centuries ago, with only a primitive infrastructure of transportation and communication; a hostile superpower on their northern border, and a heavily armed client of that hostile superpower on their southern border; a population left distrustful, cynical, and weary by decades of Maoist revolutionary upheaval.

Yet with all the problems, there is reason for the Chinese to be optimistic about their long-term future. China has enormous natural resources, including vast reserves of coal, oil, and other minerals. But more important, the Chinese have shown themselves exceptionally able people. Wherever the overseas Chinese have settled, they have been high achievers. Hong Kong and Singapore are essentially Chinese cities. Taiwan has staged a remarkable economic performance. Its per capita income is three times that of the mainland, and with less than 2 percent of the mainland's population its exports are 20 percent more. Throughout the Far East the influence and success of Chinese merchants, bankers, and businessmen is legendary. Only in mainland China itself have the Chinese failed economically, and the reasons for that failure have largely been political and ideological.

Japan offers one key to what China might achieve economically in the next century. The populations of both countries are highly intelligent and exceptionally gifted; both have ancient civilizations that combine great delicacy and grace with a fierce martial tradition; both are highly disciplined and imbued with a strong "work ethic." But in their initial encounters with the West, they responded very differently. Japan reached out to absorb Western technology; China resisted Westernization, fearing its corrupting influence. As a result, Japan was already a major industrial power before World War II, while China was still a vast, primitive agricultural preserve. But China is now beginning to do what Japan did much earlier. Japan is already on the verge of becoming the world's second greatest industrial power—and China has nine times the population of Japan, and an incomparably greater wealth of natural resources. It will take generations to bring the vastness of China fully into the modern world; even as parts of its economy advance, perhaps rapidly, others will remain far behind. But the potential is there, if the Chinese show the skill and pragmatism to develop it, and the patience to do so in an orderly way.

One reason for Japan's stunning economic success is that it never hobbled itself with communist dogma or a socialist system. But China now appears to be trying to free itself from at least some of those constraints. If this trend continues, the economic ceiling for the Chinese could be virtually unlimited; if China reverts to a stultifying Marxist ideology, it will have no chance to realize its potential.

Today's leaders have seen the mistakes of the Maoist era, and they seem determined not to repeat them. Mao died in 1976. His body was hardly cold before the new leaders moved against the "Gang of Four," which included Mao's widow, Jhiang Qing. The "Gang of Four" were dogmatists, fierce keepers of the flame of ideological purity. While not assailing Mao personally, today's Chinese leaders speak freely of the last decade of Mao's rule as a time of disastrous mistakes. The fact that they do not defend the recent past but rather emphasize the need to recover from its mistakes is the best evidence that they *can* recover. Whereas politics and ideology were the previous rulers' touchstone for virtually everything, the present rulers' assessments are far more pragmatic; they deal less in abstract theory, more in concrete observation. Deng's motto—"Seek truth from facts"—might seem elemental to a Westerner, but it is a radical departure from recent Chinese dogmatism. At the moment, moderation seems to be winning out over revolution.

Today's top Chinese leaders are self-confident, sophisticated, realistic. Hua Guofeng is a tough-minded pragmatist. He speaks softly but firmly, with a quiet assurance. Deng Xiaoping is more volatile, more dynamic; he gives the appearance of never being assailed by doubts. It seems a reasonable guess that in charting China's changes, Deng is the more aggressive innovator, while Hua quietly works to ensure that the changes are not too abrupt or too hastily considered. But both give evidence of having been liberated by Mao's death and the subsequent eclipse of the "Gang of Four," which traded on Mao's name and authority in enforcing a doctrinaire ideological purity.

Precisely what form the Chinese economy and society will take in the years ahead is impossible to predict. The Chinese are extremely subtle, which is one reason Westerners sometimes find them "inscrutable." Subtlety is one of the arts of both diplomacy and statecraft, and it often provides ways of resolving, or at least skirting, otherwise intractable differences. Already, the Chinese are showing great flexibility in their efforts to attract foreign investment and to structure joint ventures with Western companies. The officials handling this—who include business leaders of the prerevolutionary era—show a sophisticated understanding of the capitalist system and of international finance. More capitalist-style incentives are being introduced into China's own economic system. In fact, the willingness to experiment is one of the most striking features of China today, and it seems to be rooted in confidence rather than insecurity. China's leaders give the impression of being sufficiently sure of themselves and their power to be able to try new ways, and to learn from experience what works and what does not. Westerners complain that the major problem they face in trying to do business with China is the infuriating layers of Chinese bureaucracy they have to contend with. This should not be surprising, since muscle-bound bureaucracy is a common characteristic of communist and socialist regimes; ironically, it was also a major weakness of the governments of Imperial China.

The Taiwan issue continues to be one for which no easy or immediate answer appears on the horizon. The United States cannot and should not back away from its firm declaration—made in the Shanghai communiqué in 1972—against the use of force to resolve the problem. While China will predictably continue to press for bringing Taiwan under the central government in Peking, self-interest will strongly argue against any resort to military action. Despite an enormous population advantage, crossing a hundred miles of open sea and making an amphibious landing on Taiwan would be a formidable task for the mainland Chinese. To commit the forces required would weaken their capability to defend their long border with the Soviet Union and jeopardize the new American relation. It would not make sense to impose the mainland's primitive economic system on Taiwan, which has one of the most prosperous economies in Asia.

If the economic and political system of the People's Republic of China continues to change, it is possible to imagine ways in which the mainland and Taiwan might—not soon, but eventually—agree on some form of reunification.

As the differences between the two systems narrow, the bridge that has to be built between them will become shorter. For now, it is enough that the issue be postponed, with neither side accepting the status quo but with both sides living with it. Different conditions will eventually create a different situation, and it may well be one more conducive to a peaceful and voluntary accommodation between the two sides.

China's policies are dictated by what its leaders see as China's national interests. It is abundantly clear, both from talking with China's leaders and from the record of their actions, that they are far less bound today in foreign policy by abstract considerations of ideology than are most communist governments, or than they themselves were a few years ago. They do see the world—and they do discuss the world—in highly sophisticated geopolitical terms; more than the leaders of most nations, they now have a truly global view. Their chief concern is with the impact of policies on China. But they measure this impact both directly and indirectly. What weakens the Soviet lessens the threat to China; thus they support a strong NATO. Vietnam is a Soviet ally, and invades Cambodia; thus they make common cause even with the despicable Pol Pot regime, and launch their own punitive invasion of Vietnam to "teach Vietnam a lesson." The United States is the chief counterweight to the Soviet Union; thus they make overtures to the United States, and press us to strengthen our defenses.

How other countries organize their internal affairs is of infinitely less concern to the Chinese than the way they conduct their external affairs. In this respect, China has more of a traditional great-power attitude than have most of the democratic nations, and certainly far more than the U.S. State Department's division of human rights.

Looking to the future, as China develops its economy, builds its military strength, and becomes, as it may, the world's most powerful nation, the key question will be how it uses that power. The answer to this will depend, in effect, on whether it becomes more Chinese than communist, or more communist than Chinese. If for any reason the Chinese revert to their policies of the 1950s and 1960s, when they were bent on extending communist control throughout Asia and the world, they will be an enormous threat to the peace of the world and to the survival of the West. But if they continue on their present path of becoming more traditionally Chinese, then history will be on the side of optimism. Unlike Russia, whose whole history has been one of relentless outward expansion, China has traditionally been the self-sufficient, self-contained "Middle Kingdom," which had neither need of nor interest in foreign conquests. Which course China chooses may depend as much on the United States as on China. If we make it clearly in China's interest to be, in this respect, more Chinese than communist, then we will have served China's interest, our own interest, and the world's.

The unrealistic euphoria that resulted from the normalization of relations between the United States and the P.R.C., followed by Vice Premier Deng's extremely effective visit to the United States, has begun to wear off. American businessmen who flocked to Peking expecting to make a "fast buck" selling products to a billion Chinese have been disillusioned. China is short on foreign exchange. The Chinese bureaucracy moves at a snail's pace, and as Americans discovered in the Soviet Union, it is exceedingly difficult for a private firm to do business with a communist government. After a brief burst of "liberalization," the regime cracked down on expressions of dissent that threatened to get out of hand. The Soviet move into Afghanistan brought predictably sharp criticism from Peking, but Chinese leaders have made it clear in other areas that they reserve the right to pursue whatever foreign policy they believe is in their interests, rather than always following America's lead.

China has always been a mystery. The nagging question now is, how deep is the conviction that led to Peking's move toward the West abroad and away from doctrinaire Marxism at home?

It must be remembered that for five years during the 1920s Lenin's New Economic Policy encouraged and welcomed American capital and know-how. Once these had served their purpose, the Kremlin decided to go it alone and the Americans and other "capitalists" were sent home. This could happen in China unless Chinese leaders remain convinced that foreign investment is indispensable to their progress and security. This in turn will depend on whether their new friends from the capitalist world avoid the temptation to put a quick profit ahead of long-term investments that will make China's future progress dependent on continued cooperation with the West.

The future direction of Chinese foreign policy is also unpredictable, except in one respect—China will do whatever its leaders believe will serve its interests. The Chinese like Americans better than they like Russians. At present the Russians threaten them and we do not. As long as they believe we have the strength and the will to hold the ring against the Russians, Sino-American friendship will be the linchpin of Chinese foreign policy. If our conduct in Asia or in any other part of the world leads them to conclude that we are not a credible friend or ally, they will, in the interest of their own survival, seek an accommodation with the Soviet Union despite their territorial, ideological, and personal quarrels with the Russian leaders. The role the Chinese play in the future is as much in our hands as theirs.

In dealing with the Chinese, however, we only gain their contempt by appearing too eager to please them. They need us at least as much as we need them—and probably more so because they are weaker and because our common potential adversary is much closer to them than to us.

When I last visited China in 1979 the focus of its leaders' foreign policy concerns was on security, not expansion; they were interested in internal development, not foreign adventure. But they were deeply, intensely concerned with the Soviet threat and with whether the U.S. response to it would be adequate. The remarkably sophisticated global view they displayed was not that of the empire builder seeking worlds to conquer, but rather that of the world statesman seeking to maintain a global balance of power so that other nations as well as his own can be secure. If this view prevails into the next century, then China may indeed be "a great and progressing nation" and a powerful force for peace in the world. If we show that we are strong and reliable partners in maintaining security, there will be a better chance that that view will prevail.

7
Military Power

> No one in any country has slept less well in their beds because this knowledge [of the atomic bomb] and the method and the raw materials to apply it, are at present largely retained in American hands. I do not believe we should all have slept so soundly had the positions been reversed and if some communist or neo Fascist State monopolized for the time being these dread agencies.
>
> —*Winston Churchill, 1946*

> It might be to our advantage to allow U.S. superiority to fade away.... [If we had weapons superiority], I suspect we would occasionally use it as a way of throwing our weight around in some very risky ways.
>
> —*Victor Utgoff,*
> *National Security Council Staff, 1978*

In 1959 defense analyst Herman Kahn published a book, *On Thermonuclear War*, which received an extremely critical review in *Scientific American*. Kahn protested, and asked the editors to carry his reply, which he had entitled, "Thinking about the Unthinkable." Dennis Flanagan, editor of the journal, rejected the request, and replied to Kahn that he did not "think there is much point in thinking about the unthinkable; surely it is more profitable to think about the thinkable." Flanagan continued, "Nuclear war is unthinkable. I should prefer to devote my thoughts to how nuclear war can be prevented."

Perhaps the editor's preference was justified two decades ago, when the United States enjoyed overwhelming strategic nuclear superiority over the U.S.S.R. Perhaps then the American people could afford to live in blissful ignorance of the dread facts of superpower conflict and a potential nuclear exchange. Such a conflict, such an exchange, could reasonably be judged to lie outside the arena of the possible.

But the "unthinkable" has become not only thinkable, but something about which we must think. The loss of American strategic superiority requires that we understand the probabilities and consequences of a possible nuclear exchange. Further, we must understand the concept of strategic balance, which could prevent such an exchange.

Nuclear superiority was very useful to us when we had it. It will be mortally dangerous for us if we allow the Russians to get it and keep it.

The fact is that a strategic advantage for the United States and the West reduces the danger of war or defeat without war. A strategic advantage for the Soviet Union increases the danger of war or defeat of the West without war. With the spectre of strategic inferiority staring us in the face, we must act now to restore the balance of power so that we can deter Soviet aggression and retain freedom for ourselves and all free nations. And I must emphasize *now*, for the strategic balance is rapidly becoming, in the words of the chairman of the Joint Chiefs, "acutely dangerous," while our options for dealing with limited local Soviet aggression have already been reduced in most parts of the world to near zero.

The United States and the U.S.S.R. are the only two superpowers. In nuclear strength the Soviets are rapidly moving into a position of clear-cut superiority. That superiority is particularly threatening because of two deeply disturbing facts: First, it will be attained before the United States can do anything about it given present programs and funding. Second, it will be characterized by dangerous vulnerabilities in our deterrent forces and by a gross disparity favoring the Soviet Union in the ability to fight, win, and recover from a nuclear war. That means that the Soviet leaders will be able to "deter our deterrent," and threaten us more credibly with nuclear escalation than we can threaten them. At the same time, the Soviets have an enormous advantage over us in conventional ground forces and in theater nuclear forces—those designed for use within a specific region such as Europe or the Far East. Their geographical proximity to many of the prospective areas of confrontation—in Europe, the Middle East, Asia, and Africa—gives them an additional advantage. The United States has traditionally been superior in sea power, but the Soviet Union is rapidly closing the gap there as well.

These facts paint an ominous picture for the West.

Nations tend to favor those instruments they excel at, and the Soviets favor military force as an instrument of policy. Not only Russians but communists in general have consistently stressed the overwhelming importance of military might. Mao Zedong declared long ago that "political power grows out of the barrel of a gun." He also commented that "politics is war without bloodshed; war is politics with bloodshed." Khrushchev defined his policy as "Only force—only the disorientation of the enemy. We can't say aloud that we are carrying out our policy from a position of strength, but that's the way it must be."

In considering the military balance between East and West it is important to remember that the two sides arm for different purposes. The Soviets have been engaged in a determined arms race because they want strategic superiority over the United States, and every year their effort has continued to increase. Our effort has not kept pace. It has, in fact, declined. In the 1960s the United States deliberately adopted the McNamara doctrine of self-restraint, which was intended to induce a reciprocal Soviet restraint and lead to arms limitation agreements that would benefit both sides. Instead, the Soviets have taken advantage of it to further their own drive for superiority. The Soviets have raced, and the United States has not; the result has been a rapid change in strategic balance virtually unprecedented in history. Not only have the efforts of the two sides differed, but so have their views of the nature of the competition. In the West arms are maintained as a necessity of defense; in the East arms are maintained to achieve the expansion of Soviet power. So the "arms race" is not a race between two contenders with the same goal. It is now more nearly akin to the race between hunter and hunted. If the hunted wins, both live; if the hunter wins, only one lives.

This imbalance of intentions affects the balance of power. It gives the Soviets the aggressor's edge. The aggressor chooses the time and place of combat, whether in the jungles of Vietnam, a strike into central Europe, or an intercontinental nuclear exchange. We have to offset this aggressor's edge by effective deterrence, whether by the superiority of our forces or by the skill and determination with which we use them. To create an equilibrium in the conflict—to preserve our safety—we need either more power to offset their inherent advantage or clear evidence that our will to use our power to defend our interests is equal to theirs. This is the context in which we should consider the strategic balance.

For a quarter of a century American nuclear superiority kept the peace. Now that superiority is gone, and if present trends continue, the Soviets will have strategic nuclear superiority by the mid-eighties.

What is superiority? In our hands it was the safety margin that ensured that the Soviets would not risk a nuclear exchange in pursuing their goal of world domination. In Soviet hands it becomes the margin that enables them to proceed with local aggression without expecting a massive nuclear response. It also enables them to contemplate the final act in their drive toward world domination: a first strike against U.S. military targets that eliminates our capacity to respond with a counterstrike that would effectively neutralize their second-strike capability. This would then leave them in position to deliver the ultimate ultimatum: Surrender or be obliterated.

In 1972 SALT I, with the Jackson Amendment, established parity—in other words, equivalence—as U.S. policy. Parity is an uneasy condition; because of the aggressor's edge, as long as we live in a situation of parity, we live with risk. But parity is infinitely better than inferiority, and parity is something about which negotiators can negotiate. Mutually beneficial arms restraints between the two major powers can only be agreed upon on a basis of parity. Strategic parity is a situation we can live safely with—but only if it is true parity and only if we also have sufficient strength in theater nuclear weapons, if we have strong conventional forces, if we show will and skill in the use of our power, and if we successfully link things the Soviets want in the military and economic spheres with things we want in the political sphere, most particularly with curbs on Soviet adventuring. While superiority would be preferable, with those conditions, strategic parity is acceptable, but only with those conditions.

By parity, I do not mean some arbitrary and minimum "assured destruction" capability. Parity does not mean accepting wide divergencies between U.S. and Soviet capabilities. It means that our strategic forces must be *sufficient* for the tasks and purposes we set, and also that they must not be inferior to the forces of the Soviet Union. Parity means that the Soviets have *no* advantages that are not offset by U.S. advantages; no capabilities that they could expect to exploit against us either militarily or politically.

In military terms, this means that the Soviet Union must not have the capability to win a war against the United States. In political terms, it means that the Soviet leaders should not *think* that in a confrontation they would have a strategic nuclear advantage over the United States—and neither should the leaders of any other nation believe that the Soviets would have that advantage.

It is essential that the United States have, and be seen to have, at least as much flexibility and sophistication in our forces as the Soviets have in theirs—in addition to having simply as much weight, or as many total warheads, or as many missile launchers. In order to deal effectively with the

Soviet strategic nuclear forces of the future, we will require retaliatory forces in sufficient numbers and with sufficient types of weapons to survive a well-executed surprise attack on them, and then to carry out their assigned retaliatory mission in a way that will control escalation, rather than cause it. That means they must be able to penetrate Soviet defenses and destroy military targets in the U.S.S.R., with enough survivable reserve forces to constitute an adequate remaining deterrent.

With parity so defined, the Russians are not likely to launch a first strike on the United States, and they are not likely to engage in the sort of overt aggression that would be calculated to trigger a strategic nuclear response. Strategic parity gives us a good chance of keeping the nuclear genie in the bottle, and ensuring both sides that nuclear weapons will be used politically and diplomatically rather than militarily. But it does not create a risk-free environment; it does not relieve us of the necessity to maintain strong conventional and theater nuclear forces, able to preserve a local balance of power in each threatened area; it does not unburden us of the need to use power, or to deliver a credible threat to use it if challenged. The aggressor's edge must be neutralized by the power and will of those threatened by aggressors.

Parity at the strategic nuclear level makes it even more imperative that we substantially increase our general-purpose forces and improve our regional capabilities. In the past U.S. nuclear superiority compensated for regional imbalances in conventional forces. When the United States had nuclear superiority Soviet leaders had to be concerned that hostilities anywhere in the world might lead to the use of American strategic power against the Soviet Union. But strategic parity magnifies the significance of any regional Soviet superiority in conventional and tactical nuclear forces, thus increasing the threat to the security of that region.

Within an overall framework of strategic parity, the usual play and counterplay of force and diplomacy goes forward on other levels. Parity can be sufficient if we are strong enough in other areas—theater nuclear forces, conventional forces, the strength and cohesion of our alliances, the will and skill of our leaders—to check Soviet adventuring without holding a strategic advantage. If we fail in these other areas, then parity will no longer be sufficient; then we will have to resume an all-out arms race, and go all out to win. Otherwise we will lose.

From U.S. Nuclear Superiority to Parity

In the period immediately after World War II the United States engaged in a process of hasty unilateral disarmament. From 1945 to 1947 we reduced our conventional forces from 14.5 million to 1.8 million. This policy was justified in part because of our monopoly on atomic weapons.

We learned in Korea that atomic weapons are not enough to deter war waged with conventional weapons. The Korean War, and what it signified about the global designs of the Soviet Union, shocked the United States into building up both our conventional and our nuclear forces and establishing a global system of bases surrounding the Soviet Union. The Soviets still maintained far larger land armies, and in 1949 they had exploded their own atomic bomb. They lacked an intercontinental delivery system, however, and the vigorous United States effort enabled us to maintain unquestioned superiority in nuclear forces and the capability of projecting our power to any area of the world where our interests were affected. Until the early 1970s no one questioned that the United States was the most powerful nation in the world. The existence of this U.S. power deterred overt aggression and forced the communists to go under borders rather than over them.

Because of this superiority the United States was able to deter Soviet intervention in the Berlin crisis in 1948-1949, in the Mideast war in 1956, and in Lebanon in 1958, where local U.S. naval superiority also played a critical role.

In the Cuban missile crisis of 1962, the 15-to-1 U.S. advantage over the Soviet Union in nuclear weapons enabled Kennedy to face down Khrushchev.

By that time a Soviet nuclear buildup was under way; it was sharply accelerated after Cuba. Vasili Kuznetsov, the Soviet First Deputy Minister of Foreign Affairs, told his American host, John McCloy, "You Americans will never be able to do this to us again."

In spite of the threat of Soviet nuclear buildup, our own programs leveled off. As recently described by a former CIA analyst, "The U.S. approach under Secretary of Defense McNamara was one of unilateral restraint."

In 1965 McNamara gave this justification for restraint: "The Soviets have decided that they have lost the quantitative race.... There is no indication that the Soviets are seeking to develop a strategic nuclear force as large as ours." This was a massive, tragic miscalculation. It was compounded by what Dr. Fred C. Iklé, the former head of the U.S. Arms Control and Disarmament Agency, has described as a "massive intelligence failure." For eleven years during the sixties and early seventies the annual United States intelligence forecast grossly underestimated the number of offensive missiles the Soviet Union would deploy, as well as their entire strategic nuclear force effort.

The increase of Soviet military power vis-à-vis that of the United States is illustrated by a comparison of defense expenditures. The CIA has estimated Soviet defense expenditures over the last decade at 11 to 12 percent of GNP; other authoritative estimates place the Soviet defense effort in the 1970s in the 14–15 percent range, with reputable estimates of planned spending in 1980 reaching 18 percent of GNP. These higher figures are doubly sobering because of the past CIA tendency to underestimate rather than overestimate. By contrast, the United States defense budget declined from 9 percent of GNP in 1968 to 5 percent in 1978. Over the last ten years U.S. expenditures for defense in constant dollars (discounted for inflation) have fallen by a third while the Soviet Union has continued its steady increase year after year. Between 1973 and 1978 it has been estimated that the Soviet Union spent nearly $100 billion more than the United States on arms procurement and construction, and an additional $40 billion more than we did on arms research and development. The problem is not only the greatest peacetime military buildup since Hitler's in the 1930s, but also a massive U.S. build-down. As Secretary Harold Brown put it in the 1980 Defense Department Report:

> As our defense budgets have risen, the Soviets have increased their defense budget. As our defense budgets have gone down, their defense budgets have increased again. As U.S. forces in Western Europe declined during the latter part of the 60's, Soviet deployments in Eastern Europe expanded.
>
> As U.S. theater nuclear forces stabilized, Soviet peripheral attack and theater nuclear forces increased. As the U.S. Navy went down in numbers, the Soviet Navy went up.... It is worth noting, moreover, that the growth in their defense effort has correlated quite closely with the overall growth of the Soviet economy, while the U.S. military effort has steadily shrunk as a fraction of our economy.

It used to be fashionable to claim that the Soviets only wanted to catch up with us. But in 1971 they caught up with the United States in total expenditures, and over the past half decade they have outspent us by three times in strategic nuclear forces and by at least 75 percent in general-purpose forces. Since personnel and operations costs account for only about 30 percent of the Soviet military budget, compared to 60 percent for the United States, that differential is magnified when it comes to military hardware.

Looking at conventional armaments only, we now find that they have more major surface combat ships than the United States has, and twice the number of attack submarines, as well as a fleet of 70 potent cruise missile submarines—of which we have none. They recently launched a nuclear submarine that goes faster (40 knots) and dives deeper (more than 2000 feet) than anything the United States has. They also have more than twice as many men under arms as we have, and four times the number of artillery pieces. We produce 40 heavy and medium tanks a month; they produce 50 a week. In terms of strategic nuclear forces, the CIA estimated in 1978 that Soviet expenditures, exclusive of research, development, testing, and evaluation, were three times those of the United States, and had been two and a half times those of the United States for the past ten years.

Since the mid-1960s, when McNamara initiated his policy of unilateral restraint, we have not been seriously competitive with the Soviets in the development of strategic forces. Since that time seven new types of Soviet intercontinental ballistic missiles (ICBMs) have been put into service: three prior to the first strategic arms limitation treaty (SALT) and four since 1972, under the SALT I Interim Agreement. And yet a fifth generation of new Soviet ICBMs is under development. Also since the mid-1960s the Soviets have deployed four new types of submarine-launched ballistic missiles (SLBMs), three of them since 1972, three new types of strategic submarines, and the new long-range supersonic Backfire bomber, which is similar in many respects to the canceled American B-1, and three-fourths its weight. In the United States we have put only one new ICBM and two new SLBM strategic weapon systems into production since the mid-1960s: the Minuteman III ICBM, the Poseidon missile, and the Trident I missile, which is only now coming on line. Otherwise, we have stayed with the B-52 bombers of the 1950s and early 1960s, some of which are older than the pilots who fly them, and with ICBMs that reflect the design and deployment decisions of the early 1960s. We have canceled the B-1 bomber, deferred deployment of the new MX ICBM by at least three years, and slowed production of our Trident submarines.

From a position of unquestioned superiority in the early 1960s we have declined to what is at best a position of parity, and we face decisive Soviet superiority by the mid-1980s. This requires us to rethink the fundamental assumptions that lie behind the American notion of deterrence. We are now forced to think the unthinkable.

From Parity to Soviet Nuclear Superiority

For the United States and the West Mayday is the international distress signal. For the Soviet Union it is the day of annual celebration of the international communist movement. Mayday 1985 could well see these two concepts blend into one.

Paul Nitze has pointed out with regard to the strategic balance:

> Over the past 15 years it would not have profited either side to attack first. It would have required the use of more ICBMs by the attacking side than the attack could have destroyed. By the early 1980s that situation will have changed. By that time, the Soviet Union will be in a position to destroy 90 percent of our ICBMs with an expenditure of a fifth to a third of its ICBMs. Even if one assumes the survival of most of our bombers on alert, for sufficient time to launch an immediate response, and of our submarines at sea, for a much longer time, the residue at our command after a Soviet initial counterforce attack would be strategically outmatched by the Soviet Union's retained war-making capability.

In a speech at the U.S. Naval Academy Defense Secretary Brown pointed out that the Soviets have been embarked for more than a decade on a policy of building forces for a preemptive attack on U.S. intercontinental ballistic missiles. The Secretary added that by the early 1980s the Soviet Union would possess sufficient numbers of the new SS-18 and SS-19 heavy missiles to assure the destruction of the vast majority of this country's land-based Minuteman ICBMs in a surgically precise surprise attack.

By 1985, it has been estimated that with or without SALT II, the Soviets will have an advantage in their ICBM force of over 6–1 in countermilitary capability, of nearly 5–1 in throw weight, over 3–1 in numbers of reentry vehicles, over 5–1 in deliverable megatonnage, and equality in overall accuracy. The net result will be a major disparity in our first-strike capabilities, with the Soviet Union far ahead. The damage to our strategic stability and to our security will be a self-inflicted wound. By 1982, it is now conceded, our ICBM force will be thoroughly vulnerable to a first strike; our aging B-52 force (of which only 20 percent is kept loaded and on ground alert) will be vulnerable on the ground and en route to target; our strategic warning and communications system will be susceptible to attack and disruption; and Soviet antisubmarine warfare capabilities may not permit smug confidence in the survivability over time of our submarines at sea, approximately 50 percent of the force. In any case, the specter of an overwhelming Soviet strategic reserve—at least ten times our own after a first strike—would reduce the threat of retaliation from surviving U.S. forces. And Soviet active and passive defenses would reduce their impact if they were used.

As Henry Kissinger testified before the Senate Foreign Relations Committee on July 31, 1979:

> Rarely in history has a nation so passively accepted such a radical change in the military balance. If we are to remedy it, we must first recognize the fact that we have placed ourselves at a significant disadvantage voluntarily.

At the beginning of the 1960s the United States and the Soviet Union selected two fundamentally different approaches to nuclear deterrence. The United States attempted to separate deterrence and defense. But the Soviets refused to do so and oriented their planning toward the ability to fight, survive, and win a nuclear war.

In American thinking, strategic nuclear superiority and the attempt to limit damage in the event of nuclear war were replaced by theories of deterrence that emphasized the inevitability of massive civilian destruction. These theories were linked with an arms control-oriented belief that nuclear weapons beyond a necessary minimum lacked political or military utility. A theory of limitations emerged that restricted the role of nuclear weapons essentially to "deterrence only"—the threat of retaliatory punishment against an aggressor's society. This so-called assured-destruction retaliatory capability came to be measured largely in terms of population fatalities deemed sufficient to deter an initial *all-out* attack. Assured destruction did not apply to limited attacks, which was one of its major drawbacks.

It was then a short step to the assumption that Soviet leaders saw deterrence in the same way, or at least would with some help from the United States. An equally naïve belief that U.S. strategic efforts were the engine that drove Soviet responses led to the conviction that U.S. restraint would be reciprocated by the Soviet Union. If, according to this theory, U.S. action produced Soviet reaction, then American inaction was the necessary condition for reciprocal inaction. If the United States limited its nuclear capabilities essentially to the requirements of assured destruction, and if the Soviet Union were given the opportunity to match this capability, a stable situation of mutual deterrence would be created and this would encourage arms limitation agreements. For this to work, however, the Soviets would have to restrict their own strategic programs and objectives to assured destruction and refrain both from seeking superiority and from challenging the assured destruction capabilities of the United States. They did not. Instead, they used the opportunity to forge ahead toward nuclear superiority and the achievement of their own nuclear war-fighting objectives.

The Soviets reject the argument that both sides in a nuclear exchange would be losers. They believe that even nuclear wars can be fought for political objectives, that with careful preparation one side can win, and that the destruction that would be suffered by that side can be meaningfully limited. They believe that such a nuclear war-fighting, damage-limiting capability is not only the best deterrent and the best strategy in the event of war, but also the key to the effective political use of nuclear force. If a nuclear power has not prepared itself to survive a nuclear war, it cannot rationally or credibly threaten the use of nuclear weapons against another nuclear power, for this could be an act of national suicide.

• • •

There are three profound faults with the concept of mutual assured destruction (MAD). The first, of course, is that the Soviets have refused to go along with it, which alone destroys the concept. The second is that it is strategically and politically wrong. It leaves the United States with no reasonable options if deterrence should fail, and it supports no rational political or military objectives in the event of war. A rational deterrent cannot be based on irrational responses. What future American President, for example, would risk New York, Philadelphia, Chicago, and Washington to save Berlin? The third fault is that it is morally wrong. The United States should never place itself in a position where its strategy implies that the deliberate slaughter of civilians is a proper objective. Deterrence should not be based on such a threat. These two basic objections, the strategic and the moral, are linked. The Chinese strategist Sun Tzu wrote in the fifth century B.C.: "What is of supreme importance in war is to attack the enemy's strategy. . . . Next best is to disrupt his alliances. . . . The next best is to attack his army. . . . The worst policy is to attack cities. Attack cities only when there is no alternative."

While my administration sought a stable situation of mutual deterrence and parity between the United States and the Soviet Union, we wished at the same time to move away from the reliance on assured destruction that had come to dominate U.S. thinking and planning. We wished to restore the strategic and political considerations that had been lost in MAD thinking. In 1969 we established four criteria for strategic sufficiency, which in essence stipulated that an assured destruction capability was necessary but not sufficient. In addition, we required forces that could assure stability in a crisis, that did not allow the Soviets to attain nuclear superiority over the United States, and that could be used to limit damage in the event of an attack.

I tried in another way to move our thinking somewhat away from assured destruction. In my 1970 foreign policy message to Congress I asked the rhetorical question: Should a President in the event of nuclear attack "be left with the single option of ordering the mass destruction of enemy civilians, in the face of the certainty that it would be followed by the mass slaughter of Americans?"

In my 1971 foreign policy message I provided an unequivocal answer: "I must not be—and my successors must not be—limited to the indiscriminate mass destruction of enemy civilians as the sole possible response to challenges. This is especially so when that response involves the likelihood of triggering nuclear attacks on our own population. It would be inconsistent with the political meaning of sufficiency to base our force planning solely on some finite—and theoretical—capacity to inflict casualties presumed to be unacceptable to the other side." I emphasized that we needed in our strategic forces the flexibility and options to enable us to select and carry out the appropriate response without having to resort to mass destruction.

The need for options becomes even more imperative as the Soviets imminently approach the capacity to destroy U.S. counterforce capability. When they reach that goal, a U.S. President, under the MAD doctrine, will have only one option to exercise in response to a Soviet first strike—mass suicide. This "deterrent" would be ineffective and immoral. Consequently, it would lack all credibility and U.S. foreign policy would be hostage to Soviet aggression.

For years the prevailing U.S. concept has been that nuclear war could not and would not bring any meaningful form of victory, either military or political. The Soviet concept, however, has been that nuclear war—even though it would mean a disaster of immense proportions—cannot and must not be deprived of strategic meaning. However awful, nuclear war in their view must be survivable and some kind of meaningful victory attainable.

As Harvard historian Richard Pipes observes:

> The prevalent U.S. doctrine holds that an all-out war between countries in possession of sizeable nuclear arsenals would be so destructive as to leave no winner; thus resort to arms has ceased to represent a rational policy for the leaders of such countries vis-à-vis one an-

other. . . . Soviet doctrine, by contrast, emphatically asserts that while an all-out nuclear war would indeed prove extremely destructive to both parties, its outcome would not be mutual suicide: the country better prepared for it and in possession of a superior strategy could win and emerge a viable society.

Pipes puts the issue in historical perspective:

A country that since 1914 has lost, as a result of two world wars, a civil war, famine, and various "purges," perhaps up to 60 million citizens, must define "unacceptable damage" differently from the United States which has known no famines or purges, and whose deaths from all the wars waged since 1775 are estimated at 650,000—fewer casualties than Russia suffered in the 900-day siege of Leningrad in World War II alone.

The rise in Soviet power has given urgency to the differences between the two superpowers' doctrines in this crucial area. Strategic victory and survival in a possible nuclear war have become less credible than ever to Americans as the strategic power of the U.S.S.R. has grown. For the Soviets, in contrast, the growth of their strategic arms and civil defense programs has made their doctrine of victory even more plausible than it was before. Soviet leaders now seem to believe that under favorable circumstances the Soviet Union could win a war with the United States in which strategic nuclear weapons were used. And within a few short years, the circumstances will be favorable for them.

Most observers believe that it is unlikely that the Soviets will launch a massive preemptive strike against our retaliatory forces. But we must recognize that in addition to having the *ability* to do just that, they will also have the ability to do less: for example, to obliterate the American combat brigades stationed in West Germany. Their capacity to neutralize our retaliatory forces gives increased credibility to their lesser options. This means that they might reasonably believe they could launch a limited nuclear strike on our forces in Europe without the fear they have had since the establishment of NATO that the United States could and would retaliate with a strategic nuclear attack on the Soviet Union.

American strategic superiority after World War II was critically useful to us and to the free world because of our fundamentally defensive posture. It was the center of gravity of our political weight. It was the trump card enabling us to use our conventional forces to achieve political ends. It put severe constraints on the Soviets, and forced them to be careful not to provoke us where they thought we might react. If we allow the Soviets to gain and retain strategic superiority, we must face the fact that they would be greatly emboldened to employ power outside the communist bloc. If the Soviet Union holds strategic nuclear superiority and thus dominates the threat of escalation, Soviet leaders and others as well may conclude that the United States will be little inclined to oppose Soviet expansionist moves with military force, and will thus be less and less resolute in confrontations with the Soviet Union.

The greatest danger in a period of Soviet nuclear superiority is defeat without war. A voice from abroad, the London *Economist*, speaks clearly to this point:

> By the early 1980s, the growing number of increasingly accurate warheads Russia can pack into its huge missiles will put it in a position of being able to destroy virtually all of America's land-based missiles in a single half-hour cataclysm, while still keeping quite a lot of its own missiles in reserve, ready for a second blow. . . . If that Russian first strike did happen, an American counterattack against the Soviet missile system would have to depend mainly on the aircraft-carried cruise missiles permitted under SALT II which would take ten hours to trundle toward their targets—and even then would destroy not much more than half of the Soviet launching silos.
>
> This is not "parity." It is often said, quite correctly, that even with these advantages the Russians would probably not press the button for the unimaginable ghastliness of a nuclear exchange. This misses the point of nuclear mathematics. The point is that the Russians would

not have to. If they know that even a theoretical exchange of Soviet first strike and American counter-strike would leave them with more surviving missiles, which would then hold America's cities hostage, they would know that the American President would know it too; and that he would be paralyzed by his knowledge as the grizzly game of bluff and counter-bluff moved closer to the button-pressing point. This is the political reality behind the apparently abstract calculations of who-would-have-more-missiles-left.

In the Russians' favorite game of chess the queen plays a crucial role even though she may not be used. On the chessboard of international politics the queen of their chess set, nuclear weapons, can play a decisive role without ever being used.

Sir Robert Thompson puts it brutally well:

> When World War III is discussed most people think of it in terms of a nuclear exchange between Russia and China or between Russia and the United States, either of which would drag us all in, but it is quite pointless to think in terms of winning the war by that means. . . . The thesis, therefore, which I wish to propose is that we have been in World War III for the past 25 years and that the long-range Soviet goal is to win it without a nuclear exchange. This requires that eventually there should be a strategic surrender by the United States, brought about either politically and psychologically by a loss of will and purpose or politically and militarily by maneuvering the United States into a vulnerable and untenable global situation, or a bit of both.

In the 1962 Cuban missile crisis Kennedy was able to face down Khrushchev because of our decisive strategic superiority, but by the mid-1980s the positions of Kennedy and Khrushchev could be reversed. We would be doing the bluffing, and they would be calling our hand.

In political terms, as Stalin put it, nuclear weapons are things that can be used to "frighten people with weak nerves." And it is this dimension of will, nerve, and perceived will that has grown in importance as the Soviet nu clear arsenal has overtaken our own. Nuclear coercion, even more perhaps than nuclear war, is the real danger today, and it is heightened by the wide differences between the Soviets and ourselves regarding nuclear doctrine. These differences flow inevitably from the different historical and cultural experiences of the two superpowers and they mean one thing: the assumption that the strategic concepts of Russia and America are similar, which guides much of the arms control community in this country, is dead wrong.

Arms Control

When I took office in 1969 the previous administration had been devoted for some time to the idea of strategic arms limitations with the Soviet Union, and for two years had been actively seeking Soviet agreement to SALT. American strategic arms policies during that period had been SALT oriented or influenced. The message of these was that the United States was willing to forgo strategic superiority in return for a SALT-agreed mutual deterrent relationship based on parity and mutual assured destruction (MAD). This approach had the effect of inviting the Soviet Union to catch up with the United States in overall strategic capability. Unfortunately, by 1969 it was clear that Soviet forces were being developed more extensively and more rapidly than anticipated, and with characteristics that did not conform to the requirements of MAD. In particular, there was growing evidence of a future Soviet threat to American land-based deterrent forces. It was for that reason that I decided in March 1969 to reorient the Sentinel ABM program, with its emphasis on light area defense, to a new program, Safeguard, that emphasized defense of those threatened deterrent forces.

We also continued the SALT negotiations initiated by the Johnson administration—in part because we hoped to reach long-term equitable limitation agreements that would provide greater strategic stability with fewer arms. Congress and the country were clearly not receptive to costly new strategic force programs, as demonstrated by the fact that the Senate approved the Safeguard ABM system by a margin of only one vote, and it took the heaviest pressure we could muster to manage even that. We needed to buy time, and also to test Soviet intentions concerning arms limitations. If acceptable limitations could not be achieved, and if the Soviets meanwhile continued their strategic buildup, we would have the evidence that might persuade Congress to support the strategic programs we would then need. We did hope that the Soviet Union would accept truly stabilizing arms agreements. We also hoped that SALT would prepare the way for an era of improved relations in which competition would be supplemented by international cooperation and confrontation supplanted by negotiation.

Early American proposals designed to stabilize the strategic situation—to freeze the central strategic offensive systems, to establish equal ceilings on them, and to reduce them—were rejected by the Soviet Union. At the same time, Soviet strategic force levels continued to rise. By 1971 our more ambitious SALT goals had to be abandoned, replaced by the simple objective of securing Soviet agreement to offensive limitations that would halt the continuing buildup of Soviet launchers. The Soviet objective was clearly to continue that launcher construction until planned programs were completed and to limit the U.S. ABM to as low levels as possible. The Soviets were interested in curtailing the U.S. ABM, for the general reason that this was an area in which we had technological superiority, and for the specific reason that the ABM would interfere with their counterforce doctrine, since its primary purpose was defense of Minuteman.

The United States took the position that our ABM requirements were determined by the extent of the offensive threat to Minuteman; if that threat could be reduced, so could our defensive requirements. That was the principle of defense-offense linkage. In a broader sense, we were more concerned about the continued growth of Soviet offensive capabilities. Therefore, we could not agree to limit ABM without offensive force limitations. The Soviets insisted on ABM limitations only. Because of the Soviet buildup, we were unable to achieve offensive limitations consistent with the levels of defense established. But we did eventually succeed in getting an interim five-year agreement limiting offensive arms coupled with the ABM treaty.

We were not completely satisfied with that offensive force agreement. It allowed the Soviets higher levels than previously deemed acceptable, and higher than those permitted the United States. But this simply reflected the realities of the situation at that time, and we intended that the offensive agreement would last no more than five years. To emphasize this, the United States added to the treaty a formal declaration that stated, "If an agreement providing for more complete strategic offensive arms limitations were not achieved within five years, U.S. supreme interests could be jeopardized. Should that occur, it would constitute a basis for withdrawal from the ABM Treaty."

During that five years we believed that Soviet advantages would be offset by U.S. advantages, particularly in technology, and that vigorous U.S. research and development and force modernization programs would both preserve that situation and induce the Soviets to be receptive to an equitable follow-on agreement. We hoped that the SALT I agreement would thereby promote a better SALT II agreement, and also buy us time. We also hoped that it would have some moderating effect on the Soviet buildup.

SALT I itself did not freeze us into an inferior position. On the contrary, my administration welcomed and endorsed the Jackson Amendment, which required a reinvigorated American strategic effort, with aggressive modernization programs, as a condition for ratification of SALT I. It also stipulated that any future agreement should be based strictly on equality.

We moved to redress the strategic imbalance by pushing programs in all areas of the strategic triad—the MX on land, the Trident on the sea, and the B-1 in the air. None of these programs was inhibited by the agreement.

The B-1 bomber was slated to complement our aging B-52 bombers, which were designed and deployed in the 1950s and whose projected service life was to last until the 1980s.

The B-1 was intended to be able to penetrate the most sophisticated Soviet air defenses of the 1970s, and would have forced the Soviets to divert tens of billions of dollars to radically new air defense systems for the 1980s and 1990s, a diversion that could only have come out of money now programmed for more threatening offensive strategic systems aimed at the United States. The Carter administration's cancellation of the B-1 in the summer of 1977 may have been one of the greatest strategic blunders this nation has ever made.

The Trident submarine was designed to complement our Poseidon/Polaris submarine force of forty-one vessels, and eventually to replace many of the older boats. A Trident will carry twenty-four long-range missiles loaded with ten warheads each. SALT II, incidentally, would limit Trident I to seven warheads. The Trident's missiles will exceed in range, payload, and accuracy any of our present submarine-launched weapons and represent an increase to a new order of magnitude in deterrent effectiveness and invulnerability.

Similarly, the new proposed MX land-based intercontinental ballistic missile, when deployed, would provide a substantial improvement in overall power, weight, and accuracy compared with our present force of Minuteman missiles. In addition, the MX was intended to be deployed in a relatively invulnerable way, by being moved around from point to point. This would complicate the Soviets' strike plans, greatly strengthening the invulnerability of America's deterrent forces.

We also began to fund the development of cruise missile weapons, to be deployed from air, sea, or ground launchers. While it is a valuable weapon, the cruise missile is not a panacea for all our defense needs. If optimistic projections prove correct, we may have a very large technological lead over the Soviets in this form of weaponry, but advocates of the cruise missile as a substitute for heavier, more effective, and much swifter weapons should ponder the rapid deterioration of the lead we once held in MIRVing capabilities—that is, the ability to put several independently targeted warheads on the tip of a single missile. Also, while we still have no cruise missiles, the Soviets already have thousands of them deployed.

Now the B-1 bomber has been canceled, deployment of the MX missile has been delayed by at least three years, the Trident production rate has been slowed (the first boat will not put to sea until 1981), and cruise missile development has encountered unforeseen problems. The backbone of our strategic deterrent force is still the land-based Minuteman III. By comparison, the warheads on the Soviet SS-17 are four to eight times as powerful, those on the SS-19 six to twelve times as powerful, and those on the SS-18—the Soviets' supermissile—sixteen to forty times as powerful as those on the Minuteman III.

Soviet development of MIRVing technology, together with the tremendous lifting power of their huge missiles compared to the smaller size and weight of ours, means that they can mount many more warheads of much more power on each of their missiles than we can on each of ours. The SALT agreements do not limit warheads; they only limit missile launchers or airplanes. We must therefore face the grim reality that these developments have fundamentally altered the strategic equation in favor of the Soviets.

When the SALT II negotiations began early in 1973, our objective was to redress the inequalities that had been accepted by necessity in SALT I, and particularly to obtain reductions in the massive 4–1 throw weight advantage that had been permitted the Soviets. Our concern was that the Soviets would be able to convert their throw weight by the middle 1980s into a disarming first-strike option against our land-based ICBMs, our submarines in port, and our bombers on the ground. In such a situation the United States would have no response available except for the completely illogical and suicidal response of attacking Soviet cities with our small remaining force, inviting a massive, certain Soviet retaliation upon our own cities.

The Soviet leadership stonewalled us in Moscow in June of 1974. They refused to consider limitations on missile throw weight or reasonable levels of ICBM warheads. It was clear they put much political value on a first-strike capability against our land-based ICBM force. In Vladivostok in November 1974 President Ford encountered the same resistance, for the same reasons, and shifted to the less ambitious goal of negotiating equal aggregate numbers of strategic launchers, with sublimits on multiple-warhead-armed launchers. The only way in which SALT II could have meaningfully stemmed the arms race—by limiting throw weights—was dashed by Soviet intransigence and the lack of American bargaining muscle. We simply did not have the programs to offer as counters to bargain against the massive Soviet buildup. We still do not.

By the time of the Vladivostok negotiations, the strategic situation was rapidly changing, and so were American SALT expectations. Soviet momentum was increasing rather than moderating. In some cases, such as the substitution of the heavy SS-17 and SS-19 ICBMs for the light SS-11s, Soviet force modernization exploited loopholes in the SALT I agreement contrary to our understanding of that agreement. Increasingly, their overall strategic capabilities were reflecting a drive for superiority and a determination to achieve a strategic nuclear war-fighting capability that contrasted sharply with American views of deterrence. It was clear that a dangerous strategic balance was evolving and that SALT would not change that trend. The United States had to take more effective unilateral steps if it intended to avert a major imbalance in the early-to-mid-1980s. The Vladivostok limits were acceptable because they did not limit our ability to deal with the threat and because the United States then intended to go through with the programs that would do so. If arms control cannot limit and reduce the threat, it must not limit our ability to deal with it, directly or indirectly. By the time of Vladivostok the United States was determined that SALT, if it failed to do the first, at least would not do the latter.

The Carter administration tried to revive SALT with a new comprehensive proposal of March 1977, which, if successful, would have achieved some of the limits on Soviet throw weight that we had sought in 1974. The Soviets rejected the Carter proposal out of hand, and the administration quickly abandoned the effort and turned back to the Vladivostok guidelines. Unwisely, however, the administration allowed the Vladivostok framework to be expanded in ways favorable to the Soviet Union. As SALT II congressional testimony has shown, during the next two years the Carter administration gave in to the Soviet position on nearly every important point. It also abandoned or delayed those programs that would have made the strategic environment of the early-to-mid-1980s safer for the United States and more conducive to SALT agreements. Abandoned were the B-1 bomber, Minuteman III production, early deployment of the MX missile as well as the most promising rebasing mode for ICBMs, on-schedule deployment of Trident, timely and unrestricted deployment of cruise missiles, and the neutron warhead. Ironically, had the administration not abandoned or delayed those programs, it would not have encountered the opposition to SALT II that it did, despite the major flaws in the agreement.

On the basis of the record it is clear that the United States and the U.S.S.R. have diametrically opposed goals in strategic nuclear arms control negotiations. The United States seeks to reduce the danger of war, or of defeat without war; the damage to be done should war actually come; and the cost of armaments. Negotiating balanced limitations on strategic nuclear arms is a means toward these ends.

The Soviets do not seek equality. They believe strategic nuclear war might come, though they do not seek it, and they are perfectly willing to spend enormous sums of money year after year to prepare to win it. They favor arms control that will limit the United States where we are ahead, but which will not limit the Soviets either where they are ahead or where they are behind and need to catch up.

The U.S. goal during the Nixon and Ford administrations was to attempt to build a structure of peace with a negotiated equivalency in strategic nuclear arms as its cornerstone, and with sufficient strength in the other areas of national power as a part of its foundation. America has abandoned that goal, and with or without further SALT agreements the United States faces Soviet superiority by 1985, possibly sooner. This is dangerously destabilizing to the superpower relationship. One of the original premises of the SALT process was that the two sides would establish and codify strategic stability. This we have failed to do because we have not kept up with the Soviets by doing what we were allowed to do under SALT I.

Strategic nuclear arms control agreements are not an end in themselves. Just as arms are required for a purpose, so must arms control be pursued for a purpose. The Soviets arm to expand; we arm to thwart that ambition. Arms control will serve our purposes only if it achieves what some have called "crisis stability" between the two superpowers, while holding down the levels of strategic nuclear arms.

Paul Nitze has described crisis stability as "a situation where, in a crisis threatening war, there would be no significant advantage to the side striking first, preempting, or launching from under indications of attack." In effect, this means that our strategic forces must have no vulnerabilities that the Soviets could exploit by a first strike; our forces must always be able to ride out even a massive surprise attack and retaliate in a variety of ways, and still have enough left to strike again if necessary, or to preclude any Soviet postexchange advantage.

Six indispensable conditions must be met before we make any further strategic arms agreements.

1. We must establish a strong position to negotiate from, and we must bear in mind that it is better to have no agreement than to have a bad agreement. The way to avoid a bad agreement is to assure that the strategic situation is favorable to the United States during negotiation, at the time of agreement, and throughout the duration of the agreement. Arms control agreements tend to reflect the reality of the two sides' respective strength. If we want good agreements, we must establish the reality from which they

can emerge. Agreements against a background of Soviet strategic advantage will only reflect that advantage; they will not change it.

2. Any agreement we make with the Soviet Union must not inhibit us from assisting our NATO allies to develop the strength they need to help us deter Soviet use of theater nuclear weapons.

3. Our dedication to strategic arms limitations must not leave the United States, in case of attack or threat of attack on one of our allies or friends—or on our strategic defense system—with the sole option of killing millions of Russian civilians. This position would be clear inferiority.

President Carter has stated that one Poseidon submarine has the capability of taking out most of the Soviet cities in the event of a Soviet preemptive strike that destroyed most of our land-based missiles. This claim is not only wrong factually; it is incredible. Since the Soviets would then have the capacity to retaliate by obliterating every city in the United States, it is like the threat of a man who says, "Do as I say or I'll blow out my brains all over your new suit."

We must maintain sufficient land-based and accurate forces to ensure an effective second strike, not merely against the cities and population of the U.S.S.R., but also against its military targets, particularly its ICBM silos with "reload" capacity. Only through this capacity can deterrence be preserved.

4. Any SALT agreement must be strictly verifiable by national means without the cooperation of the Soviet Union.

5. Arms control must never be pursued as an end in itself, in isolation from other goals. There must be linkage between arms control and Soviet behavior in areas where they are engaging in activities that are antagonistic to our interests. Control of arms cannot be separated from the threats that require us to maintain arms. If war comes, it will be primarily because of failure to resolve political differences, combined with failure of the United States to maintain forces to dissuade aggressors from challenging our interests.

6. The SALT process must not inhibit the United

States from going forward with strategic programs that are (a) allowed under the terms of an agreement, and (b) important for the achievement of a responsible American strategic posture. We can be sure the Soviets will do everything allowed that they consider will give them superiority. We cannot deploy, use, or employ for political effect or as bargaining chips missiles we were allowed to build but did not. If the United States unilaterally makes a concession in the hope of inducing concessions on their side, the Soviets take full advantage of this stupidity and push ahead with their programs. Paul Nitze reports:

> Senator Tower asked [Soviet] academician Shchukin . . . what the Soviet side would do to reciprocate for our cancellation of the B-1. Mr. Shchukin replied, "You misunderstand us. We are not pacifists nor are we philanthropists." I am sure Mr. Shchukin had in mind a third point but was too polite to make it. "Nor are we fools."

We have been engaged in SALT for a decade and have practiced strategic arms restraint longer than we have had SALT agreements. The benefits originally expected have not materialized. In fact, our strategic situation has steadily deteriorated. Clearly, our attention now should not be on SALT, but on identifying and remedying the weaknesses in our strategic posture as rapidly as possible.

The demonstration of American will and capability to deny the Soviet leaders the strategic superiority they seek will have a more restraining influence on those leaders in the long run than a SALT agreement or anything else. It could convince them to reduce their ambitious strategic aims because the costs and uncertainties of pursuing them would be prohibitive. Consequently, taking resolute action to deny superiority to the Soviets is not only necessary to our own future security, it may also in the long run be the best means to meaningful mutual arms limitation agreements.

The question confronting us now is: What can the United States do to prevent strategic vulnerability and inferiority in the immediate future? We now have few strategic programs that will have any effect before the late 1980s.

There are some things we can do that would at least ease the situation until longer-range solutions are possible. There also are several strategic force options available for the mid-range, including accelerating some of the present long-range programs. Many of these options have been studied and presented over the past two years by a group of defense scientists and specialists, the Strategic Alternatives Team chaired by Dr. William Van Cleave of the University of Southern California. The vulnerability facing our ICBMs by the mid-1980s could be avoided by rapidly rebasing Minuteman III in the multiple vertical shelter mode, originally recommended by the air force, without waiting for development of the MX missile. The severe vulnerabilities of our bomber force could be reduced by increasing the alert rate, rebasing the force inland, and re-engining the B-52 Gs and Hs. The submarine force could be improved by fixes to its communications and by accelerating and increasing the Trident I program. Cruise missile production could be accelerated and expanded. In civil defense, studies show that inexpensive actions could be taken to improve that capability substantially within three years. I would add that in the medium term the B-1 program should be reactivated both as a penetrating supersonic bomber and as a subsonic cruise missile carrier.

Feasible, cost-effective, and timely options exist for strengthening our strategic forces and reducing their vulnerabilities more rapidly than presently planned. All it takes is the determination to implement them.

NATO and Other Theater Forces

Because Europe and Japan are geographically close to the Soviet Union and vulnerable to attack by conventional forces with or without theater nuclear weapons, they have had to rely for their security on the U.S. "nuclear umbrella." But now the Europeans and the Japanese see the spokes of that umbrella breaking, and they are questioning whether, if rain came, it would open.

Our major military problem after World War II was to defend Japan, which we had disarmed, and Western Europe, which was vulnerable to massively superior Soviet conventional forces. In Europe we established NATO, which blocked the Soviet advance to the west. In Northeast Asia we sent conventional forces to Korea to stop the communist advance, and then we kept them there to protect South Korea and Japan as well. Our nuclear umbrella sheltered both NATO and Japan and compensated for our inferiority in conventional forces. The presence of our ground troops in Western Europe and Northeast Asia made clear the seriousness of our commitment to the defense of Europe and Japan, and acted as a tripwire for nuclear escalation that effectively discouraged aggressive Soviet actions.

United States interests have not altered significantly since the close of World War II, but our ability to protect those interests has. Though geographically separated, Japan and Western Europe are two parts of one entity: that section of the industrialized democratic world that is threatened by Soviet military force. Both prospered under the protection America's former nuclear superiority provided. Both are now increasingly vulnerable to military attack and to a crippling interdiction of supplies. Both are essential elements of the Western alliance.

The Europeans will not be satisfied with general "indications" of American support, nor with "signals" of American strength, nor vague "assurances" from the State Department proclaiming strong transatlantic bonds. They will insist on a clear and steady show of American interest in maintaining the security and stability of Western Europe. We cannot afford to be fuzzy, for as Raymond Aron has commented, Europe can put up with an absurd and even an unjust situation, but it cannot put up with an ambiguous one. History has shown that the nations of Europe tend to gravitate toward a stable status quo, even if that stable situation is otherwise less favorable. They prefer it to the risks of instability. Thus they will demand a matching American move for every Soviet threat, or they will be tempted to seek accommodation with the Soviets.

As West German Chancellor Helmut Schmidt said in 1979, "Equilibrium is the main element underlying security. For many years now I have regarded balance of power as the indispensable precondition for peace and I now find that my conviction has been borne out." If America does not ensure that equilibrium, if a failure of our will leads to an alteration in the balance favorable to the Soviets, then the European nations, as well as Japan, China, and countries like Saudi Arabia, will have every reason to fear and accommodate the Soviets. Such a trend would be our fault, and ours alone.

Before my trip to Moscow in 1959 Harold Macmillan, then the British Prime Minister, astutely commented to me, "Alliances are held together by fear, not by love." Thirty years ago fear of the Soviets brought NATO into being and overwhelming American strategic nuclear superiority and allied statesmanship held it together. Today that superiority no longer exists; ironically, though, fear of a Soviet attack is less than it was when NATO was founded. But because the Soviet Union now has superiority in theater nuclear weapons and is rapidly moving into a position of superiority in strategic weapons, while at the same time maintaining its massive advantage in conventional ground forces, the threat to NATO countries is infinitely greater today than it was twenty years ago. It must be met by a drastically revised military strategy.

NATO has always been, essentially, a military alliance to deter the military threat to Western Europe posed by the Soviet Union. During the last three decades NATO's success in responding with flexibility and determination to the growing and shifting threats has been very impressive. Recently, however, three basic conditions have changed so dramatically that NATO is challenged as never before.

First, the new economic and monetary vulnerabilities of the industrial world have led many people to regard these as more urgent than the Soviet military threat. As a result, it has become more difficult to sustain public and financial support for the levels of military strength needed within NATO.

Second, former West German Chancellor Willy Brandt's *Ostpolitik,* by accepting the territorial division of Germany, seemed to lessen Soviet incentives to apply military pressures in NATO's central sector. Although the Soviet military buildup in central Europe has continued, the Europeans do not feel as threatened by the Russians as they did before.

Third, the growing Soviet strategic nuclear forces—and the resulting vulnerability of the United States to direct Soviet attack—have impaired the credibility of the American security guarantee to Western Europe. This is the central dilemma of NATO. The United States, in seeking to negotiate a stable nuclear balance, has had to moderate its security guarantee to Western Europe, which originally was based on American nuclear superiority. It is a dilemma for which neither America nor Europe can be blamed—and it is not likely we can completely escape from it. Still, the dilemma can be dealt with more effectively than it has been.

For over a decade the United States has tried to resolve the NATO dilemma by emphasizing conventional forces. With a stalwart conventional defense on the ground in Europe, it was reasoned, the Soviets would be deterred from invasion and prevented from brandishing their military prowess for political effect. To be effective, such a policy would require that any Soviet attack be non-nuclear and that NATO's forward-deployed conventional forces be strong enough to hold against a Soviet conventional incursion, so that the Soviets would have to pay a very high price for the decision to break the peace in Europe.

The Soviet military have a healthy respect for NATO's capabilities. In recent years, however, they have built up and modernized their own forces in Europe to the point where they now field the largest and most powerful military machine the world has ever seen. Moreover, as the former Supreme Allied Commander in Europe, General Alexander M.

Haig, has repeatedly warned, Warsaw Pact forces have acquired the ability to launch an attack without strategic warning. Senators Nunn and Bartlett reported to Congress in 1977 that "Soviet forces in Eastern Europe can initiate a conflict from a standing start." The same report states that "As the Warsaw Pact capability to attack from a standing start grows relative to NATO's defensive capacity, so does the likelihood that the Warsaw Pact would already be on the Rhine when the NATO decision is made to use tactical nuclear weapons."

Their geographical position gives the Warsaw forces an enormous military advantage. U.S. forces, which make up the bulk of NATO's reinforcement strength, would have to be ferried either across an Atlantic Ocean full of Soviet submarines or above the Atlantic in an aluminum air bridge that might not prove sturdy enough to bear the weight of the traffic. A 1978 computer war game simulation by the Pentagon showed that the United States may not have enough airlift and sealift capacity to get our forces to battle before it is all over. In the exercise almost all our troops assigned to be flown to Europe got there, but many of the heavy weapons they needed were stranded in the United States. Also, within the simulated exercise's first thirty days the army ran out of artillery shells, tank rounds, and several other important types of ammunition, partly because stocks in Europe drawn down to dangerously low levels during the 1973 Arab-Israeli War have never been adequately replenished. Studies have shown that some European armies would begin to run out of crucial supplies in days rather than weeks. In view of the massive numbers of Warsaw Pact and Soviet troops within striking distance of Western Europe and the Soviet emphasis on surprise and a rapid, full-scale offensive, there is a consensus that NATO's conventional forces would not be sufficient to withstand an all-out Soviet attack, even if confined to conventional weapons.

Even if NATO were to restore the balance in conventional forces, there would remain the nagging question of the nuclear role in European deterrence—or in actual fighting, if deterrence should fail. What if NATO's conventional defenses did hold against an attack by the U.S.S.R. and the Soviets found themselves stymied? Would they accept that stalemate as decisive? Would the political goals for which they had launched an invasion of Western Europe permit them to stop there? Or would they then, having gone so far, escalate to the theater nuclear level, calculating that the Americans would not launch a nuclear blow from the continental United States aimed at the Soviet Union itself? The Kremlin leaders *at that time* might well figure that we would not, for fear of a swift and certain Soviet counterblow, which would devastate the nerve center of America's military might: our land-based ICBM force plus our submarines in port and our bombers at their bases. As former Secretary of Defense James Schlesinger pointed out in a 1975 report to Congress, "The Warsaw Pact does not think of conventional and nuclear war as separate entities. Despite a recent trend to improve its conventional forces and to recognize that a conventional war in Europe need not escalate to nuclear war, the Warsaw Pact strategy, doctrine, and forces are still strongly oriented toward nuclear operations."

Even today Soviet military planning calls for the possible use of theater nuclear weapons in any war in Europe, limited to theater targets in Europe itself. Their SS-20 missile and Backfire bomber are entirely new theater nuclear systems with intercontinental capabilities, unmatched by anything in the arsenals of the West. Their improved battlefield nuclear rockets and their new attack aircraft that can carry nuclear armaments generally exceed in range, firepower, precision, and mobility the theater nuclear capabilities of NATO. The purpose of such weapons is to give Russia the nuclear upper hand in the European theater, in a situation in which U.S. strategic forces would be checkmated by the Soviets' equal or superior intercontinental might. Moreover, Warsaw Pact forces have been extensively trained for operations in a nuclear environment.

The Backfire bomber carries nuclear cruise and attack missiles and covers not only Western Europe but also the

Atlantic approaches to the European continent. With refueling it can reach the United States. The SS-20 is a mobile missile and therefore virtually invulnerable. At the beginning of 1980 the Soviets had approximately two hundred SS-20s deployed, and they are adding them at a rate of one every week. Each SS-20 carries three very accurate MIRVed warheads, and its 3,000–4,000-mile range enables it to zero in on any target in Europe—from Norway to England to Gibraltar. The SS-20 can also be converted to a mobile intercontinental SS-16 missile, capable of reaching the United States, by simply adding a third stage to the two the SS-20 already possesses.

NATO has nothing comparable to the SS-20 or the Backfire. The 108 single-warhead Pershing-2 missiles recently approved for deployment in the mid-1980s have only one-third the range of the SS-20s. If the Russians continue to deploy their new weapons at the present rate, NATO will be even farther behind than it is now in the mid-1980s—even after our new Pershings and cruise missiles are deployed. There is a clear and present need to step up the modernization of NATO's theater and battlefield nuclear forces across the board.

The effort to deploy the neutron warhead was a first, tentative step in this direction. That weapon would have been very effective against the huge Russian tank armies. But its main virtue was that it would have reduced the yield and the blast component of battlefield nuclear weapons, as well as the radioactivity problem; therefore, it would have very little effect on those not in the immediate area of its prompt radiation: its collateral damage effects would be minimal, so that political authorities would be more inclined to authorize its early use against invading tanks than they would the older and more damaging battlefield nuclear weapons now in NATO's inventory. Its deployment would have increased the credibility of our deterrent and made war less likely.

In any case, our government's political handling of the neutron bomb issue was clumsy. We told our allies we would deploy it, they took steps to prepare their publics for its deployment, and then we pulled the rug out from under them by changing our minds and declining to deploy it. This about-face was a major cause of the lessened confidence we now enjoy among those who depend on us for their protection. The episode is one of the main reasons we now have to be so careful, and so thorough, in repairing and restoring the "seamless web" of American deterrence.

In the aftermath of the neutron bomb fiasco the most important principle in dealing with all theater nuclear issues—doctrine, design, deployment, and negotiation—must be the protection of allied unity. Without NATO unity, and the restoration of greater mutual confidence, the deployment of a modern theater nuclear force will probably be impossible. Certainly any force we manage to assemble under these conditions would not impress or deter the Soviets, either militarily or politically.

The tentative alliance decision to go ahead with the deployment of the longer-range Pershing missile and the ground-launched cruise missile has political value to the extent that it represents an instance of alliance unity in the face of Soviet pressure. However, the deployment has been linked to arms control objectives, and this raises questions about its military merit. Some allies have been persuaded that the systems are needed; others see them as instruments of future arms control. This difference in perception is a potential source of alliance confusion that the Soviets can exploit.

Modernization must take place on its own merits. If we rationalize a system even partly on the basis of its arms control negotiating value, we raise justifiable doubts not only about its military importance but also about our determination to go through with the program. The military situation in NATO must be improved *before* there are any major arms control agreements with the Warsaw Pact. If we enter into arms control agreements first, we run a serious risk—approaching certainty—that those agreements will merely reflect and help perpetuate the existing imbalance.

•   •   •

The most important matter to be resolved is not the technical question of which new weapon is the most cost effective, but rather the doctrinal division within the alliance. Some—mostly Europeans—see theater forces as a way to "give a signal" of readiness to escalate and as an automatic link to U.S. strategic forces; others—mostly Americans—see theater forces as a way to defend Europe, and at the same time to control and contain a war in Europe without necessitating a nuclear exchange between the United States and the Soviet Union.

Ways must be found to reconcile these two concepts in accordance with the new realities of the strategic balance. The "European" concept plays down or ignores the fact that giving a political signal requires real military operational capabilities. Moreover, it presumes that U.S. strategic forces would immediately make up for any deficiencies in NATO theater forces. Yet the growing vulnerability of the U.S. land-based ICBM force, the proliferation of Soviet targets, and the limited growth expected in U.S. strategic force programs, together with the SALT constraints on American forces, mean that until these trends are reversed the ability of U.S.-based strategic nuclear systems to cover European military targets will continue to decrease.

In the view of many Europeans, the "American" concept puts too much emphasis on limited nuclear warfare confined to Europe, which is anathema to Europeans, and not enough on the political necessity to maintain the strongest possible link to *all* American strategic systems. For this reason many American proposals to improve NATO's theater nuclear forces—even to the extent necessary to carry out the "European" concept—appear to West Europeans to be evidence of U.S. readiness to consider a nuclear exchange in Europe without escalation to the strategic level.

Both sides should understand that the common and overriding goal is *deterrence*, both of an actual attack and of the ability of the Soviets to exploit the military situation politically. Deterrence strategies in a multinational alliance may never conform neatly to strategic military logic, but they cannot endure if they do not conform to reality. While the link to American strategic forces is not, and cannot be, as strong as in the past, it remains. The present *degree* of reliance on those forces, however, must be supplanted by a stronger in-theater defense. Deterrence of a Warsaw Pact attack aimed at seizing Western European territory must be based more on the ability to prevent the Soviets from achieving such an objective, and much less on the less credible threat of retaliation by American strategic forces. This is not American nuclear decoupling—in fact, battlefield and theater nuclear forces will remain predominantly American; nor is it merely an attempt to restrict nuclear conflict to Europe. Rather, it is an effort to strengthen deterrence.

The United States and its European allies must work out the outlines of such a doctrine and the specifics of modernization in accordance with it, with a firm grasp of our common objectives but also of the reality of the strategic situation. Certain things can be agreed upon: While there must be some deemphasis of reliance on the American *strategic* force umbrella, there must be no decoupling. In compensation, the *theater* and battlefield part of the nuclear umbrella must be strengthened. A new forward defense strategy and doctrine must be fashioned to meet modern Warsaw Pact combined arms capabilities. The starting point is to recognize the true nature of Warsaw Pact doctrine. That doctrine is oriented toward defeating NATO's defenses and rapidly seizing territory, using tactical nuclear and chemical as well as conventional weapons.

To counter this strategy we need a theater nuclear force deployment doctrine that will make absolutely clear the new relationship of theater forces to U.S.-based strategic nuclear forces at one end of the spectrum of deterrence, and to the alliance's conventional military forces deployed in Europe at the other.

At the central strategic end of the spectrum U.S. forces together with longer-range theater systems must neutralize the threat of such Soviet forces. Only the President of the United States can spell out the doctrine of limited and selective use that is needed to ensure the vital connection necessary to such neutralization.

At the battlefield end of the spectrum a modernized theater nuclear force will provide the main deterrent to massive Soviet conventional or tactical nuclear attacks. This will be so even if NATO's conventional forces are greatly improved. NATO cannot realistically expect to contain such attacks with conventional forces alone. But to be effective, the theater deterrent must be clearly able to halt a large-scale attack by the forces of the Warsaw Pact, and to prevent the loss of territory. It will require an ability to locate and destroy military targets in the field, and their support in the rear.

This requires modernization of our posture across the board: nuclear weapons and other critical military assets in the theater must be made more survivable against surprise attack; nuclear weapons must be modernized to enhance their defense capability and reduce the collateral damage from their use (battlefield variations of the neutron bomb are essential for this purpose); theater-range systems might be introduced to meet the threat of the Backfire and SS-20, but not at the expense of modernizing battlefield nuclear weapons; conventional forces need to be modernized, taking advantage of new technologies; deployment plans for combined nuclear and conventional arms must be fashioned to make credible a deterrent based more strongly on the ability to deny an aggressor his objectives. Above all, a doctrine to guide modernization and to preclude piecemeal force decisions must be devised.

All of this will be extremely difficult; more alliance cooperation than we have recently seen will be necessary. The United States will have to lead, but to do so wisely it will first have to organize its own approach. This does not mean a repetition of the mistakes of the 1960s, when our tendency was to force a strategy on our allies; the solutions must be worked out together with our allies. But wise leadership is impossible without a sense of direction, and one of the major reasons for NATO's strategic confusion today is that the United States lacks a firm sense of direction. Our tendency in recent years has been to approach alliance military decisions piecemeal. This must stop. A cooperative effort to renew and restore the reality and credibility of deterrence in Europe can help build allied unity as well as military and political strength.

The accession of Spain to NATO is vitally important. If Spain's rapidly modernizing forces and key strategic location were combined with France's growing cooperation within the alliance, NATO would have the military depth it now lacks. The United States has advocated Spanish membership since the early days of the Eisenhower administration. With the passing of the Franco regime and the evolution of democracy in Spain, the West Europeans should now be prepared to incorporate Spain into NATO. The Spanish people are hardworking, courageous, and able. The United States and the West need them as friends and allies, especially since it is NATO's political unity even more than its military posture that discourages Soviet tests and adventures.

Turkey is a time bomb that, if allowed to explode, could have a more devastating impact on NATO than even the upheaval in Iran. Turkey has no oil but it shares borders with Iran, Syria, Iraq, and the Soviet Union. It controls the entrance to the Black Sea and the eastern entrance to the Mediterranean. It provides one third of NATO's sixty-six divisions. Its 500,000-man armed forces are second in size in NATO only to those of the United States. For centuries it has been a target of Russian aggression.

Turkey's economic problems are staggering. It faces what Prime Minister Suleyman Demirel calls "the gravest economic crisis in Turkey since we set up the republic" in 1923. It is torn by religious strife and imperiled by radical political groups. Riots and assassinations are rife. Its government has long been weak and unstable. For purely political reasons, the U.S. Congress has been niggardly in providing military and economic aid. If Turkey collapses, the south hinge of NATO will be torn away and the effect on its oil-producing neighbors will be incalculable. The

NATO countries, including the United States, must urgently develop a program for military and economic assistance to ensure that this does not happen.

NATO and the Oil Lifeline

Sixty percent of Europe's oil moves by sea from the Persian Gulf. Europe, like Japan, is far more dependent on oil from Arab countries than we are. It was this consideration as much as any other that led most of our NATO allies to see the rights and wrongs of the Yom Kippur War in 1973 differently from us. Except for the Dutch, who were hit by an oil embargo for opposing the Arabs, and the Portuguese, who at that time had African colonies with oil, they were reluctant to help us help the Israelis, for fear the Arabs would punish them by withholding vital oil supplies. Thus most NATO countries denied landing and overflight rights to our air transports carrying supplies to Israel, and resisted the diversion of military equipment from central Europe.

The situation facing our Western European allies with regard to their oil supply was admittedly difficult, and their concern over diversion of NATO military stocks had legitimacy. However, in retrospect, neither consideration justified their lack of support of the United States. It is not only that their reluctance to support us in 1973 has gained them no appreciable or permanent advantage with the Arab states. Nor is it that their policies were shortsighted concerning the strategic relationship of Israel to Western European security. Their failure to support the United States when it was acting in accordance with what it believed to be a major national interest—and one common to its allies—has ominous implications for the health of the alliance. How viable is NATO if we cannot have a concerted policy to deal with major security problems beyond Europe? Economic and geopolitical considerations, particularly in the Persian Gulf, are raising problems that, while beyond the normal confines of NATO, without question concern NATO as an alliance. And so far NATO has shown itself incapable of responding as an alliance to such problems. It is urgent that we develop coordinated, effective means of dealing with such problems.

The key challenge here is not procedural or technical: it is political. The Europeans' vital and legitimate interests in the Middle East and the Gulf are more immediate to them than American interests in the region are to the United States. The United States, Western Europe, and Japan will remain heavily dependent on oil imported from the Middle East and the Persian Gulf for the remainder of this century, and the Soviets know it. Soviet oil reserves are running low and they too will soon need Mideast oil. They have an avid interest in the region for these and other reasons. As James R. Schlesinger, who was my Defense Secretary, said in his farewell address as President Carter's Energy Secretary, NATO is "insufficient" today because "it offers no protection for the energy resources on which our collective security depends." The threat is "stark," he said. "Soviet control of the oil tap in the Middle East would mean the end of the world as we have known it since 1945 and of the association of free nations."

Sooner than we would wish or might expect, it may be necessary for European nations to be ready and willing to use military force, in cooperation with the United States, in defense of the West's vital and legitimate interests in the Middle East or Persian Gulf. If so challenged, we have no choice but to do what is necessary to prevent our oil lifeline from being severed.

A Western military presence in the Middle East or Persian Gulf area need not and probably should not be a NATO presence, nor should it be under a NATO command. But there will probably be a need in the future to devise ways in which a few cooperating states could increase the readiness of their forces, after alliance consultation, without requiring the cooperation or even the assent of all.

The strategic position of the entire Western alliance hinges today, and will for years to come, on the reliability of access by Western Europe, North America, and Japan to crude oil from the Persian Gulf; on the continued credibility of United States protection and support for the key states in the area; on limiting Soviet influence in the region; and on the avoidance of war if at all possible. But these interests are not self-executing even though they are, to some extent, self-evident. It is necessary to be prepared, and to be seen to be prepared, to join together to defend them.

The United States should also have the ability to intervene unilaterally in this vital area of the world if the need arises. Strategically located bases to counter the Soviet bases in the area and a rapid deployment force would show the Soviets we are serious about countering a threat by them to our oil lifeline.

The rapid deployment idea is useful for other volatile and sensitive parts of the world as well. Senator John Stennis of the Senate Armed Services Committee has pointed out why in a colorful way. "We have more problems than just strategic threats," Stennis said, so "we've got to be prepared for more uncertainties" and have forces "that can go into the bayous" of the Third World. Rapid deployment forces, if used intelligently, would provide the United States with the necessary flexibility to respond to the needs of allies around the world.

It should be noted, however, that the capability of a rapid deployment force would depend on bases and prepositioned equipment and supplies on land or at sea. Airlift could not transport the amount of equipment needed. Above all, rapid deployment requires American control of the seas—a capability we will lose at present levels of the naval budget.

Japan

The Japanese are in a position that is strategically quite similar to Europe's. The threats that alarm the Japanese are essentially from the Soviet Union: nuclear coercion, interruption of sea-lanes between Japan and the Persian Gulf, and harassment or attack from the air. In response to these threats the Japanese can choose from three options. They could rearm, both conventionally and with nuclear weapons. They could seek an accommodation with the Soviet Union, offering to trade their technical know-how for non-aggression. Or they could continue to rely on the United States. For a few more years at least they will pursue the last course. At the same time, they can be expected to modestly increase their defense expenditures and maintain communication with the Soviet Union because our questionable stability as an ally has forced them to keep their options open.

In June 1979 during the seven-nation summit meeting in Tokyo, Japan was shocked by the arrival off Tokyo Bay of the *Minsk,* the U.S.S.R.'s new aircraft carrier scheduled for permanent Pacific stationing. This provocative gesture stole banner headlines throughout Japan from the first international summit held in Tokyo since World War II, an event that symbolized for the Japanese their readmission to the circle of global powers. Yet the presence of the *Minsk* underscored the delicacy of Japan's position. Former Prime Minister Eisaku Sato told me in 1970 that Japan was engaged in "a completely new experiment in world history," by which he meant his country was bent on taking her place as a major world power without significant military strength.

Japan allocates less than 1 percent of its GNP for defense as compared with 5 percent for the United States and at least 11 to 13 percent for the U.S.S.R.—a smaller percentage than any major nation on earth except Mexico. This free ride on defense helped spur its meteoric economic rise. Economists have estimated that if Japan had spent 6 percent of its GNP on defense over the past couple of decades, its GNP would be some 30 percent lower than its current $1 trillion—which will soon be the second highest in the world, as Japan overtakes the Soviet Union.

That same free ride has also made Japan very vulnerable militarily. Its 155,000-man army is one-fourth the size of North Korea's, its 44,000-man air force is inadequately protected, and its 42,000-man navy is vulnerable to air attack and incapable of defending the sea-lanes on which Japan depends.

Lee Kwan Yew, Singapore's Prime Minister, put his

finger on the Japanese dilemma when he told me in 1965, "The Japanese are a great people. They cannot and should not be satisfied with a world role which limits them to making better transistor radios and sewing machines, and teaching other Asians how to grow rice."

The Japanese government, however, currently defines its role as forging a wide consensus among key political actors, rather than leading them toward a clear objective. At present there is general agreement that Japan's security is slipping, but while the Japanese have made encouraging progress in strengthening their military forces, they have not yet made the very difficult but necessary decision to exceed the self-imposed 1 percent limitation on military spending. Unless there is some jolt to the international system—such as a second Korean conflict or a Sino-Soviet war—Japan's force improvements will probably be in limited areas rather than across the board.

Japan needs more defense, and it can afford it. The present constraints on defense spending are political and psychological, not economic. It may be unrealistic to expect a Japanese government in the immediate future to break through the traditional 1 percent of GNP barrier on defense expenditures. But even within that limit expenditures can and should be raised, and Japan's leaders will have to work at preparing their people for a greater military effort. Meanwhile, Japan should compensate for its virtually free ride on defense by shouldering a greater share of the free world's economic burden—in foreign aid, for example.

The cornerstone of Japan's defense, however, will continue to be its alliance with the United States. U.S.-Japanese military cooperation needs to be strengthened; this is in the interests of both countries. A close partnership between the strongest military and economic power in the free world and the strongest economic power in Asia could provide the basis for American political and military flexibility in the region and act as a restraint on Soviet adventuring.

By means of more intimate naval cooperation, the U.S. and Japanese fleets could greatly improve their coverage of the sea lines of communication south of Japan toward the

Persian Gulf area. If such cooperation were matched by similar NATO cooperation in the Mediterranean, it would be feasible to deploy a U.S. Fifth Fleet in the Indian Ocean. This could be done without involving the Japanese in international political problems for which they may be unprepared, and without lessening the essential naval presence in East Asia.

Even assuming that Japanese air-defense, sea-lane protection, and early-warning needs are met, there remains the nuclear threat from Russia. Nearly half of Russia's new SS-20 missiles are based in the Soviet Far East and cover Japan; the operational radius of the Backfire bombers based east of the Urals easily includes Japan. Although the problem in Northeast Asia is fundamentally the same as in Western Europe—a rapidly rising Soviet nuclear force buildup targeted on U.S. allies—the solution for Japan cannot be the same as for NATO, because Japan cannot yet accept the basing of theater nuclear forces on its soil. The United States could provide longer-range theater coverage of Northeast Asia by submarine-based and land-based cruise missiles deployed from bases on our own soil. One of the major deficiencies of Salt II is that the protocol would limit the range of such missiles to 600 kilometers. The United States will have to deploy long-range land-based and sea-based missiles in the Western Pacific as part of a modernized theater nuclear force.

The defense of Korea is also indispensable to the security of Japan. I vividly recall a conversation I had with Whittaker Chambers when North Korea invaded South Korea. He strongly supported the U.S.-U.N. action. He said, "What we must realize is that for the communists the war is not about Korea but about Japan." A Korea overrun by the communists would be like a dagger pointed at the heart of Japan. In view of present world developments the United States should strengthen rather than weaken its own forces in South Korea. It also should avoid the mistake we made in Iran of undermining a friendly government because it does not make progress toward American-style democracy as fast as we would like.

Finally, for East Asia as for Western Europe, it is absolutely essential that the United States clarify its strategic nuclear doctrine in ways that bolster the nuclear umbrella rather than collapse it. This strategic initiative would serve our own direct national interest, as well as the interest of our friends and allies—and at absolutely no cost to us.

If we fail to renovate and strengthen our alliance with the Japanese, we will force them either to go it alone or to seek an accommodation with the Soviets. The Japanese do not want to turn to the Soviet Union. Japan is part of the free world. The United States is an enormously larger customer for her products than is the Soviet Union. And while the United States returned Okinawa to Japan in 1970, the Soviet Union adamantly refuses even to discuss the return of Japan's northern islands, which it seized after World War II, and is even defiantly increasing its military presence on them. But above all, Japan does not want to be on the losing side again. If the Japanese lose confidence in the credibility of the American deterrent, they will be sorely tempted to make the best deal they can with the Soviets. The geopolitical impact of such a development would be catastrophic for the West.

The outcome is a question of our policy, not of Soviet policy. We possess the ability to consolidate the West's position in Asia. We must use that ability to the hilt to protect both our own interests and the interests of our friends and allies in Asia.

Naval Power

The event that dramatically symbolized the fact that the United States had become a world power was President Theodore Roosevelt's action seventy-five years ago in sending the "Great White Fleet" around the world. It is ironic that the decline of the United States as a world power may be marked by another naval milestone: by our losing our unquestioned superiority over the Soviet Union in naval power.

The United States is an "island" country and therefore a sea power; the Soviet Union, situated in the center of the Eurasian heartland, is basically a land power. As a land power, the U.S.S.R. can reasonably be expected to maintain superior ground forces along its long borders with potential adversaries. As an island sea power, dependent on ocean-going commerce and on sea lines of communication with our allies, the United States must insist on decisive superiority on the waterways of the world.

While we have not sought to challenge the Soviet's "natural" advantages on the land, they have not reciprocated by conceding our title to the seas. Instead they have vigorously pursued a naval program designed to cripple our advantage on the oceans in case of conflict—a program that gives them mobility while it seeks to deny us that very quality. Historically, the Soviet Navy has been unimportant. Now that has changed.

Just as the Soviet strategic buildup was paralleled by a U.S. strategic demobilization, the same pattern has been followed with the two sides' navies: the Soviets built, we mothballed.

From an unimportant coastal naval power at the end of World War II, the Soviet Union has grown to a major global naval power today. The Soviets now have the world's largest and most modern surface navy, its largest fleet of attack submarines, and its largest fleet of ballistic missile-carrying submarines. Recently the Soviets have doubled the size of their largest cruisers and started production of their first nuclear attack carriers, a major new step in their program of naval expansion.

Soviet warships already operate regularly, not only in the Atlantic and the Pacific, but also in the Indian Ocean, in the Mediterranean, and in the Caribbean. Not only does the Soviet Navy threaten our own naval superiority and the security of our sea-lanes; it also is becoming a central element in the U.S.S.R.'s rapidly growing capacity to project its military power, quickly and flexibly, into the most distant and remote areas of the globe. Perhaps the most telling sign of Soviet intentions is the vast expansion of their ship-yards. Only half of their shipyard capacity is now being uti-lized, which leaves room for huge increases in shipbuilding in the future.

Even as the Soviets were building and deploying a pow-erful counterforce to our navy, the United States was saving them much of the trouble. In the last decade we cut the number of our ships by more than half, from 976 in 1968 to 453 in 1978. Admiral James L. Holloway, then chief of naval operations, reported in 1978 that in a sea war "which involved Soviet combatants in both the Atlantic and Pacific our prospects for success for sea control would be margin-al."

The commander-in-chief of the Soviet Navy, Admiral Sergei Gorshkov, boasts, "The flag of the Soviet navy flies over the oceans of the world. Sooner or later the United States will have to understand that it no longer has mastery of the seas."

Gorshkov may overrate his own accomplishments and underrate our superiority in carriers. But the fact remains that the Soviet Navy has soared to a position of second best in the world, and is moving rapidly toward becoming num-ber one. This would be a disaster for the United States, and there is no time to lose if we are to avert it.

In a foreword to the 1979-1980 edition, the editor of the authoritative *Jane's Fighting Ships* warns of the signifi-cance of these developments. He says that failure to counter Soviet moves into countries "in which there can be no rea-son for their presence other than plans for expansion and eventual control" is allowing the U.S.S.R. to establish a se-ries of bases remarkably similar to those used by the British empire at the turn of the century. He concludes:

> By dropping the shield of maritime security the Western leaders have so weakened their own position that they are moving towards a position of vulnerability to blackmail.
>
> The results of the blackmail? Deprivation of raw

materials, markets and the freedom of those friends who
are not strong enough to guarantee their own security.

The Soviets are prepared to maintain at least a 775-ship
navy for the foreseeable future. The U.S. target for the mid-
1980s is only 525 ships. While the U.S. Navy is barely managing to avoid further budget cuts, the Soviets are building
four new cruiser classes, at least two new aircraft carriers,
and every six weeks a new submarine. The United States
does not have to match the Soviet Union ship for ship; we
have major seafaring allies and they do not. It should be
noted again, though, that we have a significant problem in
obtaining those allies' cooperation in areas where they are
reluctant to be seen to be involved with us—as in the Mideast in 1973. And the U.S.S.R. has one unique advantage:
its fishing fleet and merchant marine are integrated with its
navy. "Nonmilitary" Soviet trawlers have traditionally
served as the eyes and ears of the Soviet Navy off our coasts.

For all these reasons, we have to make a very substantial effort to increase the size of our naval forces and to
modernize them. A recent Atlantic Council study demonstrated that a U.S. shipbuilding and aircraft procurement of
an additional $10 billion annually would be required to sup-
port a 600-ship navy. This figure is probably the minimum
that would be needed. The study also showed that the other
members of the alliance should collectively be able to maintain another 600-ship navy for approximately $6 billion ad-
ditional annually, after a period of modernization. These
levels appear consistent with total alliance defense spending
and should provide combined navies capable of handling the
775-ship threat of the Soviet Navy, if that should ever become necessary. We need a single policy that clearly speci-
fies for each alliance country the future role and mission of
its navy, a strategy for carrying it out, and a commensurate
construction program for the next ten to twenty years.
Nothing short of that will be adequate.

The allied nations have a common area of interest in
that we all depend on open sea-lanes for our continued pros-

perity, indeed for our very survival. The interconnected one-world ocean, that body of water that makes the earth look blue from space, links America and Europe and provides contact between the West and the rest of the world. As Harold Macmillan has said, Asia and Africa are the two great lungs by which Western culture breathes; the oceans of the world are the arteries that carry the life-giving oxygen from these lungs to us.

The artery that leads directly from these twin lungs is the Indian Ocean. Many Americans, if asked to name the five oceans that go with the seven seas, would not get much further than the Atlantic and the Pacific. Another ocean we should start thinking more about is the Indian. In 1968, within a month after the British announced they were withdrawing from "East of Suez," Admiral Gorshkov was in India testing the political waters. Soon afterward the Soviet Navy began making itself at home in the Indian Ocean, and by 1976 the Soviets were spending five times as many ship-days there as we were; in 1979 they maintained eighteen to twenty ships in these waters.

The Indian Ocean contains many of the key choke points through which the commercial and military ships of the world must pass. The Straits of Hormuz control traffic in and out of the Persian Gulf; the Suez Canal and the Bab el Mandeb Straits control transit to the Mediterranean; the Straits of Malacca, passage to Japan and the Pacific. With Soviet-backed groups sweeping to power all around the borders of the Indian Ocean's "crescent of crisis," and Soviet ships steaming back and forth across its expanses, the Indian Ocean may one day become a "Red Sea."

America has permanent fleets in the Atlantic, the Pacific, and the Mediterranean—all areas of vital and legitimate interest to the United States. In view of the British pullback and the heightened importance of the Indian Ocean, we must, in league with our allies, work out an arrangement to station an American Fifth Fleet there. This, together with the British, French, and Australian navies, would be a stabilizing force in the area.

The West—and the United States unilaterally—must

build up its naval strength to be able to defend those sea routes that are vital to it.

The Nixon Doctrine

More nuclear bombs, unquestioned military superiority, and massively superior economic strength will not deter revolutionary war, terrorism, or other forms of communist aggression that fall short of conventional war. The United States, our allies, and friends must develop power commensurate with the power being used against us. It makes no sense to try to use a sledgehammer to kill a fly. That kind of enemy calls for a less powerful but more effective weapon—a fly swatter.

In these situations it is not the balance of power in the arsenal that counts, it is the balance of power on the battlefield. If we are relatively equal to the Soviet Union in nuclear arms, but the Soviets have 5,000 Cubans, or even 500 agitators and terrorists, where we have no countervailing force, then the balance of power on the scene is massively on their side. Local defense forces are the ones best equipped to deal with these low-level threats, but if the aggressor is receiving aid from outside, those defending their freedom must also have access to aid from outside.

The Nixon Doctrine provided that the United States would supply arms and assistance to nations threatened by aggression, *if* they were willing to assume the primary responsibility for providing the manpower necessary for their defense.

Some Americans have an almost theological aversion to having the United States sell arms abroad. But those who argue against supplying our friends with the arms they need to defend themselves ignore one very important point. There is almost no case on record since World War II in which arms provided by the United States have been used by the country receiving them for purposes of aggression. Soviet arms are the ones that have been consistently used to break the peace.

Whether we like it or not, most countries need arms, and this is especially true of those in the path of Soviet ambition. Many of these nations have unfriendly neighbors. In much of the world democracy is weak or nonexistent and the army is essential to internal stability. These simply are facts of life. Another fact of life is that the Soviets are willing arms merchants, wherever arms sales can give them a foot in the door.

The Soviets cannot match the West in terms of the promise of economic progress, and their ideology has little appeal. But if the leader of a threatened or unstable nation finds that the only way he can retain power is to turn to them, he will do so. Some leaders who have broken with the Soviet Union may be forced to return to the Soviet fold if the United States does not provide them with an alternative source of arms. We must not leave such leaders with that sort of Hobson's choice.

Now that the Soviet Union is pouring Russian arms and Cuban troops into Africa, some in the West argue that we should not aid the targets of this new aggression because in the end the Soviets will dig their own graves in Angola, Ethiopia, Afghanistan and elsewhere. But this will not happen. The Soviets are ruthless in the use of power; they are expert at digging graves for others. Even the staunchest local resistance cannot hold out indefinitely against an aggressor who is better armed.

Colin Legum, a British expert on Africa, writes, "A new phrase is creeping into the language of Marxists in the third world: 'superior arms.' The argument among those advocating revolutionary change is that, in choosing your 'strategic allies,' it is necessary to be sure that they possess 'superior arms.'"

Reliable delivery of military supplies is of crucial concern to the leaders of Third World nations. The Soviets stand by their friends in this regard. It is both stupid and dangerous for the United States to curtail arms sales to our friends while the Soviets supply the enemies of our friends.

It is ironic that the Soviets have had enormous success

since World War II with their own version of the Nixon Doctrine. In Vietnam, they helped their allies by providing the arms; we helped our allies by providing both the arms and a large proportion of the men. More than 110,000 Americans were killed as a result of wars with Soviet-supported communist forces in Korea and Vietnam. The Russians suffered no casualties in those conflicts.

The interests of the United States and of our friends and allies require that we provide threatened nations with the aid they need to defend themselves. World conditions still require that the basic elements of the Nixon Doctrine be fully implemented. We must have the strategic nuclear power to hold the ring against the Soviets whenever they seek to extend their domination. We must keep our treaty commitments by having adequate conventional and theater nuclear power. When the Soviets resort to indirect aggression by support of revolutionary war, we can avoid more Vietnams by providing military and economic assistance to our friends so that they will be able to defend themselves without our assuming the burden of fighting the war for them.

Meeting the Cost

The notion that government spends more for arms than for social programs is a myth. The total defense budget today is less than 5 percent of our GNP and less than 25 percent of the federal budget compared with peaks of 12–13 percent and 61 percent, respectively, at the height of the Korean War. While defense spending has gone down since 1965 from 7 to 5 percent of GNP, federal, state, and local spending on social welfare programs has gone up from 12 percent to 21 percent—four times as much as we spend on defense.

As Michael Novak has pointed out, "Free societies are not natural to this planet. They have arisen only rarely in human history and commonly they have collapsed in the face of superior barbaric force. . . . The alleged superior morality of the statists—who desire more funds for the bureaucracy of poverty and less for the bureaucracy of defense—may not be as moral as the statists like to believe."

Dr. Fritz Kraemer, Henry Kissinger's early mentor, graphically illustrates the problem. "It is a question of priorities," he once told me. "If I have a house in the valley and there is a leak in the dam in the mountains, repairing the leak must come before adding a room or buying a Picasso for my house."

Marshal of the Royal Air Force Sir John Slessor put this "question of priorities" in capsule form: "The most important social service a government can render its people is to keep them alive and free."

In the mid-1980s, assuming present projected defense spending in the United States and the U.S.S.R., the West will face a situation of maximum danger. The Soviets will have unquestioned superiority in strategic and theater nuclear weapons, overwhelming superiority in ground and air forces, and at least equality in naval forces.

The current administration's proposed 5 percent increase in defense spending, even if a real 5 percent, is totally inadequate to meet that threat. Rather than fixing on such arbitrary and minor percentage increases, we should examine our military requirements and determine the funding necessary to meet them, given a reasonable and coherent set of priorities. But even a cursory summary of our needs demonstrates that a 5 percent increase is far too little at this late stage.

With or without further SALT agreements we must increase our strategic nuclear power so that after a possible first strike we have enough ground-based missiles to liquidate the remaining Soviet ground-based missiles, destroy all important military targets, and still have a survivable reserve force equal or superior to that of the Soviet Union. In addition, we must improve our capability to protect our civilian population. Otherwise we will be blackmailed into surrender since the option of mutual mass destruction of civilian populations will not be credible.

We must restore parity between NATO's and the Warsaw Pact's theater nuclear and conventional capability, and assure that our key forces can survive even a surprise attack.

We must provide the arms and assistance needed by our friends and allies to meet threats they face from forces supplied by the Soviet Union and its allies, whether those threats are internal or external.

As a land power with two fronts, the Soviet Union may be expected to have overall superior conventional land forces. But we are a sea power, and therefore we must strengthen our navy to ensure that we will have unquestioned superiority at sea. Our own security, and that of every nation using the world's sea-lanes, depends on that superiority.

We cannot do what is needed without cost, both socially and financially.

I considered the end of the draft in 1973 to be one of the major achievements of my administration. Now seven years later, I have reluctantly concluded that we should reintroduce the draft. The need for the United States to project a strong military posture is now urgent, and the volunteer army has failed to provide enough personnel of the caliber we need for our highly sophisticated armaments. Its burden should be shared equally by all strata of society, with random selection and as few deferments as possible. Even so, it will cause hardships, and whatever its form, the draft is inherently unfair; it can only be justified by necessity. But as we look at the 1980s, necessity stares us in the face: we simply cannot risk being without it. To put off that hard decision could prove penny wise and pound foolish; our reluctance to resume the peacetime draft may make us weak enough to invite war, and then we will find ourselves imposing a wartime draft instead.

To meet the requirements for restoration of a balance of power adequate to deter war and avoid defeat without war will require an increase in our defense budget of at least $30 billion—in 1980 dollars—annually for five years. This means a real increase of more than 20 percent over present levels. This is a substantial sum, but it would amount to barely more than 1 percent of our GNP. It is necessary life insurance—for our life as a nation and for the lives and freedom of the more than 2 billion people living in the noncommunist world. This is the most important social service we can provide.

8
Economic Power

Our policy is directed not against any country or doctrine but against hunger, poverty, desperation, and chaos. Its purpose should be the revival of a working economy in the world so as to permit the emergence of political and social conditions in which free institutions can exist.

—*George C. Marshall, 1947*

And what do Soviet people say about "rotting capitalism"? "It may be rotting, but what a lovely smell!"— and they inhale voluptuously.

—*Vladimir Bukovsky, 1978*

Just as military power provides the muscle, economic power provides the lifeblood for a successful strategy for victory in World War III. Economic power not only enables us to maintain the levels of military power we need; by itself it is a powerful weapon that, used skillfully, can advance our interests. It brings prosperity, not destruction. We should stop being apologetic about having it and reticent about using it.

The plain truth, evident to anyone willing to see it, is that the West in general and the United States in particular have created the greatest economic machine known to man. Communism, the system that promises wealth for all, has in practice turned plenty into scarcity, surplus into shortage, and wealth into poverty.

Tsarist Russia used to be a major grain exporter, and was known as the breadbasket of Europe; now its agriculture is a basket case. Although over 30 percent of its labor force is employed on farms as compared with 3 percent in the United States, it must import tens of millions of tons of grain in order to feed its people. China's "economic miracle," which naïve reporters in the West extolled for years, has now been revealed to have been a paste-on job. The Peking *People's Daily* has admitted that it published many false and misleading reports in the past in order to make things seem better than they were. China now acknowledges that its people are getting less grain than they were twenty years ago. In Cambodia, the Khmer Rouge's "purification" campaign led to the destruction of virtually all forms of modern civilization, a literal return to barbarism. The numbers of Cambodians sacrificed on the altar of ideology ran into the millions, even before Vietnam's latest invasion of that tragic country.

Wherever there is a divided country, the free side prospers. West Germans are twice as rich as East Germans. Free Chinese are three times as rich as communist Chinese.

The United States produces twice as much as the Soviet Union. Overall, the West produces four times as much as the Soviet bloc. The Soviet Union's neighbor, Japan, with less than half its population, one-sixtieth its territory, and hardly any natural resources, is well on its way to surpassing the Soviet Union in production.

The economic bankruptcy of communism has forced it to turn to the West for assistance. Though the Soviets have long boasted of their economic achievements, the U.S.S.R. has been economically dependent on the West since the 920s. Confronted with postrevolutionary economic chaos, Lenin himself invited Western firms to set up industrial concessions—a move hailed as "peaceful coexistence" in the West, but explained differently by Lenin himself, who told Communist Party meeting, "Concessions—these do not mean peace with capitalism, but war on a new plane."

Western firms took the bait, flocking eagerly to exploit what they saw as a rich new market. More than 300 "concessions" were granted, and by 1930, according to one exhaustive analysis, every major industrial process in the Soviet Union had derived from Western technology. But as soon as the Soviets had extracted the capital and technology they needed, they forced Western firms out of the country; by 1933 there were no foreign manufacturing concessions in the Soviet Union. Yet in that short period of economic "coexistence" America's contribution to Soviet industrialization was so large that in 1944 Stalin himself commented that two-thirds of the large industrial projects in the Soviet Union had been built with American assistance.

American assistance continued during World War II when the United States sent $11 billion worth of Lend-Lease aid to Russia.

After World War II reconstruction of the U.S.S.R. was accomplished in large measure by looting defeated Germany. Industrial plants worth $10 billion were disassembled, carted off to Russia, and reassembled there. Included were such plums as the Karl Zeiss factory (precision optical instruments), the Opel auto works and the V-2 rocket plant at Nordhausen, which provided the basis for the Soviet Sputnik programs. All told, Stalin carried off more than 40 percent of Germany's 1943 industrial capacity. The Soviets took Germany's creative talent as well—6,000 scientists, engineers, and their families, 26,000 people in all, were spirited away on a single night.

But when it must stand on its own, the Soviet Union is an economist's nightmare. In 1969 Brezhnev sent a confidential letter to the Central Committee detailing the desperate situation of Soviet industry. Oil, which provides almost half of its foreign exchange, is drying up; Siberia, potentially rich in resources, remains inaccessible and forbidding. The rate of growth of the Soviet labor pool is shrinking, and many of those now coming of age are less educated Moslems from Soviet Central Asia. Signs point toward a slower rate of economic growth in the future.

The highly centralized communist economic system, with its limited incentives, is incapable of generating creative new technologies at the rate the West does.

Soviet Economic Warfare

The Soviets treat economic transactions as matters of state. They apply the same discipline and tactics to them that they would to an exercise on the battlefield. Not only do they use trade to try to skim the cream of Western technology for themselves; they also seek to weaken the West by means of economic warfare, one of their most effective weapons in World War III.

As analyst Richard T. McCormack has pointed out:

> The Soviets appear to have discovered various ways to harass and damage the economic and political systems of the West. They do this by such instrumentalities as Western communist parties which they subsidize on a fairly large scale, by fomenting terrorism, encouraging conflict and war outside the East Bloc, and launching skillful propaganda efforts aimed at Western multinational companies, among others.

Nothing is more chilling to those who make decisions about long-term investment in other countries than reports of terrorist activities there, or kidnappings or murders of businessmen. In a less dramatic but equally effective way communist-led unions can also create an unfavorable climate for investment.

In Italy the postwar economic boom was halted in the late 1960s by massive communist-led strikes that resulted in crippling wage increases of up to 50 percent. According to Dr. McCormack, "Economists have calculated that these wage increases actually damaged the Italian economy more than the subsequent OPEC oil price increase by weakening her international competitiveness and by sapping needed money from the investment pool." Since terrorism by the Red Brigades has been added to the witch's brew, private investment in Italy has virtually dried up. Without new investments, living standards are sure to decline, creating further discontent, which the communists will be able to turn to their purposes.

Local Communist parties, by leading strikes, by de-

manding excessive wage increases, by calling for nationalization of industries, and by sponsoring terrorism against
businessmen, can damage the investment climate in a country so badly that money will stop flowing into it. This, by
itself, can have a major impact on whether a country remains free or not.

In tiny El Salvador leftist guerrillas have mounted a
crushing offensive against the country's economy. The leader of the largest leftist group, Rafael Calente, has declared,
"If we can stop the crop collection, we can vanquish the
capitalist enemy more thoroughly than with a hundred
bombs." Coffee accounts for nearly 70 percent of El Salvador's income. Calente's followers recently occupied seven of
the largest coffee plants and forced the mill owners to agree
to a crippling 100 percent wage increase, throwing the economy into a tailspin. "The idea isn't to bargain and concede,"
Calente says. "The idea is to upset and destroy." The guerrillas have also been kidnapping business executives; by late
1979 they had collected nearly $50 million in ransom pay-
ments. As a result, most American companies have evacu-
ated their non-Salvadorean managers. Tourism, construction, and industry have all been crippled by the guerrillas,
who have been placing themselves in a position to take over
if the economy breaks down.

The communists have now hit on the oil weapon as a
means of striking at the vital economic underpinnings of
Western society. Communist-led strikes in the European
coal industry in the aftermath of World War II led to an increased dependence on oil from the Middle East. Then, as
early as the 1950s, the Soviets quite deliberately set out to
make it difficult for the West to import oil from the Middle
East. Recently, Premier Kosygin himself spearheaded the
Soviet pressure on the Arabs to use the oil weapon against
the West. The Soviets' forays into Africa are motivated in
large measure by the enormous economic stakes involved.

During World War II the United States recognized the
importance of the economic battlefront by setting up a powerful Board of Economic Warfare. Since then several attempts to coordinate international economic policy,

including one in my own administration, have foundered because of bureaucratic infighting among the government departments involved. Now time is running out. A modern-day equivalent of the Board of Economic Warfare is needed to fight the economic battles of World War III, and it should be established under the direct control of the President. Policies on trade, foreign aid, loans, and support of international lending agencies must be coordinated to serve U.S. foreign policy interests. Only strong presidential leadership and direction can accomplish this result.

Trade with the Soviet Union

An area that urgently needs new direction and heightened attention is trade with the Soviet Union. The Soviets are using every possible weapon to cut the economic lifelines of the West in Africa, the Mideast, and other critical areas; we should not throw them a lifeline to rescue them from their sinking economy—except for a price.

In 1922 British Prime Minister David Lloyd George said of Russia, "I believe we can save her by trade. Commerce has a sobering influence. . . . Trade, in my opinion, will bring an end to the ferocity, the rapine, and the crudity of Bolshevism surer than any other method." Such ideas may have been excusable fifty years ago, when Soviet communism was an unknown quantity. But there is no excuse for such wishful thinking now. The fashionable theory that a fat communist is less dangerous than a lean one is nonsense. Khrushchev was certainly well fed.

Whether directly or indirectly, trade with the Soviets strengthens them militarily. Even trade in nonstrategic items frees resources for them to use in other ways. We must never forget that doing business with the Soviets includes these costs; it is only justified when the benefits outweigh the costs. Trade with the Russians must be used as a weapon, not as a gift.

In 1972 the United States signed a number of commercial agreements with the Soviet Union as part of a larger whole, in an exercise of linkage. In 1972 we wanted Soviet help in extricating ourselves from Vietnam; we were negotiating an arms control pact; we were expanding people-to-people contacts and trying to establish a pattern of mutual restraint in which both superpowers would resolve conflicts by negotiation instead of confrontation. Trade was one of the principal things we had to offer in return for political and diplomatic concessions. We were also quite deliberately creating a network of interdependencies that would give us more leverage in future crises. We wanted the Soviets to think twice about the potential economic costs of provoking us by troublemaking adventurism.

In my television address to the Soviet people during the 1974 Moscow summit, I compared the reaching of our various trade, arms, and other agreements to the weaving of a cloth: "Just as a cloth is stronger than the threads from which it is made, so the network of agreements we have been weaving is greater than the sum of its parts. . . . Thus each new agreement is important not only for itself but also for the added strength and stability it brings to our relations overall."

Since then, however, the deterioration of America's military posture and the crippling effect of congressional restrictions on providing support for anti-Soviet forces in Southeast Asia, Africa, and other trouble spots have placed on trade more of a burden than it can bear. Trade must be the carrot and military power the stick. Without the stick, the Soviets simply pack the carrot in their picnic basket while they continue to forage in Angola, Ethiopia, or Afghanistan. As long as the Soviets continue on their present aggressive course—and they will do so until we present them with unacceptable costs—we should remember that trade is something they want which we can give or deny, depending on their behavior.

We should be especially careful about high-technology transfers that directly strengthen the Soviet military. The latest computer technology is absolutely vital to many modern weapons systems. We should not be so naïve as to suppose that high-technology items the Soviets request for their consumer sector are necessarily destined for that sector. Silicon chips with integrated circuits etched on them can be used for pocket calculators—or for the guidance systems of intercontinental ballistic missiles. Under no circumstances should a technology transfer that directly affects our national security be permitted.

With regard to less sensitive technology, we should structure our deals with the Soviets as much as possible so that we retain leverage. Modern plants that are dependent on a steady supply of spare parts or that need sophisticated maintenance create opportunities that we can exploit to our benefit. Wheat or other grain sales can be held back or canceled to induce positive behavior. We must recognize, however, that if limiting trade is to be effective as an instrument of policy, U.S. unilateral action is a very weak reed. The Russians, or other countries whose policies we are trying to affect, can fill their needs from other industrial nations—all of whom are allies of the United States. United action on the economic front by the United States and its allies is as essential as a coordinated military policy if we are to deter aggression.

Many trade deals—turn-key plants, for example—have a crucial disadvantage in that they have no value as a bargaining chip once the deal has been made. Once a plant has been built in the Soviet Union we cannot take it back, nor can we require the return of technology already transferred.

Most favored nation status is an economic lever we can use for diplomatic purposes. MFN status is something we routinely extend to nearly all our trading partners. In essence, it provides that in such matters as tariffs and trade regulations we will treat that country as favorably as we do any other country. MFN status has the effect of reducing import duties on goods from those countries extended it; it is something the communist bloc countries want very much. As of 1979, only four communist countries had MFN status: Poland, Romania, Yugoslavia, and Hungary; China was given it early in 1980.

As long as the Soviets continue to be actively engaged in aggressive policies around the world, we should under no circumstances grant them this status, for that would send a signal that aggression pays. On the other hand, neither should we say they will never get it. We should hold out MFN status as an incentive to moderate their behavior in the future.

Trade with Eastern Europe

The overwhelming majority of the people of Eastern Europe, and even their communist leaders, are anti-Russian. They resent the presence of an occupying power. Eastern Europeans have had significant exposure to the ideas of freedom and democracy, something the Russians have never had. They are courageous people who have borne a tremendous burden since 1945. They face difficult years ahead and they deserve our support, both spiritually and materially.

In general, it is in our interest to expand the choices Eastern Europeans have about where they can buy their goods. The Soviets use their economic stranglehold over their satellites in Eastern Europe to keep them in line politically. Any alternative the West can provide lessens Eastern Europe's dependence on the Soviets.

Trade lessens the Eastern Europeans' dependence on the Soviet Union; it also keeps open the bridge between East and West. The Eastern Europeans are starved for contact with the other half of Europe, so the human contact that results from trade has a more significant leavening effect on them than it does on the Russians. It is a mistake to look at East-West trade solely in bilateral U.S.-Soviet terms. In the long run the less spectacular contact between the two halves of Europe, Eastern and Western, may prove much more important.

Of course, our trade with Eastern Europe has to be limited by the fact that most of what we transfer there can become available to the Soviet Union. Especially with regard to high technology, we can expect that whatever we crate and send to Prague or Warsaw will eventually be unpacked in Moscow.

We must also be discriminating in providing favorable trade terms to Eastern European countries. Countries such as Poland or Romania that are not engaged in adventurist foreign policies should get favorable treatment from us. Those such as East Germany, which openly participate in aggression around the world, should not.

Finally, we must recognize that the peoples of Eastern Europe will not become independent of the Soviet Union overnight. Trade and contact with the West will inevitably lead to more economic independence for the satellite nations, but we must not ask or expect them to assert their political independence prematurely. The tragic experiences of the Hungarians in 1956 and the Czechs in 1968 showed that the Soviets will not allow themselves to be pushed too far too fast.

Trade with China

Soviet domination of China would be a potentially mortal blow to the free world. A weak China invites Russian aggression; therefore it is in our interest to bolster the Chinese economy.

China may now be at an important turning point. The People's Republic is in desperate shape economically and its leaders are finally acknowledging that they could use help from the West. The internal convulsions of the period when Mao and the extreme leftists tried to run the world's largest country on revolutionary rhetoric have now ended, at least temporarily. The present Chinese leaders are trying to tackle China's greatest task—modernization—in a more sensible way. They openly acknowledge that they can learn from the West. The success or failure of their effort over the next few years to bring some measure of modernization to the Chinese people may determine whether China continues in its more moderate stance or reverts to revolutionary chaos, isolation, and belligerence. It is obviously in our interest that the Chinese remain open to Western ways. The boost that trading with the West, especially with Japan, gives to their modernization plans will be crucial to the decisions they make about their future path. That is why we are justified in giving MFN status to China and denying it to the Soviet Union. The Soviet Union threatens us; China, as of now, does not.

Whether dealing with China, the Soviet Union, or Eastern Europe, we should ensure that the bottom line in our trade policy is its impact on our geopolitical objectives. We should make a deal with the Soviets only when it involves a significant diplomatic or political payoff for us. As much as possible, we should seek arrangements that allow us to withdraw advantages if the Soviets do not keep their end of the bargain. We should not put our faith in their future goodwill. We should use our economic power to give the Eastern Europeans an option and to encourage them to pursue independent and nonadventurist foreign policies. We should use our economic power to help build a less vulnerable China and—by making it in their own interest to do so—to encourage the Chinese to follow the path of moderation.

Trading with the communist countries can backfire on us if we do not use our power in a very precise, surgical manner, on a case-by-case basis. Still, we must be willing to take some risks in the hope of creating a more peaceful and prosperous world. If we do not use the tremendous advantages our economic power gives us, or if we throw those advantages away by giving trade away, we will be squandering one of our most valuable resources in World War III.

Aid for Our Friends

The task of harnessing our economic strength to our foreign policy goals is quite different when we deal with allies instead of adversaries.

From 1946 to 1976 the United States provided over $180 billion in foreign aid for 137 nations around the world. Much of it was wasted, some of it did not advance our interests, but on the whole it was a massively expensive but worthwhile investment in our goal of building a peaceful and better world for ourselves and all peoples.

The most dramatic use we made of our economic power came in the wake of World War II, when we helped Europe back onto its feet with the Marshall Plan. Britain's Foreign Secretary Bevin said our aid was "like a lifeline to sinking men." With it, we did more than prime the pump for European economic recovery. By showing the Europeans how important they were to us, we catalyzed the energies of an exhausted continent. Our generosity toward Germany, Italy, and Japan enabled them to make the transition from enemy to ally without resentment toward us. Never before had a victorious nation financed its defeated enemies back into competition with it.

We acted as trustee for all of Western civilization in those crucial years, and the dividends that have accrued for all mankind have proved the worth of our investment. Then we were helping industrial nations recover from war. Now our aid has a broader range of purposes.

First, American aid must be used to strengthen the economic base of nations, such as South Korea, to which we provide military assistance. Second, we must aid nations that face a threat from within, which need foreign aid to stabilize their economies and thus deny the revolutionaries a "cause" that will enable them to overthrow the government. Third, we must continue to be generous in providing purely humanitarian aid to victims of natural disasters such as earthquake, famine, and flood. Disaster victims suffer regardless of the kind of government they have, so they should be helped regardless of the sort of government they have— as we recognized when we sent relief to earthquake victims in Romania in 1977. In the case of a ruthless communist regime such as that in Cambodia, however, we should ensure that our aid goes directly to the people, not to the government to keep itself in power. Fourth, two-thirds of the world is underdeveloped; we have a practical as well as a humanitarian stake in aiding its development. But this stake is shared by the other advanced nations, which should also share in the tasks of development. Those nations we helped rebuild after World War II should now help others to build. Fifth, aid can sometimes be used to great effect in achieving specific diplomatic gains, as it was in bringing about the Egyptian-Israeli accord in 1979.

When I first traveled in the Far East in 1953, some of the "old China hands" told me, "Give every Asian a bowl of rice and there will be no communism." This was not true then and it is not true today. Poverty does not produce communism; communism produces poverty. Communists can find other issues besides poverty to exploit. But advancing countries are less vulnerable than stagnant countries, and even if communism were not a threat to the world, helping people escape the bonds of poverty would be something we should do because it is right, just as helping people preserve freedom is something we should do because it is right.

We cannot aid all nations equally and we should not apologize for singling out for special economic assistance countries whose security is particularly important to us. The Soviets are not shy about providing aid where they think it will best advance their purposes. Outside the communist world, almost half of Soviet economic aid between the years 1954 and 1976 went to four countries: India, Egypt, Afghanistan, and Turkey. In each of these countries the Soviets had a tremendous geopolitical stake. Egypt provided the first foothold the Soviets had in the Middle East, although they have since lost influence there. Afghanistan has now fallen under their control, and Turkey is developing into a major economic battleground.

Before World War I Turkey was known as the "Sick Man of Europe"; now it is almost a terminal case. Inflation has been running at nearly 100 percent, unemployment at 20 percent, and Turkey's foreign exchange earnings have not been enough to cover its oil bill. Yet with Turkey desperately in need of our aid, Congress, because of pressure from the Greek lobby, cut it back. There is an old saying: A Turk will burn his blanket to kill a flea. If we anger the Turks further with our spiteful behavior, they may burn their bridges to the West. The Soviets are waiting for this to happen. As we have cut back our aid to Turkey, they have stepped up theirs, providing over $1 billion in recent years. They will not hesitate to fill the vacuum in Turkey if we bow out. Cuba is costing the Soviets $3 billion a year and Ethiopia has cost them at least $2 billion already, but they are willing to bid high for countries they want.

In providing economic aid there are three rules we should follow.

First, just as a banker does a borrower no favor by making a bad loan, we do countries no favor by providing aid that only perpetuates inefficiencies. We should not insist that recipients adopt our political system. But we should tie aid to sound economic policies, insisting that it go for projects that have a good chance of success. By being firm about this, we can help developing nations learn the easy way lessons that other nations have learned the hard way about what works and what does not.

Second, we should resist the clamor to channel more of our aid through multinational agencies such as the World Bank. The charters of these organizations do not allow them to discriminate among nations on a political basis. It hardly serves the United States' interests to pay a third of the bill for the World Bank while the World Bank provides a fifty-year 1 percent loan to Vietnam in spite of Vietnam's continued aggression against its neighbors. The answer is not for us to pull out of the World Bank, but we should recognize reality and concentrate more of our available aid money in bilateral programs where we can use it effectively to advance our foreign policy purposes.

Third, we should use our aid to further our policies, and to further the cause of peace and stability in the world. It should not be simply a handout to whatever country needs it. Countries that slap us in the face on issues of vital interest to us—by refusing to support us, for example, on an issue like Iran's seizure of American hostages in violation of every principle of international conduct—should not expect us to ignore this when they ask us for aid.

In the long run one of the greatest advantages we derive from the economic power of the West may come not through our direct use of it, but through the attraction it holds for people around the world. Although many Third World leaders are more interested in guns than in butter, some are not. President Gaafar Nimeiry of the Sudan spoke for these others recently when he said, "We say to the Soviet Union and its allies: 'Get your hands off Africa. The continent needs tractors, not guns.' "

In 1958, speaking in London, I said, "What must be made clear and unmistakable for all the world to see is that free peoples can compete with and surpass totalitarian nations in producing economic progress. No people in the world today should be forced to choose between bread and freedom."

The free nations have demonstrated their superiority in achieving and exporting economic progress. The danger now is that we have not proved as effective in protecting freedom as the Soviets have in advancing tyranny. When the leaders of frail countries around the world see that we are determined to hold the ring against the Soviets militarily, then the economic attraction of our system will have the conditions it needs to work its magic.

Preserving Economic Power

A major strategic goal of the Soviets in World War III is to weaken and destroy our economy. Conversely, if we are to prevail in World War III, one of our first priorities must be to keep the American economy strong, sound, productive, and free.

Short of actual war America's economic power cannot be destroyed by the Soviet Union. But we can destroy it ourselves. The primary danger in this regard is not from recession. However painful, recessions are ills from which the patient recovers. Rather, the major danger is from the creeping anemia of taxation, regulation, nationalization, socialization; of government-itis; of what in recent years has come to be called "the English disease."

Before World War II British intellectuals nurtured the

doctrines of democratic socialism; they were enormously influential in spreading those doctrines around the world. After World War II British politicians increasingly put those doctrines into practice. The result should be a warning to the world, and especially to the United States.

Labour Party leader Aneurin Bevan once said of Britain, "This island is almost made of coal and surrounded by fish. Only an organizing genius could produce a shortage of coal and fish in Great Britain at the same time." After years of socialist economic management there were shortages of both. By 1976 the government was spending $63 out of every $100 circulating in Great Britain. Nationalized British industries were turning belly-up in world markets everywhere. Until recently personal incomes were taxed at rates up to 83 percent, up to 98 percent for "unearned" income. As a result, incentives were eroded and many of Britain's most productive people left—65,000 professionals in 1975 alone—creating a "brain drain" that further debilitated the economy. Britain's nationalized health service is a disaster. At the end of 1974 over half a million people were on waiting lists for "noncritical" surgery. In 1979, with the economy tumbling toward chaos, Conservative Party leader Margaret Thatcher pledged to turn away from smothering statism and return Britain to the era of individual incentives. Britons voted for the change she promised, and Prime Minister Thatcher has an enormously difficult but urgently important challenge to restore Britain's economic vitality.

Unless we too reverse the trend, the United States is headed toward socialism in everything but name.

When the communist world is turning to the West to save it from its economic follies, it is absurd for the West to be lurching in the other direction. Yet the United States has been doing just that. The promise of statist remedies for every real or imagined social ill holds an irresistible appeal for both populists and demagogues. Demands that government "do something" may bring relief in the short run. But the cumulative impact of all these government interventions will be to destroy the base on which all else is built.

Even John Maynard Keynes, the architect of liberal

economics, warned that a level of public spending over 25 percent of GNP would have dire consequences. The budgets of our state, local, and federal governments now amount to 32 percent of the gross national product, up from 21 percent as recently as 1950. The federal budget alone for 1980 is bigger than the gross national product of all but three of the world's 159 other nations. The 1980 budget for the Department of Health, Education and Welfare—nearly $200 billion—was more than that of any other organization on earth except for the governments of the United States and the Soviet Union. The big growth has not been in defense, but in social programs and income transfers. In real, constant-dollar terms, despite the enormous increase in the Soviet threat, the government is spending less on defense in 1980 than it did in 1960. In the twenty-five years from 1950 to 1975, by contrast, federal expenditure on social-welfare programs rose, in 1975 dollars, from the equivalent of $32 billion to $169 billion; from 26 percent of the federal budget to 54 percent.

The government now consumes more goods, spends more money, employs more people, and is more heavily in debt than any other segment of our society.

As government grows, bureaucracy grows, and the strangling web of government rules tightens around everyone else. The United States today is overlawyered, overlitigated and overregulated, and every year it gets worse.

It now costs the federal government $6 billion a year just to operate its regulatory agencies, a seven-fold increase since 1970. Former Treasury Department official Murray L. Weidenbaum estimates the cost to the public of complying with federal regulations at $121 billion a year—more than $500 for every man, woman, and child in America.

There are crippling hidden costs as well: in ideas not pursued, businesses not started, inventions left undeveloped because the government has been suffocating the entrepreneur under an avalanche of paper. Innovation is the spark that fires economic growth; productivity is the engine that drives prosperity. Overregulation kills both.

American productivity—that is, actual output per

worker-hour—is still among the highest in the world, but its rate of increase has shown alarming declines. For the years 1947–1965, productivity rose at an average annual rate of 3.2 percent a year. By the mid-1970s, this had dropped to percent a year; in 1979 output per worker-hour was actually falling. Productivity is the cushion between prices and wages; it determines how fast the standard of living can rise. Without a rising level of productivity, we will be doomed to standing in line in a standstill economy.

We need to take the regulatory shackles off the entrepreneur, spur innovation, and provide incentives for people to save so that business will have the huge sums it needs to invest in order to rebuild the nation's industrial plant and restore our competitive position in the world economy.

Erecting tariff and trade barriers to keep lower-priced foreign goods out of the U.S. market will provide short-term relief for American producers and long-term disaster for the American economy and consumer. The only sound approach is to give American companies a chance to become competitive again by removing the shackles of excessive government regulation, and by providing incentives for U.S. industry to modernize and replace obsolete equipment. Our present tax system is a major culprit in the decline of productivity in the American economy. Any proposed tax relief for corporations is immediately attacked by political demagogues as helping the rich at the expense of the poor. This is economic hogwash. What all people, poor as well as rich, need first of all is a job, and if our tax system continues to discourage incentive and reward indolence, jobs will become increasingly hard to find as American industry inevitably becomes noncompetitive at home and abroad.

We must above all else bring inflation under control. Vermont Royster points out:

> Inflation is counter-productive to every other aspiration, including the needs of the poor, the black, the sick, the young. It undermines our economic prosperity. It costs us our position in the world. It weakens our ability to defend ourselves or our interests abroad. It puts its heaviest burdens on the poor and the middle class. And—here is

the tragic irony—it puts beyond reach those very social programs, such as a workable national health plan, so avidly sought by those who profess themselves "liberals."

Inflation can only be overcome by attacking the problem at its roots: too much government, mortgaging the future by spending beyond our means, overregulation, inflationary monetary policies, tax policies that penalize initiative, disincentives for saving and investing, and low productivity. What will not work is treating the symptoms of inflation by imposing wage and price controls.

On August 15, 1971, I did something that went against my every instinct about what is good for the American economy: I imposed a ninety-day nationwide freeze on wages and prices, to be followed by a gradual return to decontrol. History told me that while controls might be politically popular, they would be economically disastrous. Imperial Rome imposed wage and price controls in A.D. 300. They proved unworkable and were a contributing factor to Rome's economic decline. A contemporary historian wrote that "the people brought provisions no more to markets, since they could not get a reasonable price for them and this increased the dearth. . . ."

Over my protests, an opposition-controlled Congress had given me the power to impose controls. With inflation worsening, there was a swelling chorus of demands in Congress and the media that the power be used. The clamor grew so great that Secretary of the Treasury John Connally, who disliked the idea of controls as much as I did, bluntly told me, "If we don't propose a responsible new program, Congress will have an irresponsible one on your desk within a month."

When controls were imposed in August 1971 the nation stirred with excitement and sighed with relief. In the first day's trading, the Dow Jones average on Wall Street rose thirty-three points. But it was a false euphoria. In the short term, controls provided relief; in the long term, they made the situation worse. Once in place, they were more difficult to get rid of in an orderly way than I had expected. The longer they stayed in place, the more they compounded economic imbalances for which the piper would have to be paid later. The best thing they did, if the lesson has been learned, was to demonstrate dramatically that controls do not work.

Price controls can do one of two things: create surpluses or create shortages. Price floors for farm products created grain surpluses; price ceilings on oil and gasoline have created gas shortages. When the government pays more for a product than consumers are willing to, producers will come up with more of it than the consumer wants. When the government puts a ceiling on prices so that consumers are not allowed to pay as much as they would be willing to for a product, producers will not supply enough of it to satisfy the public's demands. There may be circumstances in which creating surpluses is justified; our grain surpluses, for example, helped keep the price of wheat stable for twenty years. But there is no justification for creating shortages in basic industrial materials.

Wage and price controls throughout an entire economy create thousands of separate spot shortages and surpluses. There may be more lumber than anybody wants but not enough nails; there may be more cars than people want but not enough gasoline; there may be a huge surplus of wheat in the Midwest but no railroad cars to get it to market.

The best economic advice I can give to my successors in office is to resist firmly political pressures to impose wage and price controls, however strong those pressures may become. Controls will not solve the problem of inflation. They may give short-term relief but inevitably they produce long-term disaster. The only answer to inflation is for government to spend less and for people to produce more.

What we do with the American economy is important not only at home but also abroad. The American economy produces over $2 trillion worth of goods and services—one-quarter of everything produced in the entire world. Seventy percent of international trade is transacted in dollars. The old adage that when the U.S. economy sneezes, the economy of Zaire gets pneumonia is still true, and today we are running a high fever.

There once was a time when "sound as a dollar" was a description, not a joke. If the dollar continues to lose value, international trade will become a guessing game. The money markets of the world will be places where speculators will prosper and businessmen suffer.

There is no rising economic and military power that can take over the international economic burdens of the United States. We have to set things in order. We not only owe it to ourselves, we also have a responsibility to the rest of the world. The way to restore faith in the dollar abroad is to reestablish its soundness at home. Until we do so, the spectre of runaway worldwide inflation and new trade barriers will haunt businessmen everywhere and inhibit the trade that is the lifeblood of the international economic system.

As Irving Kristol has noted, our foreign policy and economic policy are inexorably linked:

> It is an inescapable fact that the American economy is a vital organ of a larger world economy. The one cannot survive, and certainly cannot prosper, without the other. The wealth of nations today is indivisible. Our economic growth will henceforth be as dependent on our foreign policy as on our economic policy. And if we fail to establish the conditions for such growth, our democracy will itself unravel, as economic pressures give rise to political polarization, at home and abroad. . . . What few seem to realize is that a prospect of economic growth is a crucial precondition for the survival of any modern democracy, the American included.

Energy

Along with inflation, energy is the most urgent problem facing the American and world economies today. Ener-

y is basic to the world economy; all other industries depend
n it.

Wood was the fuel of the preindustrial world; coal was
he fuel of the first industrial revolution, which began in the
ighteenth century; oil has been the fuel of the second indus-
rial revolution, which continues to this day. Other energy
ources, including nuclear and solar, will fuel the industrial
dvancements of the twenty-first century. Nothing is more
atural than a depletion of one energy resource, its gradual
ise in price, and its replacement by a new source. In our
ay, however, that transition has turned into a crisis.

Three candidates are usually put forward for the role
f villain in the present energy debacle: the oil companies,
)PEC, and the government.

It has been especially popular among politicians to
ake scapegoats of the oil companies. But the oil companies
id not create the energy crisis. They are, in fact, one of the
onsumer's best allies in trying to solve it. From 1950 to
970, when the oil companies were at the height of their
ower, the price of gasoline rose from 27 cents a gallon to
6 cents a gallon, and half of that rise was due to an increase
 taxes. In the 1970s, when OPEC and the federal govern-
ent had stripped the oil companies of much of their power,
e price of gasoline went from 36 cents per gallon to over
1 per gallon.

On January 1, 1970, OPEC was charging $1.80 for one
arrel, or forty-two gallons, of crude oil; in late 1979 they
ere charging around $30 for the same amount, more than
fteen times as much. It is OPEC's price hikes, not an oil
ompany conspiracy, that have caused higher prices at the
ump. In addition to price increases, political instability in
e Persian Gulf has made the supply of oil uncertain. As
ng as the West is dependent on oil from the Gulf there will
e crises or the possibility of crises. In this situation govern-
ent has a role to play, but the role it has chosen to play
as turned the energy crisis from a manageable drama into
 Greek tragedy.

·   ·   ·   ·

I was the first President to propose a wide-ranging energy program. I did so nearly a decade ago, in 1971. In my last State of the Union address, in January 1974, I described energy as our number-one priority.

Like my successors, I encountered frustration after frustration in trying to get Congress to act on my proposals legislative roadblocks to the Alaska pipeline, inaction on proposals for coal conversion, natural gas deregulation, fast breeder reactor development, and other needed measures The goal of my energy policy—which I named Project Independence—was, in the long run, to stimulate the production of energy from renewable sources such as nuclear power, and, in the short run, to cut back our dependence on unreliable foreign suppliers of oil. The United States is uniquely qualified to do these things. Ill-considered government policies, however, have had the opposite effect; they have actually increased our dependence on foreign oil.

At the present time conventional fuels supply 90 per cent of our energy needs. Oil, half of it imported, supplie 45 percent; coal, 20 percent; and natural gas, 25 percent. By boosting production from these sources and increasing conservation, while at the same time gearing up to increase our energy supply from renewable sources, we could probably have managed the "energy crisis." As it is, we are making things worse than they were before.

Government policies of price controls, high taxation and overregulation have discouraged the use of our domestic energy resources, encouraged waste, and increased our vulnerability to OPEC's price hikes and supply interruptions. Price controls on oil and a nationalized allocation system, which I regret I did not remove before I left office in 1974, have created spot shortages and surpluses in a checkerboard pattern all over the country. Former Treasury Secretary William Simon, who also served as my energy administrator, has aptly commented on the allocation system: "The kindest thing I can say about it is that it was disaster."

The best way to encourage conservation is through the free market. When waste becomes too expensive, people will find ways to eliminate it, and in a much more efficient manner than the government could ever devise, much less manage. The government could back up its strong words on conservation by taking one simple action: decontrolling all oil and natural gas prices once and for all.

Decontrol of prices would not only cut consumption, it would also boost production. For twenty-five years price controls on the interstate sale of natural gas have made it uneconomical to sell gas from gas-producing states to other parts of the country where the gas was needed. In the winter of 1976-1977 thousands of factories were closed and over a million people thrown out of work because of fuel shortages—shortages caused by controls such as those that kept natural gas from crossing state lines.

High taxation on "windfall" profits has a similar effect in discouraging production. Unless the energy producers of this country can make an extra dollar from their extra efforts, there is no incentive for them to solve the energy problem. It makes no sense to provide incentives for new oil production by removing price controls and then take away the incentives by punitive taxation. What "windfall profits" taxes really produce is a windfall for the government, paid by the consumer.

Coal is our most abundant energy resource. At the 1973 rates of consumption we have enough coal to last 800 years. But overly stringent environmental constraints have prevented us from using it to decrease our dependence on imported oil; in recent years the percentage of our energy needs supplied by coal has actually decreased. It makes no sense to sit on half the free world's reserves of coal and not use them. Environmental laws that were passed in a time of energy abundance need to be reexamined.

The Department of Energy employs 20,000 people and has a budget of $8 billion a year. It should be abolished. Its primary achievement to date has been to prevent the free market from solving the energy crisis. As long as the government is running the energy business we will have an energy crisis. The whole dismal history of government interference, whether in Britain, the Soviet Union, or the

United States, points to one conclusion: politics is harmful to the economy's health.

Looking to the future, we have to prepare for the day when conventional fuels will become too scarce and expensive to remain the principal source of power for our industries. At that point renewable energy sources should have come on line, supplying us with a virtually inexhaustible reservoir of energy. Solar, geothermal, and other research programs should be strongly supported, as I urged in 1973 and as President Carter did in 1979.

But none of these renewable sources offers more promise in both the short term and the long term than the power of the atom. Unfortunately, the issue of nuclear power has become extraordinarily politicized, polarized, and emotionalized. Opposition to nuclear power has become the new "cause" of the political Left. Panic-mongering modern Luddites have carried their ideological crusade against it into the streets in an attempt to cut off reasoned debate. Already companies trying to move forward in this area are inhibited by what William Simon calls a "crazy-quilt of environmental regulations" that threatens to destroy the economic viability of nuclear power. The latest nuclear power plant built in the United States took sixteen years to construct; in South Korea it takes less than five years. As a result, even before the latest OPEC price hike, in South Korea electricity from nuclear power plants was only half the cost of electricity from oil-fired plants.

There are risks in nuclear power, as there are with any energy source, and there is room for disagreement about the extent of those risks. But we should strive to keep that disagreement within informed and reasoned bounds, rather than letting our energy future be swept away in a sea of placards. If our ancestors had consulted only their fears, America would never have been discovered and the modern world would never have been built.

From my office in San Clemente I can daily view the white domes of the San Onofre nuclear power plant. These domes do not threaten me with radiation. They do not remind me of death or destruction. If they did, I would not have set up the Western White House virtually next door to them in 1969.

Rather, these domes represent heat and light for me and my neighbors and thousands of jobs for those working in plants dependent upon the electricity they produce. They represent the growth of an expanding economy and a rising standard of living. They represent the most abundant, and potentially the cheapest, source of energy, and one which Dr. Edward Teller describes as "the safest, cleanest way to generate large amounts of electrical power." We need this energy for the nation's future. As former Energy Secretary Schlesinger has put it, "Quite bluntly, unless we achieve greater use of coal and nuclear power over the next decade, this society just might not make it."

Seven years have passed since we began Project Independence, but we are no closer to energy independence now than we were in 1973. Indeed, we are farther from it. We must begin now to prepare to protect our interests in the oil-producing regions of the world. At the same time we must reject the fuzzy negativism of "limited growth" and continue to press for vigorous progress in developing our abundant energy resources. Only thus can we be assured of our viability as the world's greatest economic and military power. If we don't follow this course, we will face growing darkness with each passing year as surely as twilight follows the sunset.

Ceiling Unlimited

The economy is not just the realm of accountants. It is also the realm of the spirit. We fulfill ourselves in work, enriching our lives and the lives of others. Most important, there is a direct relationship between human liberties and a free economy. As Nobel Prize-winning economist Milton Friedman has noted, "Historical evidence speaks with a single voice on the relation between political freedom and a free market. I know of no example in time or place of a society that has been marked by a large measure of political freedom, and that has not also used something comparable to a free market to organize the bulk of economic activity." Conversely, when economic freedom disappears, political freedom dissolves with it.

The struggle between the American Revolution and the communist revolution is a struggle between a free society and a controlled society. The communists are materialists, but they have failed to match the material achievements of capitalism. What socialism promised, capitalism delivers. What utopians have predicted, capitalism provides. What dreamers have dreamed of for centuries, capitalism has produced and continues to produce: freedom and wealth, together, for the many.

The cult of the guilt-ridden has imbued us with the notion that we must be apologetic and defensive about our wealth; that because ours is a rich society, it is therefore an evil society. Giving credence to this nonsense is a disservice to America and the rest of the world. The plain fact is that ours is a rich society because it is a productive society, and unless we accept and proclaim that fact, the example we set for the needy nations of the world will be a false one.

Poverty oppresses. The best antidote to poverty is productivity, and the greatest productivity occurs when the economy provides incentives and rewards for hard work, for extra effort, and for increased investment.

The great majority of the world's people want change. But they want change for the better. Communism offers it, and then imposes a system that produces change for the worse. Capitalism, by contrast, is the greatest instrument of progressive change in the history of civilization. It produces more prosperity, more abundantly shared and with more freedom of choice, than any other economic system.

Two hundred years ago, at the start of the industrial revolution, the average per capita income in the world, in 1979 dollars, was $200. Today it is $2,000. Futurist Herman Kahn predicts that it will rise to $20,000 in the twenty-first century. Kahn says we are at the midpoint of an economic revolution as significant as the one that transformed man from a hunter to a farmer some 10,000 years ago. "Two hundred years ago," he writes, "almost everywhere human beings were comparatively few, poor and at the mercy of the forces of nature. Two centuries hence, barring some combination of very bad luck or bad management, they should be numerous, rich, and in control of the forces of nature."

What distinguishes these last 200 years from the thousands that preceded them is industrial capitalism. As recently as the 1780s four-fifths of French families spent 90 percent of their income on bread alone, for the sole purpose of staying alive. With the dawn of industrial capitalism the chains holding people to the land were broken, and peasants by the thousands flocked to the cities in search of a better life. Millions willingly put up with the hardships of early urban life to escape the even more gruesome lot of a peasant.

As it was for those peasants 200 years ago, the future is a vast unknown for us today. Man has always approached the future with a mixture of hope and fear. Now those fears are being fanned by the apostles of a new cult that is antigrowth, antitechnology, antibusiness, antiprogress. Sociologist Robert Nisbet warns: "I can think of no intellectual change that has come over America in the latter part of the 20th century that is more pregnant with institutional and material consequence than the almost complete disappearance—among intellectuals, not yet perhaps the majority of the people—of faith in progress."

There have always been prophets of doom, men of little minds and smaller faith. Pundits of Columbus's time advised the King and Queen of Spain that his proposed voyages were unlikely to yield any good result. In 1835 railroad experts dismissed as "extremely improbable" the development of any system of transport that could move at a rate exceeding ten miles per hour. One week before the Wright brothers flew, the New York *Times* ridiculed the idea that man would ever get off the ground. Again and again, timid pessimists have said it cannot be done. Again and again, courageous men have proved them wrong. If we do not fall captive to our fears—more specifically, to the fears of a vocal minority—we will again shatter all preconceived notions about the "limits" of growth. We will enter an era of "ceiling unlimited."

Our current economic problems all share a common solution: increased productivity. This is our challenge: to use the economic power of the West to produce a global flowering. It can be done, but only if we preserve the powerful dynamic of industrial capitalism.

It is typical of the day that a military thinker and an expert on Soviet strategy, Sir Robert Thompson, has framed one of the most compelling economic questions of our time. Thompson notes that the main Soviet targets have been large agricultural countries such as India. This is a matter of grave concern, he says, "because it could lead to a situation where perhaps three-quarters of the population of the world, through adopting a Marxist economy, is starving beyond even the capacity of North America to feed it. . . . It is alarming to think what the American aid bill may be if it has to feed a collectivized world. . . . It is even more alarming to think what might happen if the United States does not feed them." "Ceiling unlimited" for a free world or unlimited demands upon the United States are the alternatives we face in the century ahead.

The West towers over the communist world by a four-to-one margin economically, yet the Soviets have equalled us in military might. It is clear that they are channeling their economic resources into activities they think will enable them to win World War III. We must use our greatest advantage, our economic power, to match or better their military efforts, and at the same time to bring a new life of peace and prosperity to the peoples of the world.

Richard McCormack again states the challenge clearly:

> Our strategy should be to unlock private capital on a worldwide basis and get it back into growth and development. To do this, we must systematically begin to attack and overcome the fear, instability and economic policies which collectively are strangling investment, and with it the hopes for worldwide economic growth and development. This will involve helping to provide greater

physical security for societies now being preyed upon by
the Soviet Union, terrorists, guerrillas and Cubans.

If we do thus use our economic power, we will be fighting World War III according to our rules; then we will be
winning it, and the world will also win.

9
Will Power

The crocodile is a more primitive zoological speci-
men than the human being: but if a man steps blindfold
and naked into a crocodile's river, it is the crocodile who
will prevail.

—*Hugh Seton-Watson*

One of the lessons of history that one has to learn,
although it is very unpleasant, is that no civilization can
be taken for granted. Its permanency can never be assumed; there is always a dark age waiting for you around
the corner, if you play your cards badly and you make
sufficient mistakes, and we must never think that this
can't happen to us. It can happen to us, as it has happened four or five times in the history of the world....
I've no doubt at all that America has not only the
physical resources, but equally important, the moral resources to reassert its leadership of the world and to pursue that leadership role vigorously.... I think America
has to make a tremendous act of will, and the sooner it
makes it, the easier it's going to be.

—*Paul Johnson*

Not long ago I asked Dr. Edward Teller, the nuclear physicist who is often called "the father of the hydrogen bomb,"
what he thought things would be like in the United States
in the year 2000. He thought for a long while, and then re-

plied that he believed there was a 50 percent chance that the United States would not be in existence. I asked whether he meant physically or as a system of government. He said, "Either—or both."

This may seem apocalyptic. But as Samuel Johnson once said, "When a man knows he is to be hanged in a fortnight, it concentrates his mind wonderfully." Our task today is to concentrate the mind sooner, and thus to avoid the hanging.

One characteristic of advanced civilizations is that as they grow richer and fatter, they become softer and more vulnerable. Throughout history the leading civilizations of their time have been destroyed by barbarians, not because they lacked wealth or arms, but because they lacked will; because they awoke too late to the threat, and reacted too timidly in devising a strategy to meet it.

Optimists, unable or unwilling to confront the magnitude of the challenge, assume that the West will somehow survive; that free societies, having withstood so many past challenges, will withstand this one as well. Pessimists see the advance of "socialism" as an inevitable tide, with resistance ultimately futile. Both prefer not to think about nuclear war. Pessimists willingly trade a country here, a country there, for a few more years of ease and comfort. Optimists speak of the perfectibility of man, and suppose that if we smile enough at the Soviets, their hearts will melt and their policies will mellow.

A colder-eyed appraisal would see neither victory nor defeat as inevitable. Both sides are immensely strong. Each has a lot to fight for. Each has different strengths and different weaknesses, just as each has different goals.

One thing we should not expect is that the Soviet Union is going to mellow, or that Soviet values and ambitions in the next twenty years are going to be markedly different from what they consistently have been during the sixty-plus years since Lenin seized power. The Soviets have made clear what they want. We know what the United States and its allies want. We know the means by which the

Soviets pursue their goals. We know the resources each side has at its disposal. The crucial uncertainty is not in the Soviet thrust, but in the West's response. As Winston Churchill II recently wrote, "The days of effortless supremacy for the West are now gone."

The U.S.-Soviet contest is a struggle between two opposite poles of human experience—between those represented by the sword and by the spirit, by fear and by hope. Their system is ruled by the sword; ours is governed by the spirit. Their influence has spread by conquest; ours has spread by example. This struggle is not new. It did not begin with the end of World War II, or with the Russian Revolution. It is as old as civilization. And history gives no sure guide to the outcome, for it shows us that through the centuries first one side has prevailed, and then the other. The struggle is as old as the drive of rulers to impose tyranny and of people to escape it; as old as the effort of one nation to conquer and of others to resist. Tyrannies have risen and fallen; so have democracies. Man has struggled against oppression and won; oppressors also have won.

Edith Hamilton, a historian of ancient Greece, once wrote, "To the Greeks of that day their most precious possession, freedom, was the distinguishing mark between East and West. . . . 'You do not know what freedom is,' Herodotus reports a Greek saying to a Persian. 'If you did you would fight for it with bare hands if you had no weapons.' " Freedom is still the distinguishing mark between East and West.

Gandhi once said, "No society can possibly be built on a denial of individual freedom." But as a young dissident Soviet historian, Andrei Amalrik, observes, the ideas of self-government, of equality before the law, and of personal freedom "are almost completely incomprehensible to the Russian people. . . . As for respecting the rights of an individual as such, the idea simply arouses bewilderment."

To most Americans, the Russian experience is similarly incomprehensible. The illusion is widespread that because the Soviet way of life is unnatural to Americans, it is unnatural to Russians; that if only the Soviet people were exposed to the ways of the West, they would quickly change. The Westerner believes the Soviet system is bound to change simply because people cannot live that way. But they do, and this is the point that the West must grasp. We can hope that the Soviet system eventually changes, but we act at our peril if we expect it to change and base our policies on that expectation.

The Soviet sword has been annealed in the fires of centuries of suffering. To the Soviets, the greatest brutalities are not unthinkable, because they have been part of their experience. We know freedom, liberty, hope, self-indulgence; they know tyranny, butchery, starvation, war, and annihilation. Those qualities that make Soviet victory so frightful a prospect for the world are the same ones that make it possible.

Throughout its first 200 years the United States has had a rare luxury. Protected by two oceans from the swirling conflicts of Europe and Asia, we could develop the dream that inspired our creation. We could concentrate on taming a continent, on building the most powerful industrial machine the world had ever seen, on improving our democracy and making it a beacon to the world.

We could caustically examine our own shortcomings while ignoring those of older—and newer—nations, because our own were the ones for which we were responsible. We did not have to measure ourselves by reference to the rest of the world. The rest of the world was distant, almost irrelevant. From time to time it encroached on us; in two world wars we had to step in, after those wars had begun, in order to ensure that the side of freedom won. But we remained essentially apart. When new barbarisms appeared, other nations were first in their line of march. Others bore the brunt of aggression, while we moralized from afar. André Malraux once commented to me that the United States was "the only nation ever to become the most powerful in the world without seeking to." Because we did not seek that power, we were unprepared for its exercise when we assumed its responsibilities.

Now we ourselves are on the front line, and the adversary we confront is tough.

Those who get to the top in the Soviet system do so by being more cunning, more brutal, and more ruthless than their rivals. Leon Trotsky wrote that "Lenin, at every passing opportunity, emphasized the absolute necessity of terror." Lenin himself declared bluntly in 1920 that the "scientific concept of dictatorship means neither more nor less than unlimited power, resting directly on force, not limited by anything, not restricted by any laws, nor any absolute rules. Nothing else but that."

Stalin killed nearly a million people per year in the quarter century of his rule. Khrushchev and Brezhnev both served their apprenticeships under Stalin, not by distributing food stamps or serving in a Peace Corps, but by efficiently eliminating those whom Stalin saw as threats to his power. Khrushchev was sent to the Ukraine by Stalin in 1938 to conduct a political housecleaning. Within a year 163 of the 166 members of the Central Committee there had been liquidated. Khrushchev was then promoted to full membership in the Politburo.

The Darwinian forces of the Soviet system produce not only ruthless leaders, but clever ones. Former Ambassador Foy Kohler writes of Khrushchev:

> To me he came to be the embodiment of the almost untranslatable Russian adjective *khitryi.* . . . According to the dictionary it means sly, cunning, artful, intricate or wily. But it really means more than this; it also means unscrupulous, smart, clever, quickwitted. Roll all these adjectives into one and you have the *khitryi* Khrushchev—a bootlicker or a bully as circumstances required, a demagogue and opportunist always.

Often we in the West are overly impressed by the style, manner, and education of leaders of other nations, forgetting that elegant manners do not make a strong leader. Education may strengthen the brain but weaken the backbone.

At first, many American experts on the Soviet Union

tended to downgrade Khrushchev, noting that he was poorly educated, spoke bad Russian, drank too much, and had boorish manners. But they missed the point. John Foster Dulles saw through the façade. At a National Security Council meeting just after Khrushchev took power he put it sharply. "Anyone who survives and comes to the top in that communist jungle," he told Eisenhower, "is bound to be a strong leader and a dangerous enemy."

Dulles was right. Anyone who gets to the top in the Soviet Union has climbed over a lot of corpses to get there. He would not have made it unless he gave others reason to fear him more than he feared them. By going through the fires of purges, intrigue, and cutthroat competition for power, the Soviet leaders come out as tempered steel.

If the Soviet leaders are tough, so are the people. Every suffering the leaders have inflicted, the people have endured. Adversity is a good teacher, which makes the Soviet people well schooled indeed. Noting that he knew people who had lived through the Revolution, the farm collectivization, Stalin's terror, and the German invasion in World War II, Soviet dissident Lev Kopelev commented to an American, "Think how much more experienced we are than you."

All of this is not to say that the Soviet people, or even necessarily the leaders, are inherently bad. There is an old saying that "I can hate the sin, but never the sinner." I like the Russian people. I like the Chinese people. I hate communism and what it does to people. The communist leaders are products of a cruel system and inheritors of a harsh tradition. They act by instinct, just as the man-eating tiger or the piranha does.

By and large, the people of the Soviet Union are warm, generous, good, and very able in many respects. They have suffered brutally, both before and since the Revolution. They tend to get along extremely well with Americans. Many of the Soviet leaders are capable of behaving with great charm, and they can become genuinely emotional when they discuss their hopes for the next generation or the devastation their people suffered in the war. In 1973 I gave a small private dinner for Brezhnev at my home in San Clemente. I delivered a warm, personal toast. Tears came to his eyes as it was translated, and he rose impulsively from his chair and folded me in a Russian bear hug. But later that same night he brought Gromyko and Dobrynin to my study and launched into a brutal three-hour attack on our policies in the Middle East.

The fact that the Soviet leaders can be personally very friendly even while they plot the destruction of the other person's country is a dichotomy, but not a contradiction. They operate on several levels at once. They can be as warm and effusive as individuals as they are ruthless as wielders of state power. For that is the way the Soviet system is. Generosity, love, tenderness, charity of spirit, all have their place in the Russian soul, but not in the actions of the Soviet government. This is a distinction too few Americans seem able to make.

The totalitarian nature of the Soviet system is at once its chief strength and its chief weakness. Interestingly, it was Benito Mussolini who introduced the word "totalitarianism." Writing in 1932, he gave this authoritative interpretation of the fascist system:

> The Fascist system stresses the importance of the State and recognizes the individual only insofar as his interests coincide with those of the state. . . . The Fascist conception of the State is all-embracing; outside of it no human or spiritual values may exist, much less have any value. . . . For Fascism the State is absolute, individuals and groups are admissible insofar as they act in accordance with the State.

Mussolini's description of fascism reads like a charter for communism.

The strength of Soviet totalitarianism is that the government can concert its efforts in every field: military, economic, propaganda, scientific, education. A pluralistic free society cannot do this. Most of its economic decisions are made in the marketplace, its education system goes its own way, its press is free. Our government can subsidize certain kinds of scientific research, and thus, for example, speed the development of selected new weapons or new technologies, but the great bulk of our research is directed by the private sector for private purposes.

The corresponding weakness of the Soviet system is that this central, bureaucratic control stifles creativity and limits incentive. Our freer system provides incentive and encourages creativity, and thus we *produce* more: more goods, more ideas, more innovations. They *concentrate* their more limited production in those areas they believe will best serve their central purposes.

Just as Stalin exported butter by the ton and grain by the shipload while millions of peasants died of starvation, today's Soviet Union can, in effect, strip the shirts from its workers' backs in order to build more and bigger missiles. In cold military terms this is one of its great advantages, for it enables the Soviet leaders to spend on their military more than twice the percentage of GNP that the United States does. They can tell their workers where to work, for what hours, at what pay, and they have no fear of strikes.

As a result of our different systems, marshaling the nation's will is a more difficult task in the West. But it also is more important. In the Soviet Union the state speaks and the people obey. In the West the people speak with a cacophony of voices and go their own ways. Soviet leaders command. Western leaders must lead.

In America, the spirit is there, if only the spark can be found to light it. As Churchill once said, "We have not journeyed all this way across the centuries, across the oceans, across the mountains, across the prairies, because we are made of sugar candy."

America's greatest strength in this global contest is America itself—our people, our land, our system, our culture, our tradition, our reputation. American history is full of archetypal heroes: the stony Vermont farmer, the Pennsylvania coal miner, the Southern gentleman farmer, the Texas oilman, the Las Vegas gambler, the California gold miner, the Oregon lumberjack—the list is extensive. Cow-boys, robber barons, pioneers, traders, roughnecks, and horse thieves—all share a common trait that is cherished in American folklore: individuality. We have always prized and encouraged the individual. The acceptance of individual differences has been our hallmark.

Americans also are a generous people. We have shown ourselves willing to help others anywhere on the globe. We have extended aid and encouraged development in the rest of the world, because we have been conditioned by our history to see good in growth. We want independent, self-reliant neighbors and prosperous trading partners, nations joined with us in the sort of common interest that benefits us all. This is why the United States has friends and allies, while the Soviet Union has subjects and satellites.

From George Washington's Neutrality Proclamation through the Monroe Doctrine and the Marshall Plan runs an American impulse that disdains war and instead seeks to spread freedom and prosperity. We have a natural respect for the individuality of others, and a concern for their well-being. These instincts make for a constructive foreign policy, one that commands the genuine respect of other nations—*if* we also show the resolve required of a great power.

And there, precisely, in that "if," lies our greatest potential weakness, and the greatest danger to the West. There is no question that if there is to be an arms race, we can win it. There is no question that if there is to be an economic race, we can win it. There is no question that if there is to be a contest for the "hearts and minds" of the world's people, we can win it. But there is a question whether we can win the contest we are actually going to be engaged in: a test of will and determination between ourselves and the most powerfully armed aggressive power the world has ever known.

William F. Buckley, Jr., once remarked that he would rather be governed by the first 100 names in the Boston telephone book than by the faculty of Harvard University. This reflects a shrewdly perceptive analysis of American strengths and weaknesses. The people as a whole often lack sophistication, but they have a good, gut common sense, and when necessary they can draw on an enormous reservoir of courage and will. But too many of America's intellectual and cultural elite have shown themselves to be brilliant, creative, trendy, gullible, smug, and blind in one eye: they tend to see bad only on the Right, not on the Left. Extremely sophisticated about ideas in the abstract, they can be extremely simplistic and naïve about the realities of the actual global conflict we find ourselves engaged in. "War" is "bad," "peace" is "good," and posturing with words is everything.

The nation's immediate problem is that while the common man fights America's wars, the intellectual elite sets its agenda. Today, whether the West lives or dies is in the hands of its new power elite: those who set the terms of public debate, who manipulate the symbols, who decide whether nations or leaders will be depicted on 100 million television sets as "good" or "bad." This power elite sets the limits of the possible for Presidents and Congress. It molds the impressions that move the nation, or that mire it.

America lost in Vietnam because this power elite persistently depicted first Diem and then Thieu as corrupt and dictatorial and the war therefore as not worth fighting—ignoring how much worse the alternative would be. The Shah of Iran and President Anastasio Somoza of Nicaragua met the same fate, with the United States greasing the skids for their downfall. While still our U.N. ambassador, Andrew Young nominated the Ayatollah Khomeini for sainthood and praised Cuban troops as providing "stability" in Africa. Television romanticizes revolutionaries, thus greatly increasing the chances that Soviet-backed revolutionary wars can be waged successfully—just as the New York *Times'* romanticizing of Fidel Castro two decades ago was a major factor in legitimating his revolution and securing his victory.

This complex of attitudes is nothing new. Reinhold Niebuhr once pointed out that communism was more dangerous to the West than the naked fascism of the Nazis, because "Russia comes to every nation, which it intends to subjugate, as a 'liberator' from 'fascist' and 'imperialist' oppression. . . . A corrupted ideal may be more potent than a frank defiance of all ideal values. The proof of that higher potency is given by the fact that Russia's 'fifth columns' in the Western world are composed not of the miserable traitors who constituted the Nazi-dominated 'Bund,' nor yet of mere Communist party hacks. They contain thousands of misguided idealists who still think that Russia is the midwife of an ideal society, about to be born." Communism's greater subtlety would not make it more dangerous than Nazism if the leaders of Western thought were more discerning.

Even though Mussolini's definition of fascism was a perfect description of Soviet communism, fascism has been identified as right-wing and therefore "bad," while communism has been identified as left-wing and therefore, if not actually "good," at least to be viewed in a sympathetic light that points up its promise while obscuring its crudities.

The forced collectivization of Soviet agriculture in the 1930s was one of the most monumental atrocities of human history, in many ways the model for the genocidal tragedy of Cambodia in our own time. Families were torn apart, peasants were slaughtered for trying to hold onto a pig or a cow; millions, their few possessions confiscated, were packed into cattle cars and sent to die in the frozen wastelands of Siberia. Children, orphaned or separated from their parents, wandered the countryside starving and homeless. But in the West the leaders of intellectual fashion were so infatuated with the romance of revolution that they closed their eyes to its gore and saw only its glory. Thus George Bernard Shaw, in the midst of the horror, could tell a press conference in Moscow that he was "more than ever convinced" that capitalist countries "must adopt Russia's methods," and write in his hotel guest book, "There is not a more interesting country in the world today to visit than Soviet Russia, and I find travelling there perfectly safe and pleasant. . . . Tomorrow I leave this land of hope and return to our Western countries of despair."

Reflecting on his days as a Moscow correspondent for

the *Manchester Guardian* during the Stalin era, Malcolm Muggeridge recently recalled "the extraordinary performance of the liberal intelligentsia, who, in those days, flocked to Moscow like pilgrims to Mecca. And they were one and all utterly delighted and excited by what they saw there. Clergymen walked serenely and happily through the anti-god museums, politicians claimed that no system of society could possibly be more equitable and just, lawyers admired Soviet justice, and economists praised the Soviet economy." It was this, he said, that "touched off my awareness of the great liberal death wish, my sense that Western man was, as it were, sleep-walking into his own ruin."

William Pfaff of *The New Yorker* notes that those "who believed in Russian Communism, and went enthusiastically to Moscow a half-century ago to see what they wanted to see, and no more, were not negligible men. They included John Reed, Bernard Shaw, André Gide (for a time), Theodore Dreiser, John Dos Passos, Julian Huxley." More recently, he argues, "With Stalin dead and the Soviet Union discredited as a society of reform, the communisms of Mao Zedong and Ho Chi Minh assumed the function of 'Beau Ideal' for a new generation of European and American idealists." These people "see in the political character and accomplishments of other countries what they need to see. . . . For admiring foreigners, Vietnam and China were too often countries that existed mostly in their heads. Since they were imaginary countries, they were preserved from the corrosion of existence, the wear of life. Faith in them could remain; they could be stubbornly believed societies of justice, warm human cooperation, mutual support, simple honesty, truth-telling."

A comparable blindness in one eye exists with regard to Africa. Long before his fall the brutalities of Uganda's Idi Amin were revealed beyond the capacity of any apologist to pretend they were anything but the most savage sort of butchery on a vast scale. Yet the hypocrisy of those African leaders who elected him president of the Organization of African Unity while hurling moral thunderbolts at the West was ignored. Harvard students demanded boycotts of the

Union of South Africa, not of Uganda or communist-dominated Mozambique. In South Africa blacks are consigned to certain areas and forbidden certain forms of fraternization; in Uganda the heads of black Ugandans were beaten in with hammers, their legs were chopped off, and they were forced to eat the flesh of their fellow prisoners before they too were put to death. But fashionable outrage is directed against apartheid, not against savagery.

Longshoreman-philosopher Eric Hoffer has commented:

> One of the surprising privileges of intellectuals is that they are free to be scandalously asinine without harming their reputation. The intellectuals who idolized Stalin while he was purging millions and stifling the least stirring of freedom have not been discredited. They are still holding forth on every topic under the sun and are listened to with deference.... The metaphysical grammarian Noam Chomsky, who went to Hanoi to worship there at the altar of human rights and democracy, was not discredited and silenced when the humanitarian communists staged their nightmare in South Vietnam and Cambodia.

There is none so blind as he who will not see—and this has been the condition of much of America's intellectual establishment through much of this century. Unfortunately, as Hugh Seton-Watson points out, "Nothing can defend a society from itself if its upper 100,000 men and women, both the decision makers and those who help to mold the thinking of the decision makers, are resolved to capitulate."

Too many of those who should be most jealously preserving and defending what America represents have instead been paralyzed by a misplaced sense of guilt, which has led them to abandon faith in our own civilization. As *Commentary* editor Norman Podhoretz has put it, "The forces that have prevented both the strengthening of our military power and the energizing of our economic capacity seem to be based on the continuing conviction of many that the kind of society and civilization we have are not worth maintaining—neither worth defending by military means nor perpetuating by economic means."

If America loses World War III, it will be because of the failure of its leadership class. In particular, it will be because of the attention, the celebrity, and the legitimacy given to the "trendies"—those overglamorized dilettantes who posture in the latest idea, mount the fashionable protests, and are slobbered over by the news media, whose creation they essentially are. The attention given them and their "causes" romanticizes the trivial and trivializes the serious. It reduces public discussion to the level of a cartoon strip. Whatever the latest cause they embrace—whether antiwar, antinuclear, antimilitary, antibusiness—it is almost invariably one that works against the interest of the United States in the context of World War III.

These trendies are ready with an opinion at the drop of a microphone, and their opinions are treated as news—not because they are authorities, but because they are celebrities. Their minds are impervious to argument, and their arguments are impervious to fact. Posture is all. Some see their posturing as a conspiracy, and suspect that it is directed from Moscow. But this misses the point. It is not a conspiracy, but a conformity. If it were a conspiracy, it would be easier to deal with. The trendies are an army of the gullible, steering by the star of fashion, drawn to the sound of applause. They call themselves "liberal" because "liberalism" is in fashion; but they have lost touch with the classic spirit of liberalism. As Michael Novak points out, "The liberal spirit believes in the potent energy of the individual spirit. It believes in a free economy in a free polity. . . . Liberals must begin to strengthen the mediating institutions of society which alone, as social organisms, can check the power of the state."

There is a sort of Gresham's Law that applies to public discussion: bad ideas drive out good, and attention given to empty posturing shuts the door on serious debate.

In a less hazardous age we could afford to indulge the prancing of the trendies on the stage of public debate. But now our national survival depends on learning to distinguish between the meaningful and the meaningless.

The issues that confront us are complex and the answers are by no means all clear. But this increases rather than decreases the need for calm, rational examination of alternative courses and alternative consequences. It also increases the need for the most meticulous care in ensuring that we decide on the basis of fact, not fantasy.

The defining characteristic of today's intellectual and media elite is that it swims merrily in a sea of fantasy. The world of television is essentially a fantasy world, and television is today's common denominator of communication, today's unifying American experience. This has frightening implications for the future.

Ideas that fit on bumper stickers are not ideas at all, they simply are attitudes. And attitudinizing is no substitute for analysis. Unfortunately, too often television is to news as bumper stickers are to philosophy, and this has a corrosive effect on public understanding of those issues on which national survival may depend.

Only in very recent years has the notion taken hold that life is meant to be easy. Coddled, pampered, truckled to, a generation of Americans has been bred to believe that they should coast through life—and that any disparity between American society as it is and a gauzy, utopian ideal is evidence that society is corrupt. The principal threat to a highly developed society is not that overconsumption depletes its resources, but rather that insulation from the hardscrabble challenge of basic existence dulls its sense of reality and leaves it prey to the barbarians who are always at the gates. Where abundance comes easily, it becomes too easy to assume that security comes with comparable ease. "Street smarts," jungle savvy, that edgy wariness that comes naturally to those whose precarious existence keeps them ever on the alert—these atrophy in the cushioned luxury of a life in which ease and deference are taken for granted.

Given the choice, most people would rather cruise the

Caribbean than drill with the militia. It thus becomes very tempting to consult our hopes rather than our fears, and to drape an optimistic view of human nature with the cloak of moral virtue. It becomes much easier, much more indulgent, to denounce as alarmists those who tell us we must prepare for the worst in order to preserve the best. It takes an effort of will to rouse ourselves from lethargy, to put aside the pursuit of pleasure, to defend our liberty. Laxity is the affliction of the comfortable, and this is why every past civilization that has achieved comfort has been destroyed by another less advanced. Our task is to make sure that this does not happen to us.

If the West loses World War III, it will have been because of an unwillingness to face reality. It will have been because of the compulsion to live in a dream world, to infuse the public dialogue with romantic fantasies and to imagine that cold steel can somehow be countered with simplistic moralisms.

The key thing to recognize about America's decline in will is that it has not been a failure of the people; it has been a failure of the leaders. Robert Nisbet notes: "We appear to be living in yet another age in which 'failure of nerve' is conspicuous; not in the minds of America's majority but in the minds of those who are gatekeepers for ideas, the intellectuals." Alexander Solzhenitsyn has pointed to "a decline in courage" as the most striking feature of the West: "Such a decline in courage is particularly noticeable among the ruling groups and the intellectual elite, causing an impression of loss of courage by the entire society. . . . Should one point out," he asks, "that from ancient times decline in courage has been considered the beginning of the end?"

America is a sleeping giant. It is time to wake up that giant, to define his purpose, restore his strength, and revitalize his will. Nothing less will save the West and the institutions of freedom around the world from the merciless barbarism that threatens us all. As Solzhenitsyn has also argued, "no weapons, no matter how powerful, can help the

West until it overcomes its loss of will power. In a state of psychological weakness, weapons become a burden for the capitulating side."

The war in Vietnam was not lost on the battlefields of Vietnam. It was lost in the halls of Congress, in the boardrooms of corporations, in the executive suites of foundations, and in the editorial rooms of great newspapers and television networks. It was lost in the salons of Georgetown, the drawing rooms of the "beautiful people" in New York, and the classrooms of great universities. The class that provided the strong leadership that made victory possible in World War I and World War II failed America in one of the crucial battles of World War III—Vietnam.

They had their excuses. They said it was the wrong war in the wrong place (as if any war were ever the right war in the right place). They said Thieu was a corrupt dictator. They said that by aiding South Vietnam, we were only bringing death and destruction. They said South Vietnam was unimportant and not worth saving. Since then the flood of refugees from Vietnam and the tragic fate of the people of Cambodia have torn at the consciences of many. Now they have both an obligation and an opportunity to help restore the strength of America's leadership, and thus to ensure that such tragedies are not repeated on an even larger scale.

The greatest institutional change in America's leadership class has been the development of enormous new power in the hands of the media. But the failures of the leadership class go beyond the intellectual and media elite. The leaders of "big business" once were a bastion of support for American strength, just as they once were rigorously independent. Now, with some admirable exceptions, they have become timid, reluctant to roil bureaucratic waters or offend consumer spokesmen; as huge corporations have become huge bureaucracies, corporate leaders themselves have become bureaucratic. There are few big business leaders I would have put in the ring with a healthy Brezhnev. A George Meany or a Frank Fitzsimmons, however, would have held his own. When the chips were down, when America's future was on the line and I needed support for the really tough decisions, I seldom got it from the corporation chairmen or university presidents. I did get it from labor leaders, from smaller businessmen, from "middle America." They had the strong heart, the solid will, the guts, that have saved America before and will save it again.

Now that the passions of Vietnam have subsided and the Russians are brazenly using the Red Army itself to absorb countries directly into their empire, there are stirrings among the intellectual elite of a new awareness that the Soviet challenge is real. France, where the Left was so long ascendent in intellectual circles, is now producing some of the toughest and most realistic thinking in the West. I hope that this is a trend throughout the West and that those in America whose natural function is to lead will soon begin once again to lead in those directions that national survival requires.

America must come to grips with the realities of power. It must accept power, accept its existence, accept its exercise, and accept the ambiguities of result that are sometimes inherent in its use in a conflict-ridden, imperfect world. The time has passed when we could afford to temporize, to equivocate, to hesitate, when we could indulge the luxury of moralistic pettifogging as an excuse for keeping our feet out of the muddy waters. In today's world, purity is no excuse for pusillanimity. Every day lost in mounting our own strategic counteroffensive narrows an already perilously thin margin of safety.

Perhaps a nation that equates celebrity with wisdom, that looks to rock stars and movie actresses as its oracles, deserves to lose; and yet there is more to America than that. There is more backbone, more common sense, more determination—if only the public can be wakened to what the reality is. And make no mistake about it: If the American people do wake up one day to find themselves confronted with the stark choice between war and slavery, they are going to fight. They are going to fight with missiles, with airplanes, with ships, with tanks; they are going to fight, if need be, with sticks and stones and with their bare finger-nails.

Americans have not known suffering on such a scale as the Russians have. But we have known it, and we have overcome it. The frontier was not a garden party. World Wars I and II were not Woodstocks. The immigrants who came to our shores in prewelfare days scrabbled for existence, and they grew strong in the process. We have not confronted suffering on the Soviet scale because we have not had to. But we have shown time and again that what we had to do, we could do, once we recognized the necessity for doing it.

If those who have never known the absence of freedom are slow to recognize how much it means to them, it is equally true that those who have never lived *in* freedom may underestimate the strength of a free people's gut determination to preserve it. Faced suddenly with the prospect of its loss, they are going to discover its value. And this, in the final analysis, is what must give the Kremlin leaders pause.

Meanwhile, we must underscore that basic truth with actions that drive its meaning home. We must show the Kremlin that its drive for military supremacy is ultimately futile. We must recognize that what we are engaged in is a war, even if not in the conventional sense in which our history books have defined it. If this war is not to escalate to the level of an actual armed clash, we must fight it effectively on the nonmilitary level.

The crucial element in developing a strategy to win victory without war is willpower. Military power and economic power are necessary, but they are useless without willpower.

It has been said that where there is a will there is a way. As we have so often proved in the past, by summoning up our will we can find the way.

10
Presidential
Power

Presidents must have a will to power or they will not be successful presidents. They must constantly search for power, building it, if necessary, out of every scrap of formal authority and personal influence they can locate. They must constantly guard whatever power they have achieved. They must hoard power so that it will be available in the future.

—*James MacGregor Burns*

When to pause, lower one's voice; when to thrust out one's jaw in defiance?

—*Hugh Sidey*

When I first entered Congress more than thirty years ago Truman was in the White House, Stalin was in the Kremlin, MacArthur ruled Japan, and Europe lay in ruins. Since then I have watched nations advance and decline, and have seen leaders succeed and fail. America has been through seven presidencies. It has confronted many crises, fought two wars, and narrowly averted fighting others.

As I have watched the unfolding of world events over these years, it has become clear to me that the one factor most crucial to the strength and cohesion of the West, and to the chances for peace, is the leadership provided by the President of the United States.

269

The President has great power in wartime as Commander-in-Chief of the armed forces. But he also has enormous power to prevent war and preserve peace. Having had both responsibilities, I know that the latter can be even more important than the former. It can also be more difficult to exercise effectively, especially in this era of a "war called peace."

Americans prefer to conduct their peacetime contests in the international arena by Marquis of Queensberry rules. For the Soviet leaders, however, the same rules apply in peace as in war, and those are the rules of the street-fighter: anything goes. To meet their challenge, the American President must use all the power at his command in an effective and responsible way. "Responsible" here includes the specific responsibility that he alone bears for ensuring the nation's survival and the free world's future.

This requires that he think realistically, not naïvely; that he be a skilled diplomat; that he know when to go to the summit and when not to go, and what to do when he gets there; that he never give our adversaries something they want unless he gets from them something we want; that while respecting the principle of openness when feasible, he preserve secrecy when necessary; that he recognize that gathering intelligence and conducting covert activities are justified as much to prevent war as to wage it; and finally that he accept the reality that moral perfection in the conduct of nations cannot be expected and should not be demanded. A President needs a global view, a sense of proportion, and a keen sense of the possible. He needs to know how power operates, and he must have the will to use it.

The effective use of power, especially on the world scene, is a skill that only experience can teach. But we can learn from the experience of others. We can draw on the wisdom of others. In the heyday of the British Empire young Englishmen grew up with their eyes on the far corners of the earth. The British had a national tradition of ruling a vast empire from a small island; this is one reason they were so adroit at it. A global view came naturally, and so did a familiarity with the exercise of power and with the ways of the world. In the postwar world America has assumed global responsibilities; we must try to prepare our next generation to carry them. We must understand that while the President is chosen by Americans, that choice can determine the future of free people everywhere.

If I could carve ten rules into the walls of the Oval Office for my successors to follow in the dangerous years just ahead, they would be these:

1 Always be prepared to negotiate, but never negotiate without being prepared.
2 Never be belligerent, but always be firm.
3 Always remember that covenants should be openly agreed to but privately negotiated.
4 Never seek publicity that would destroy the ability to get results.
5 Never give up unilaterally what could be used as a bargaining chip. Make your adversaries give something for everything they get.
6 Never let your adversary underestimate what you *would* do in response to a challenge. Never tell him in advance what you would *not* do.
7 Always leave your adversary a face-saving line of retreat.
8 Always carefully distinguish between friends who provide some human rights and enemies who deny all human rights.
9 Always do at least as much for our friends as our adversaries do for our enemies.
10 Never lose faith. In a just cause faith can move mountains. Faith without strength is futile, but strength without faith is sterile.

Having laid down these rules, I would also suggest that the President keep in his desk drawer, in mind but out of sight, an eleventh commandment: When saying "always" and "never," always keep a mental reservation; never foreclose the unique exception; always leave room for maneuver.

"Always" and "never" are guideposts, but in high-stakes diplomacy there are few immutables. A President always has to be prepared for what he thought he would never do.

Private Diplomacy

By its nature, diplomacy must be conducted beyond the range of cameras and microphones if it is to succeed. Diplomacy is not the raucous haggling of an Oriental bazaar, but rather a quiet, often subtle process of feeling out the differing degrees to which various elements of the other party's position are negotiable, and of trying varying combinations of give-and-take. Negotiators have to be able to advance tentative proposals, to explore alternatives, and to test the other side's reactions. They can only afford to do this if they can do it in privacy. Genuine negotiation is a search for some form of accommodation that advances the general interests of both parties by compromising on the specific interests of each. In such an agreement each side gets something, and each side also gives something. Premature exposure of part of the agreement—or even of tentative proposals that might later be abandoned—can destroy the whole agreement. Privacy in negotiations advances agreement. Publicity defeats it.

Frequently results can be achieved through quiet diplomacy that could never be achieved through public diplomacy. A classic illustration of this occurred during my first term, in 1970. In the fall of that year U-2 flights over Cuba revealed that a base was being constructed at Cienfuegos which could be used for submarines armed with nuclear missiles. This violated the 1962 U.S.-Soviet agreement on Cuba. But instead of confronting the Russians publicly with our knowledge of this violation, we decided to use quiet diplomacy so that they could withdraw without losing face publicly. Henry Kissinger informed Soviet Ambassador Anatoly Dobrynin that we were aware of the base under construction, told him unequivocally that we considered it to be a violation of our agreement, and let Dobrynin know that we were keeping things cool deliberately so that the Soviets could withdraw without a public confrontation.

Two weeks later Dobrynin handed Kissinger a note reaffirming the 1962 understanding about Cuba and stating that the Soviets were doing nothing to violate that understanding. U-2 flights showed that construction had slowed down at the sub site. After some face-saving delays it stopped altogether and the base at Cienfuegos was abandoned. Our strategy had worked. The Russians had decided to take advantage of the maneuverability our low-profile strategy afforded them. By denying that the violation had ever existed, they backed away from the crisis and still saved face. Quiet diplomacy supported by steady nerves and a still-superior arsenal had prevailed. We had not forced the issue into the open where the Russians could retreat only at the cost of a great deal of prestige. We made it easier for them to retreat, thereby averting another confrontation at the brink over Cuba.

This episode proved the wisdom of Liddell Hart's dictum:

> It is an elementary principle of strategy that, if you find your opponent in a strong position costly to force, you should leave him a line of retreat—as the quickest way of loosening his resistance. It should, equally, be a principle of policy, especially in war, to provide your opponent with a ladder by which he can climb down.

Our low profile proved to be the ladder the Soviets used.

In the 1978 meetings at Camp David with Egyptian President Anwar Sadat and Israeli Prime Minister Menachem Begin President Carter also dramatically demonstrated the benefits of negotiating in an atmosphere free from the baying of press hounds. His private meetings with Sadat and Begin proved absolutely essential to the breakthroughs that paved the way to the Egyptian-Israeli peace accord.

There are, of course, times when going public becomes a useful tactic to advance a negotiation, to rally support, to bring pressure on the other side, or to counter enemy propaganda. In January 1972 I disclosed publicly that for nearly

two and a half years Henry Kissinger had been periodically
traveling in secret to Paris and conducting negotiations
there with representatives of North Vietnam, and I also disclosed the proposals we had secretly made. North Vietnam
had been cynically exploiting the secrecy of those negotiations; we were being accused of intransigence, when in fact
we had advanced extremely forthcoming peace proposals
and had been stonewalled by the North Vietnamese. In this
case, with North Vietnam clearly hoping to wear down
America's will by blaming us for the lack of progress and
thus fanning heightened antiwar sentiment, it became important to make the record public. As I put it then, "Just
as secret negotiations can sometimes break a public deadlock, public disclosure may help to break a secret deadlock."
Even in a case such as this, however, the public disclosure
is a tactic; the negotiations themselves still have to proceed
in secret.

The British diplomat Sir Harold Nicolson put the case
for private diplomacy perfectly in his book *Diplomacy*. He
said that while a foreign policy must be openly proclaimed
and subjected to the closest scrutiny of the public, the negotiations that are necessary to carry on that policy must be
kept secret or else the policy itself will be sabotaged. Commenting on Woodrow Wilson's secretiveness during the negotiation of the Treaty of Versailles, Nicolson noted that
even "the highest apostle of 'open diplomacy' found, when
it came to practice, that open negotiation was totally unworkable." Wilson, he declared, had failed "to foresee that
there was all the difference in the world between 'open covenants' and 'openly arrived at'—between policy and negotiation."

The "Hole Card"

Diplomacy often requires a delicate and intricate balancing of ambiguity and straight talk, the unpredictable and
the very predictable. A complex game is played out between

adversaries, a game that involves, or should involve, the least amount of guesswork on the part of the American, and the greatest amount of guesswork on the part of the other side.

In this respect international relations are a lot like poker—stud poker with the hole card. The hole card is all important because without it your opponent—the Soviet leader, for instance—has perfect knowledge of whether or not he can beat you. If he knows he will win, he will raise you. If he knows he cannot, he will fold and get out of the game.

The United States is an open society. We have all but one of our cards face up on the table. Our only covered card is the will, nerve, and unpredictability of the President—his ability to make the enemy think twice about raising the ante. If we turn that card up, it is no contest. We must, of course, have good cards showing. But we must also make the Russians think that our hole card is a very good card indeed. The Russians are masters at disguising their hole card—they are masters of the bluff. More often than not, that is all their hole card is, a bluff.

Nevertheless, we can never make that judgment with certainty, so we must exercise caution in our negotiations with them or with their surrogates. To be on an equal footing with them, our "up" cards must be as good as theirs, and our "down" card—the President—must be every bit as unknown as theirs.

Many examples from recent years illustrate the danger of turning all our cards up, as well as the benefit of keeping one down.

In 1950 the United States had overwhelming nuclear superiority. But when Secretary of State Dean Acheson announced an American view of vital international interests, he excluded South Korea. The North Korean communists thought that our intentions were face up on the board, and that they did not include the defense of South Korea. So they attacked, confident of both Soviet and Chinese support. It was a miscalculation by them, based upon a misrepresentation by us. Had Acheson's statement left doubt in the minds of the communists, the war in South Korea might have been avoided.

During the course of the war Truman again turned up a card by announcing his intention to refrain from using tactical or strategic nuclear weapons in the conduct of the war. The North Koreans, Chinese, and Soviets once again gained full knowledge of our hand, so they felt comfortable continuing to pursue the war at the conventional level. Only when Eisenhower assumed power did the card again become a mystery. Eisenhower was a proven, strong military leader. They had ample reason to wonder about his intentions, and Eisenhower gave them no reason to believe he would not use our strategic superiority. On the contrary, his Secretary of State, John Foster Dulles, sent strong hints through diplomatic channels that he might. With mystery restored to the equation, the communists began to negotiate seriously and the war was soon ended.

When French and British forces moved into Egypt at the height of the Suez crisis, Soviet Premier Nikolai Bulganin proposed to President Eisenhower that the Soviets and Americans engage in a joint military action to stop the fighting in Egypt, a proposal the White House immediately branded as unacceptable. As the fighting increased, however, and it appeared possible that the Soviets might take some unilateral action, Eisenhower ordered the Joint Chiefs to put American military units on alert. Even after a cease-fire was declared, the Soviets continued to threaten to send "volunteers" into Egypt. While Eisenhower's answer to this was diplomatically worded, NATO Commander Alfred Gruenther was authorized to be blunt: a communist attack on the West would result in the Soviet bloc being "destroyed . . . as sure as day follows night." As Eisenhower noted in his memoirs, "The Soviet threat proved to be nothing but words." However, it was clear that Eisenhower's credibility as a strong military leader, combined with our overwhelming nuclear superiority, was the decisive factor that deterred Soviet intervention.

Two years later, in 1958, when the United States confronted Chinese communist threats to take over the Nationalist-held islands of Quemoy and Matsu, Eisenhower explained to me his version of the concept of the hole card. Reflecting on his own experience as a military commander, he said that "You should never let the enemy know what you will do, but it's more important that you never let the enemy know what you will not do."

If the adversary feels that you are unpredictable, even rash, he will be deterred from pressing you too far. The odds that he will fold increase greatly, and the unpredictable President will win another hand. By contrast, statements that appear to rule out the use of force, while perhaps meant to be nonprovocative, will in fact provoke an antagonist to push for more.

Even when you are strong, it is bad strategy to let yourself appear weak. This can lead to a dangerous miscalculation on your adversary's part. The 1961 Vienna Summit between Khrushchev and Kennedy led to such a miscalculation. Perhaps Kennedy was confident of his own resolve, but he did not project that confidence to Khrushchev. As James Reston has since written, "Kennedy went there shortly after his spectacular blunders at the Bay of Pigs, and was savaged by Khrushchev. . . . I had an hour alone with President Kennedy immediately after his last meeting with Khrushchev in Vienna at that time," Reston reported. "Khrushchev had assumed, Kennedy said, that any American President who invaded Cuba without adequate preparation was inexperienced, and any President who then didn't use force to see the invasion through was weak. Kennedy admitted Khrushchev's logic on both points."

Khrushchev later called Kennedy's hand by putting missiles into Cuba. A dangerous confrontation with nuclear overtones resulted, one that could have been prevented had Kennedy's conduct in Vienna given Khrushchev a greater impression of strength and determination.

In 1973, when the United States and the Soviet Union were roughly equal in nuclear capability, Brezhnev demanded that the United States join the Soviet Union in sending troops into the Mideast during the Arab-Israeli war. This would have created a potentially explosive situation. And Brezhnev threatened that if we did not agree to joint action, he would send in Soviet forces unilaterally.

When we ordered a military alert Brezhnev backed down. The alert might not have had this effect had Brezhnev not concluded from his conversations with me in June of that year, and also from the strong actions we had taken to protect our interests in Vietnam in 1972, that I might back up my strong words with strong actions. He was not willing to take that risk.

In 1979 the Carter administration's relatively mild reaction to previous Soviet moves may well have led Brezhnev to conclude that he could send the Red Army into Afghanistan without provoking a strong U.S. response.

Public statements that we will not let the Russians push us around are not effective. They dismiss these as bravado, primarily because they engage in that sort of bluster so much themselves. They must always have very serious questions about what a President will do. For example, we should not make statements that we will never launch a preemptive strike. Whether or not we would ever exercise that option, we should always leave open the possibility that in extreme circumstances we might.

The demonstrated will, nerve, and unpredictability of the President become even more important in a period when the Soviet Union moves from inferiority to superiority in nuclear arms. If the Soviets fear that the President might react strongly, they will be less likely to put him to the test. If they conclude that they can predict his response, and that it will be a weak one, they will test him. Then, if they turn out to be right, they will win. If they turn out to be wrong, they will have made the kind of miscalculation that could lead to a major conventional or even nuclear war. The lesson of history is that wars more often than not come from this kind of miscalculation.

•   •   •

The Uses of Secrecy

Secrecy is a *sine qua non* in the conduct of international relations, whether dealing with allies or with adversaries. Without privacy—and the assurance of privacy—there is little hope of accomplishing anything.

The freedom a leader feels to exchange information and ideas candidly with his allies is in direct ratio to the faith that he has in their ability to keep what he tells them confidential. American Presidents have generally had exceptionally open relationships with their British counterparts, and one of the reasons is that the British keep a confidence. I never knew of an occasion in which any of my private discussions with British leaders was leaked. The same has been true of some of our other allies. Unfortunately, it has not been true of all, and even where it has been true of personal talks between the heads of government, it has not always been true of discussions at other levels.

I was able to have very candid discussions with Charles de Gaulle when he was President of France, but only when we were alone, with just an interpreter present. It even mattered who the interpreter was. De Gaulle talked freely in the presence of his own personal interpreter, but not with the interpreter from our State Department, whom he did not know. However, when I brought my old friend General Vernon G. Walters, who not only is one of the world's most skilled interpreters but also was personally known and trusted by de Gaulle, de Gaulle was delighted and again spoke freely.

Where we have not felt free to share critically important items of information with allies, the damage to our relationships has sometimes been severe. This has been true even where the fear of leaks was indirect, where we could not tell one without telling another.

The announcement on July 15, 1971, that I was going to visit China stunned Japan; it was described as a "Nixon shock." The Japanese thought, quite reasonably, that as our principal ally in Asia they should at least have been informed that such a momentous policy shift was under way. They should have been, and in an ideal world they would have been. But if word of the move had leaked, it might have jeopardized the whole China initiative. Thus we could not risk informing any ally that might leak it, and if we informed one without informing others, and this became known subsequently, it would have been bitterly resented.

We can share particularly sensitive information with allies only when we have confidence that they will not leak it; conversely, they can share sensitive information with us only when they have confidence that we will not leak it.

Secrecy is particularly important in dealing with the leaders of communist countries. They are products of a system that values secrecy, which is why I could talk so candidly with the Chinese—they never leak. By the same token, they expect us to keep secrets. If we fail to do so, the chances for negotiating with them in any meaningful way will be substantially reduced and may be totally destroyed.

Unfortunately for the nation, breaches of security created especially difficult situations during my administration. The most dramatic of these came in June 1971, when the so-called Pentagon Papers were suddenly made public. These were 7,000 pages of classified documents relating to the Vietnam War, including material that was still sensitive not only for the United States but also for a number of our allies. They had been leaked to the New York *Times* months earlier. The *Times* went to extravagant lengths to keep an absolute lid of secrecy on the fact that it had them, until it was ready to spring them on us—without even a moment's advance notice, and without giving any responsible official a chance to read them, much less to advise the *Times* on what parts might be particularly sensitive. I have always had great respect for the New York *Times* as one of the world's finest newspapers, and I still do. But I considered this one of the grossest acts of journalistic irresponsibility I had encountered in a quarter century of public life. In his dissenting opinion in the Pentagon Papers case Chief Justice

Warren Burger wrote of the *Times'* failure to consult the government:

> To me it is hardly believable that a newspaper long regarded as a great institution in American lives would fail to perform one of the basic and simple duties of every citizen with respect to the discovery or possession of stolen property or secret government documents. . . .
> This duty rests on taxi drivers, justices, and the *New York Times*.

The next month, on July 23, the morning before we were to present our formal, opening position at the SALT talks in Helsinki, the New York *Times* carried a front-page story detailing what was allegedly our fallback position.

These events took place just as Kissinger was making his first secret trip to Peking, the SALT talks were starting, and the war in Vietnam was at a critical juncture. By fall the CIA reported that we were in the midst of the worst outbreak of leaks in nearly twenty years, since 1953. Trying to conduct effective international relations in such an atmosphere, much less to lay the cornerstone for a durable structure of peace, was a nightmare and threatened to become an impossibility.

When I made my trip to Peking in 1972 the Chinese leaders were particularly concerned about the possibility of leaks. In December 1971, during the war between India and Pakistan, columnist Jack Anderson published verbatim minutes of a high-level discussion of our policy with regard to the war. Referring to the Anderson leak, Chinese Premier Zhou Enlai commented to me that "the records of three of your meetings were made public because all sorts of people were invited." He was politely suggesting that he would not like to see the transcripts of our talks suffer the same fate. This was not a farfetched possibility. In the course of tracking down the Anderson leak we discovered that a memo of Kissinger's conversation with Zhou during his first secret trip to Peking had been copied and passed along to others who, fortunately, had not made it public. But the danger remained. I sensed clearly that unless the Chinese were assured that our talks would be kept in confidence they would be hesitant about revealing how far they might be willing to go to reach an accommodation with us. I assured Zhou that where the fate of our two countries—and possibly the fate of the world—was involved, we would be able to talk in complete confidence. Only then were we able to make progress in our negotiations.

In retrospect I am sure that the opening to China in 1972 and the development of our relationship since could not have been achieved had there not been absolute secrecy both in setting up the trip to Peking and in the conduct of our talks there.

A nation unable to protect its own vital secrets will certainly not be trusted with another nation's crucial information. As Cord Meyer has pointed out, "Even the most friendly ally must hesitate to cooperate with the United States if it has to fear exposure of its sources." The Western alliance weakens as a result, with no member losing more than the United States.

"Freedom of information" has become a sacred cow. Secrecy is considered sinister and wrong. Yet common sense ought to tell us that publicity that leads to bad results is not necessarily good, and that secrecy that leads to good results is not necessarily bad. We need more effective legal sanctions to discourage harmful disclosures. Even more important, we must quit making national heroes out of those who illegally disclose top-secret information. Our Presidents *want* publicity, but above all, they want results. We should applaud rather than condemn them when they resist the insatiable demands of the media in order to do the job they were elected to do.

The "Black Arts"

The kinds and quality of intelligence information available to a President can be crucial to success or failure in his role as world leader. So, too, is the availability of means short of war to project American power or advance American interests in volatile and threatening situations—and this often means the use of covert action.

There has always been a strong ambivalence in American attitudes toward intelligence. When Americans do not feel threatened, they tend to regard such activities as immoral or un-American. When they do feel threatened, they wonder why we do not have better intelligence. During all our wars we built up excellent intelligence services, only to dismantle them as soon as the war ended. Today our leaders have to make almost instant decisions, often for extremely high stakes. If they have no warning of impending dangers, they will be far less likely to make the right decisions.

Espionage and covert operations are as old as mankind. Both have existed alongside the system of international law as long as there has been a system of international law. All nations, with the possible exception of some of our modern mini-states, have engaged in them; only the United States has adopted the curious doctrine that they should be performed in public. In Great Britain, where modern democracy began, even publishing the name of the head of the Intelligence Service can land a citizen in jail. Acts that Americans insist on protecting under the banner of freedom of speech would, in such other democracies as Sweden or Switzerland—neither of which bears the world responsibilities the United States does—result in long prison sentences.

In this country we seem to have evolved the strange doctrine that it is the duty of government to keep its secrets, and the equally sacred duty of the media to expose them. For the future we must find an accommodation between freedom of the press and the requirements of national survival in a threatened and uncertain world—in a way that enhances survival.

Failures of intelligence can be disastrous. In the 1960s and early 1970s, for eleven years in a row, the Central Intelligence Agency underestimated the number of missiles the Russians would deploy; at the same time the CIA also underestimated the totality of the Soviet strategic program effort and its ambitious goals. In 1976 the CIA estimates o

Russian military spending for 1970–1975 were doubled overnight as errors were discovered and corrected. Throughout the critical period of the mid-1960s, when McNamara decided to curtail unilaterally U.S. nuclear programs and the Russians moved massively to catch up, and in the early 1970s, when the first concrete steps toward arms control were taken, American Presidents were being supplied by the CIA with figures on Russian military spending that were only half of what the agency later decided spending had been. Thanks in part to this intelligence blunder we will find ourselves looking down the nuclear barrel in the mid-1980s.

The real question before the American people is this: Can we afford to stumble like a blind and deaf giant into the last twenty years of this century, until one day we face the alternative of surrender or total destruction? If we lack proper intelligence, we will, as former Marine Corps Commandant General David M. Shoup has said, "be in the ring blindfolded."

There is a vast difference between the quantity and quality of information readily available from the closed Soviet society and from our open one. The Soviet military budget is announced in one figure and eight words, and the Soviets reveal nothing of the debates that produce that budget. If they published only the equivalent of the annual unclassified report of our Department of Defense, and if it were equally reliable, we would know far more than we do about Soviet military programs. Beyond this, congressional hearings multiply greatly the amount of useful information we give the Soviets free of charge, detailing not only the extent of opposition to particular arms programs but also the nature of the uncertainties in our defense posture. Soviet embassy personnel can sit in on those hearings; we have no such privileges in Moscow.

We also depend on our intelligence agencies for covert, or hidden, operations that are meant to help one's friends or make the task of one's enemies more difficult. Here too Americans have had ambivalent feelings. Since the beginning of history almost every country has sought to influence events in other countries in ways favorable to its own interests. This is accepted practice. Countries tolerate propaganda from abroad through publications, radio broadcasts, and even television appearances by foreigners.

A fundamental purpose of every embassy in the world is to influence events in the host country in ways favorable to the country the embassy represents. Today the Soviet Union subsidizes and controls local Communist parties all over the world, which give Moscow an often powerful means of exercising pressure within other countries.

Even more serious have been the arms, training, and supplies of all kinds that the Soviet Union regularly sends to support so-called people's wars of liberation, a euphemism for the establishment of pro-Soviet control of a country. To the Soviets, intervening in another country to bring about the triumph of their friends is a holy duty. We must have the means to help our friends in other countries where their freedom is under attack and their survival is threatened.

Here again, the issue is not the simple moralistic one, "Is it right to interfere in the internal affairs of another country?" Rather, it is whether the United States will have the ability to help its friends in another country resist an armed threat to their freedom by means short of intervening with our armed forces. Without such means, we would have no options between a diplomatic protest and the direct use of our armed forces. Our friends must not be left with the assumption that regardless of what the enemies of freedom may do, we shall offer them no help. Improved covert capabilities could also help in combating some forms of terrorism, and might give us additional options in case the rights of the United States and its citizens are again flagrantly violated as they were in the hostage seizure in Iran.

Most covert actions are not armed actions. Many times they consist only of helping a democratic newspaper to survive economic action against it, support for cultural activities, or paying the fares of young people to some world gathering so that they can speak out for freedom.

The Soviets suffer no qualms about the morality of their actions. They use the Communist Party of the Soviet Union as an instrument for subversion, then deny government responsibility, even though the Communist Party and the Soviet government are virtually one and the same. We do not have that option. But what we can do is to give covert support to indigenous political organizations that support our position and oppose a communist takeover.

The scope for covert action in peacetime is more restricted than it is in wartime, the need for it is not so unambiguous, but the payoffs may be just as large. Unless we restore the covert capabilities of the CIA we are going to get rolled by the Soviets in country after country. The proportion of the CIA's budget that goes for covert actions has fallen from over 50 percent to less than 5 percent. In an effort to clean up abuses—and alleged abuses—we have come close to throwing out the baby with the bathwater. The Freedom of Information Act lets anyone—including enemy intelligence agents—rummage through CIA and FBI files at taxpayer expense. According to CIA officials, the agency has spent more man-hours filling Freedom of Information requests than "on any one of several areas of key intelligence interest." In addition, opening these files has a chilling effect on those who would be ready to risk their lives and their reputations to help the United States in sensitive areas or operations. With the CIA reporting its covert activities to eight separate committees whose members comprise one third of Congress, as well as the staff members, we might as well send out news releases to our opponents. This requirement restricts the CIA, as Senator Daniel P. Moynihan has put it, to "doing research that might as well be done in the Library of Congress." Foreign intelligence agencies and individual agents are no longer willing to risk exposure by cooperating with the CIA—and our operations are crippled. The "black arts" should, as the London *Economist* puts it, "be restored to dimmer light, or to darkness, where they can thrive."

Throughout history people have tended to think of intelligence as an instrument of war. Today it is an essential instrument of peace. The more we know about the Soviets, the less likely we are to underestimate or miscalculate what they may do. The knowledge that we have an effective intelligence community that can follow whatever they do will lessen their temptations.

We have castrated the CIA and other intelligence agencies. We must restore their ability to keep the President and our other leaders informed, ready, and able to respond to danger. We must give them the means to do their job.

Summit Meetings

Harold Nicolson, in *Diplomacy,* sounded a warning about the dangers of summitry. "Such visits," he wrote, "arouse public expectation, lead to misunderstandings, and create confusion. The time at the disposal of these visitors is not always sufficient to allow for patience and calm deliberation. The honors which are paid to a minister in a foreign capital may tire his physique, excite his vanity, or bewilder his judgment."

A summit meeting presents other pitfalls as well. When a President negotiates personally, he deprives himself of three major assets:

He loses some of the enormous prestige of his position as head of state *and* head of government by talking as an equal with the head of government from another country. Frank I. Cobb made this point in a memo to Colonel House in 1918: "The moment President Wilson sits at the council table with their prime ministers and foreign secretaries he has lost all power that comes from distance and detachment. . . . He becomes merely a negotiator dealing with other negotiators."

He reduces the mystery, which is one of his greatest

weapons in diplomacy; a President may appear more powerful and less predictable from a distance than in face-to-face encounters.

Probably most importantly, he loses flexibility: an ambassador, or even a foreign minister, can put forth positions that a President can later modify or even repudiate. For example, Dulles, with Eisenhower's approval, would often take a hard line, which would later allow Eisenhower to act as the conciliator. Kissinger, on the other hand, with my approval, would profess to want to be more conciliatory, and use the prospect of my harder line for negotiating leverage. As a veteran British ambassador observed, "Sometimes the function of a diplomat is to fail in a negotiation or to make little or no progress. But when a head of state gets involved, his need to look like a winner can do serious damage to a delicate process."

Against these costs must be balanced two benefits that might be produced from a summit meeting:

In U.S.-Soviet relations a meeting at the summit allows each leader to take the measure of the other and thus may reduce the possibility of miscalculation in the event of a future confrontation. For example, my very heated discussion on the Mideast with Brezhnev in San Clemente in June of 1973 helped to give credibility to the alert I called a few months later during the Yom Kippur War.

Summitry can also provide an opportunity for a President to exercise the powers of personal persuasion. President Carter's Middle East negotiations vividly illustrate this point.

But a President should go to a summit only if the stakes are worth the risks, and if the meeting is thoroughly programmed in advance. No American President should go to a summit with an adversary unless he knows what is on the other side of the mountain.

The highly publicized formal summit meeting may seem like the ultimate forum for high-level discussion of state-to-state relations. This is not the case. Many people attend the main official meetings and the press is always buzzing around trying to pry out some detail for tomorrow's headlines. In such circumstances the diplomatic rule of thumb about not broaching sensitive matters in public comes into play. At the formal meetings, where more people are present, I have found the Soviet leaders to be less forthcoming than when we meet informally or alone with just a translator. The larger the group, the less free the conversation, especially when the group consists of high-ranking communists. In the formal sessions everybody is talking for the record and talking like a record, carefully watching what he says. Real progress is more likely to be made in small, informal sessions—not those that are given over to social amenities, but the private working sessions that allow higher degrees of both candor and concentration.

It is disastrous to play to the press during a summit meeting. When either leader does this he is tempted to take heroic positions that do not lend themselves to realistic accommodation later on. Bargaining stances openly proclaimed are difficult to back away from. Better results are produced in diplomacy when the leaders talk to each other instead of to the press.

Creation of a willowy euphoria is one of the dangers of summitry. During my administration excessive euphoria built up around the 1972 Peking and Moscow summit meetings. I must assume a substantial part of the responsibility for this. It was an election year, and I wanted the political credit for what I believed were genuinely major advances toward a stable peace. Further, some of our summit agreements faced tough opposition in Congress, and in order to win approval for them we tried to present them in the best possible light—emphasizing the great hopes we might realize if both sides adhered to both the letter and the spirit of the agreements. I did make efforts to keep expectations from getting out of hand: for example, I warned in a televised speech to a joint session of Congress on my return from Moscow that we did not "bring back from Moscow the promise of instant peace, but we do bring the beginning of a process that can lead to a lasting peace." I cautioned that "Soviet ideology still proclaims hostility to some of Ameri-

ca's most basic values. The Soviet leaders remain committed
to that ideology."

The events themselves were so dramatic, however, that
unrealistic expectations were raised. Many people embraced
the naïve notion that in the new era of détente the Soviets
would suddenly abandon their ambitions and we would all
live happily ever after. When Soviet adventurism continued,
they then turned around and said détente was a failure. The
euphoria also made it more difficult to gain support for the
decisive actions and strong military forces that were needed
to make détente succeed. Euphoria is dangerous in dealing
with the Soviets, or with any adversary. Euphoria is a harmful illusion that eventually breeds disillusion; it also invites
irresolution.

Linkage

There is one cardinal rule for the conduct of international relations: Don't give anything to your adversary unless you get something in return. At the summit there
should be no "free rides" for the Kremlin leadership. We
should never engage in summitry for the sake of summitry
and for the fleeting "spirit" of cooperation that these meetings customarily produce. Such "spirits" often gain very little for the United States, and a great deal for the Soviets.

It was during the transition period between my election
in 1968 and my first inauguration in 1969 that Henry Kissinger and I developed what is now widely called the concept of linkage. We determined that those things the Soviets
wanted—the good public relations that summits provided,
economic cooperation, and strategic arms limitations agreements—would not be gained by them without a quid pro
quo. At that time the principal quid pro quos we wanted
were some assistance in getting a settlement in Vietnam, restraint by them in the Middle East, and a resolution of the
recurring problems in Berlin.

In SALT negotiations they wanted an agreement limiting defensive weapons only, an area in which we were

moving ahead faster than they were. We insisted there should also be a limit on offensive weapons, in which they were moving ahead faster than we were. Here, congressional approval of the ABM program was indispensable. In diplomacy, as in other walks of life, you can only get something you want if you can give your opponent something he wants. Unilateral concessions on our part—to prove our "goodwill"—are stupid and dangerous. As Henry Kissinger puts it, "As a general rule the Soviet Union does not pay for services that have already been rendered."

We "linked" our goals to theirs, and though it took two years for the Kremlin to accept this policy in the SALT I negotiations, it finally did.

Linkage remains a viable strategy. The Soviets still want arms control agreements and economic cooperation, and the United States must again insist on a balance. We have great reason to be concerned over the Soviets' African adventurism, the conduct of their ally Vietnam, their support of Castro's "Hessians," their aggressive use of the Red Army outside of the Soviet bloc, and their attempts to gain control of the Persian Gulf and to intervene in the Middle East. All these concerns are legitimate interests of the United States. We should not be shy or apologetic about linking what we want in these areas with what the Soviets want in other areas, any more than we should be apologetic about insisting that American interests be sufficiently safeguarded by the terms of arms control agreements themselves.

There are no hard and fast boundaries that separate one form of Soviet imperialism from another. They are linked by a common thread that leads to the Kremlin. The Soviets know this, and if compelled by the leadership in the United States to accept linkage, they will do so. They have done so in the past. They will do so again.

They will not accept linkage, however, out of an unselfish concern for preserving peace in the world. If we do not demand it, we will not get it. The Soviets do not like American determination to see justice done, but they will respect it. Linkage is a just concept. If pursued vigorously and from a position of sufficient strength, it will produce fair results.

The primary purpose of arms control is to reduce the danger of war. But arms control by itself cannot do this. Political differences, not arms, are the root causes of war, and until these are resolved, there will be enough arms for the most devastating war no matter how many arms control agreements are reached.

Trade by itself will not reduce the danger of war. In World War I and World War II nations that had traded with each other went to war against each other because of political differences.

Trade and arms control must be linked with the settlement of political differences if the danger of war is to be reduced. Only if we use linkage in this way will we be attacking the root causes of war.

Dealing with Our Allies

During the first 150 years of our history it was often said that the President wore four hats—as chief of state, head of government, Commander-in-Chief of the Armed Forces, and head of his political party. Since World War II the President has worn a fifth hat, as leader of the free world.

The Soviet Union has subjects and satellites; the United States has allies and friends. The Soviet Union dictates to its satellites; the United States does not dictate to its allies. But it is our responsibility as the strongest and wealthiest free world nation to lead. The President of the United States is the only one who has the power and prestige to provide this leadership. This is often more difficult than his other four roles, for it requires a combination of toughness, subtlety, decisiveness, and skill.

Diplomacy can be used either as a sword or as a needle—as a weapon or an instrument of union. In dealing with allies the President is chiefly engaged in mending tears and strengthening seams.

America remains powerful, but not all-powerful; our

allies need us, but we also need them. This mutual interest is what brings alliances into being. One of a President's chief tasks is to nurture that sense of common interest.

In some ways good personal relations are more important in dealing at the summit level with allies than with adversaries. With adversaries, personal cordiality is not going to make opposing national interests disappear, though it can keep irritations from becoming unnecessarily inflamed, and it can sometimes help in the search for those conceptual breakthroughs that make it possible to bridge gaps that had seemed unbridgeable. But with allies, relations can be conducted on an entirely different level of trust and confidence. Two leaders who know each other, who trust each other, who respect each other's judgment, and who share common goals can establish a working relationship that transcends normal diplomacy and that greatly benefits both nations. The partnership between Roosevelt and Churchill in World War II is a prime example. My own friendship with de Gaulle helped greatly, when I first took office, in repairing the previously strained relations between the United States and France. And de Gaulle, whose eye was always fixed on the long view, offered me wise counsel on dealing with America's global responsibilities, particularly with regard to the Soviet Union and China. West Germany's Konrad Adenauer had a similar long perspective; though he died before I became President, I carried his counsel with me. I frequently had very helpful discussions with British leaders; with Harold Macmillan before meeting Khrushchev in 1959, for example, and with Harold Wilson and Edward Heath before my visits to Peking and Moscow in 1972. French presidents Georges Pompidou and Valéry Giscard d'Estaing both had special expertise on international economic issues, which made my talks with them both educational and constructive.

The counsel of trusted allies can be particularly helpful in dealing with those parts of the world they know better than we do. Discussions with Japanese leaders like Nobusuke Kishi, Eisaku Sato, and Masayoshi Ohira gave me insights into Asian issues I could not have gained from Europeans or Americans. And the French know more about black Africa than we do, or probably ever will; so do the British, the Belgians, and others. The British, as a result of their imperial days, have a vast store of knowledge and understanding about South Asia, the Persian Gulf, and many remote but strategically important places around the world. Some leaders of small nations are intimately familiar with their parts of the world and wise about the whole world. Singapore's Prime Minister Lee Kwan Yew is in my view one of the world's premier statesmen, even though his own stage is too small for the full exercise of his talents.

The difference between meeting with friends and meeting with adversaries can best be summarized this way. When you talk to your adversaries you learn *about* them. When you talk to your friends you learn *from* them.

We often tend to overlook the vital importance of maintaining and strengthening our ties with countries that are not major powers, some of which, like Australia and Brazil, because of their vast resources, are destined to be great powers in the future. If I were to advise a young man where to go to seek his fortune in the twenty-first century, I would recommend Brazil or Australia. Brazilians fought courageously side by side with U.S. troops in Italy in World War II, and I witnessed first-hand the bravery and dedication of Australian and New Zealand troops in the South Pacific. They were magnificent allies in war and we should seek their advice and assistance in maintaining the peace.

Canada, our staunch ally to the north, should not be taken for granted simply because we share the longest unguarded border in the world. The Canadians are our best customer, buying 20 percent of our exports. But living next to an industrial giant like the United States can be difficult. Their understandable desire to lessen American control of their business enterprises should be respected and encouraged.

The United States is fortunate to have genuine allies and not satellites. We should treat all of them as such—recognizing that they are as important to us as we are to them and that their judgment on great issues may at times be better than ours.

As long as alliances are needed, maintaining the strength of those alliances will remain one of the President's chief responsibilities. Success or failure will often depend on the President's personal skills in dealing with allied leaders, and their personal assessment of the caliber of his leadership.

The "Bully Pulpit"

Presidents, particularly in this century, have often used the Oval Office, in the words of Theodore Roosevelt, as a "bully pulpit." The power of the President as moral leader of the free world is immense, but to be effective, a President must use this power with great skill. Most importantly, he must use it only when the stakes are high and worthy of his commitment. The area of human rights is one in which that power, properly used, can be immensely effective. But it must be used selectively, with a discriminating awareness of the many distinctions that exist in the real world.

The tragedy of Iran is a case history of what happens when the United States fails to distinguish between authoritarian and totalitarian regimes, between those that provide some human rights and those that deny all, between those who are our staunch allies and friends and those who are our potential enemies.

I first met the Shah in Tehran twenty-seven years ago when I was forty years old and he was only thirty-four. He had just been restored to his throne. He was only reigning, however, not ruling. Power was being ably exercised by General Zahedi, the father of the Shah's last ambassador to the United States. I found the Shah to be intelligent, dignified, quiet, and not too sure of himself. However, he was a good listener, and he demonstrated a profound understanding not only of the problems in his own country but of the world around him as well. Iran's deposed, left-leaning anti-Western Prime Minister Mossadegh had left the Iranian economy in shambles. Eighty-five percent of the people were illiterate. Women had no political rights whatever. Iran was still in the nineteenth century.

Since then, I have met with the Shah on a number of occasions. We became friends. I saw him grow in power and in wisdom. While I was out of office, during the 1960s, I made four trips to Tehran to see him. By then he had matured into a world leader of the first rank. What was even more important and exciting, he had made a revolution in Iran. In less than twenty years he had brought Iran into the twentieth century. Before he came to power, well over half of Iran's lands had been held by less than 1 percent of its people. He initiated a massive land-reform program, which included a wholesale divestiture of Crown lands as well as forcing the wealthy landowners and Moslem clergy to give up much of theirs; for Iran's peasants, this meant their first chance ever at owning their own land. He launched an imaginative plan to give Iran's workers a share in the economy, first through profit-sharing, and then by encouraging workers to buy stock in the enterprises they worked for; he even had the government lend them the necessary capital to buy it. To help the rural poor, long one of the most poverty-stricken and disease-ridden populations in the world, he organized young Iranians into a Literacy Corps, a Health Corps, and a Reconstruction and Development Corps—as alternatives to military service—and sent them into the countryside. The number of schools and colleges skyrocketed; the level of illiteracy plummeted; eventually, with the Shah's help and encouragement, more than 40,000 young Iranians were also studying abroad. Enormous strides were made in health care. In what amounted to a revolutionary change in Moslem Iran, women were given full political rights over the bitter opposition of traditional Islamic leaders.

Even before the oil boom that began in 1973, Iran's economy was growing at an impressive rate of 9 percent a year. Unemployment and underemployment nearly vanished. The Shah told me that Britain's Labor Prime Minister

Harold Wilson once commented that under the Shah's leadership Iran had done more in achieving the goal of socialism—more prosperity equally shared—than had Great Britain. The Shah also developed substantial military strength and was filling the vacuum left by the British when they withdrew from the Persian Gulf area.

He did not provide as much progress in political rights as most Americans would have wished. Iran had no tradition of democracy, and his government still used what by Western standards were harsh measures to keep its political opposition in check. But the people of Iran had made far more progress in political and human rights than any of their neighbors except Israel. Under the Shah, Iran was advancing internally and was secure externally. In one of the last comprehensive studies of Iran done before the upheavals of 1979, under the auspices of Stanford University's Hoover Institution, the Shah's rule was rightfully judged to have been one that oversaw "Iran's transition from weakness to strength, from backwardness to progress, from poverty to wealth."

When I saw him in Cuernavaca, Mexico, in July 1979 I found that the Shah had lost none of the dignity, character, or courage that were his trademarks when he was in power. But he was deeply depressed. Tears welled up in his eyes as he spoke of the savage slaughter of his friends and supporters by the new regime. But he was not sorry for himself. He was sorry for his country. The clock had been turned back a hundred years for the Iranian people. Women had lost their rights. The economy was in shambles. Four million people were unemployed. Inflation was running at 40 percent. Iran was no longer the staunch friend of the West holding back the forces, internal and external, that threatened to cut our oil lifeline.

The Shah was hard on himself, admitting that he made his share of mistakes. But he had tried desperately to do his best. He still has great affection and respect for the United States. He finds it difficult, however, to understand the policy of the U.S. government toward him during his ordeal.

Despite the economic progress that had been made during
his reign and the slow but sure movement toward more democracy, the United States, both privately and publicly,
pushed him to do more. He tried to comply. But, as he reflected, he feels now that he may have tried to do too much
too soon—both economically and politically. The more the
people got, the more they wanted. He had antagonized the
Moslem leaders by forcing them to give their lands to the
peasants, as he had done with his own lands, and by eman-
cipating women. He had enormously increased the availability of higher education; but then thousands of educated
young Iranians—particularly those who had gone to school
in the United States—joined his opponents and insisted that
he abdicate so that democracy and human rights, American
style, could come immediately to Iran.

Instead of rights, they got an Islamic dictatorship.

He found it difficult to understand the attitude of the
French. Iran had been a friend to France, and even had contracts to purchase at least $10 billion worth of goods from
the French. Yet the French government allowed the Ayatollah Ruhollah Khomeini to set up what was in effect a gov-
ernment-in-exile outside Paris and to use it as a forum to
attack him from abroad and to direct and incite the mobs
in the streets at home.

As he sees it now, the crucial mistake the United States
made was not in giving him support or failing to give him
support, but in being indecisive. One day, he would receive
public and private assurances of all-out support. The next
day, a story would be leaked to the effect that second-level
U.S. emissaries were in contact with his opposition. The day
after that, a statement from the White House would indicate
that the United States, in the event that the Shah was overthrown, would accept any government the people wanted. A
vacillating United States government could not seem to decide whether to support the Shah unequivocally, force him
to compromise with his enemies, or leave him free to maneuver without its support.

The Soviets did not vacillate. They beamed inflammatory radio broadcasts to Tehran and other major cities. They supported the small but well-organized Communist Party and other dissident groups. They did not expect to bring Iran into the Soviet camp immediately. But they knew that chaos in Iran was their ally, and if they could generate enough of it, over a long enough period of time, Tehran would cut its Western ties, become neutral at the very least, and perhaps move toward the Soviets. Their strategy worked.

The Shah became a man without a country, hounded from one refuge to another. American diplomatic personnel were taken hostage, and Iran's Ayatollah Khomeini thumbed his nose at the UN and the rest of the civilized world. While demands that the Shah be forcibly returned to Iran have been refused, the way he was treated by many of his erstwhile friends once he fell from power contrasted shabbily with the way he had stood by them in their own times of need.

The United States and the West have lost a staunch friend in an explosive area of the world where we desperately need friends who will act as a stabilizing force. Countries in the area, such as Saudi Arabia, that have the will to assume that stabilizing role lack the military power. Those, such as Iraq, that have the power may not seek the same kind of stability. The Soviet threat looms larger. Now the United States and our Western allies must fill the vacuum, or have it filled in a way detrimental to us.

Iran has lost an effective leader. The world has lost one of those leaders who, far from being parochial, have a better understanding of the great forces that move the world than leaders of most major countries. When I saw him in Mexico the Shah gave me, at my request, an hour-long appraisal of developments in the Soviet Union, in China, in India, in the Mideast, in Africa, and in Latin America. His knowledge was encyclopedic and his wisdom was incisive.

There are lessons for the future in this tragic development.

Especially when a key country like Iran is involved, we

must never forget that our choice is usually not between the man in power who is our friend and somebody better, but rather between him and someone far worse.

We must not set higher standards of conduct for our friends than for our enemies.

We must not insist on forcing American-style democracy on nations with different backgrounds and different problems. They must move in their own way at their own pace toward the goals that we in the West have taken hundreds of years to achieve.

Above all, in the future we must stand by our friends or we will soon find that we have none. After seeing what happened to the Shah in Iran and how he was treated by the United States after he left Iran, other rulers in countries that are very important to us—such as Saudi Arabia—now wonder if the same thing will happen to them if they come under attack from foreign-supported internal revolutionaries.

As the *Wall Street Journal* observed:

> The United States needs friends. And more often than most allies the shah was willing to help, for example in fueling U.S. warships in the midst of the Arab oil embargo. If his reward for this is infamy even in the U.S., how many future rulers will take risks for the U.S. side? We can be sure that the fate of the shah is carefully watched by Prince Fahd controlling the oil taps, King Hussein sitting next to the West Bank and King Hassan holding one side of the straits of Gibraltar. To the extent the shah is ill-treated by the U.S., it is one more incentive for them to cut the best deal they can with the anti-Americans.

We must grasp the distinction between "totalitarian" regimes, which deny all freedoms, and "authoritarian" regimes, which may severely limit political rights but allow personal liberties—for example, the right to free choice in education, religion, employment, marriage, friends, workplace, and family life, and in some cases the protection of a system of jurisprudence, which while not as advanced as ours, is nevertheless far more meaningful than the purely paper legality of the U.S.S.R. or the Koran's protection in present-day Iran.

Many Third World countries are governed by authoritarian regimes run by dictators, often military men. The Shah's father was a military man who seized power and made himself the new Shah; Franco was a general who prevailed in the Spanish Civil War; the Greek colonels ran an authoritarian regime; so does the Chilean junta.

One thing we should recognize about these and similar regimes is that they are not run by zealots determined to impose their iron will on every aspect of their citizens' personal lives. For these authoritarian rulers, political repression is an expedient to enable them to hold power and maintain order. By contrast, the Cambodian bloodbath was a brutal effort to transform a society and to destroy everyone who resisted change. In this it differed only in degree, not in kind, from other communist regimes.

We must also grasp the distinction between those regimes that threaten their neighbors and those that do not. As one British writer put it, "We should distinguish between those systems, usually totalitarian, that wish to *export* their repression and those, usually authoritarian, that don't. Even the simpleton understands that no matter how obnoxious they may be, neither Chile nor South Africa has submarines lurking around the oil fields in the North Sea." He might have added that unlike Cuba, they are not exporting communist subversion to their neighbors in Latin America, or sending their troups to serve as Soviet Hessians in wars of "liberation" in Africa.

Exerting more pressure on friendly regimes that provide some rights and do not threaten their neighbors than we exert on hostile regimes that provide no rights and do threaten their neighbors is not only hypocritical, it is stupid. Alliances are arrangements of convenience. Allies do not have to love one another or even admire one another; it is enough that they need one another. Being joined in an alliance neither obliges nor entitles us to deliver condescending lectures in political morality to our partners. The "moral imperialists" who insist that other nations be re-created in our image as the price of our friendship do freedom no favor.

I do not suggest that we abandon our commitment to "human rights" in our relations with our friends. But to be effective, we need to adopt a policy of realism. And to do this we must make a simple but crucial differentiation in our minds between the long view and the short view, between the ideal goal and what is immediately feasible.

In the long term we should hold high the banner of the American Revolution as the standard to which man aspires. But in the short term—in the immediate, real world we must deal with—we must recognize that for much of the world this is still a distant dream. It took centuries for Western Europe, with its relatively advanced civilization, to evolve democratic forms, and even some of these countries have at times lapsed back into authoritarian rule. American-style democracy is simply not suited for many countries, and if they tried it, it would not work. Democracy is like heady wine—some can handle it and some cannot, at least not right away.

In the world contest one of the West's most powerful weapons is the idea of freedom. The communist nations have proved that they can equal us militarily. Economically, they will continue to try to match us. But in terms of human aspirations, it is no contest—the West wins hands down.

As the free world's leader, the President must use that weapon—the idea of freedom—to the hilt. But he must use it precisely and effectively. It would be tragic if we misused this powerful weapon, flaying about with it at random, hitting our friends and foes alike and ultimately injuring ourselves. The "bully pulpit" is a place for moral leadership, not for moral imperialism.

11
No Substitute for Victory

Russia fears our friendship more than our enmity. The Soviet dictatorship could not stand free intercourse with the West. We must make Moscow fear our enmity more than our friendship.

—*Winston Churchill*

The object in war is to attain a better peace. . . . Victory in the true sense implies that the state of peace, and of one's people, is better after the war than before.

—*B.H. Liddell Hart*

Nearly thirty years ago as a junior senator from California I heard General Douglas MacArthur tell a joint session of Congress that "in war, there is no substitute for victory." The members rose to their feet. They cheered. Grown men cried. The nation was then mired in a war in Korea. MacArthur, the hero of the Pacific in World War II, had been fired by President Truman from his command in Korea. MacArthur had wanted to carry the war to the enemy. Truman was determined to contain the war and to achieve a negotiated truce.

Historians and strategists will argue over which was right in the circumstances of that time. But as we look across the balance of this century and beyond, as we think

303

of the stakes involved, we must conclude that in World War III there *is* no substitute for victory.

Victory requires knowing when to use power, how, and where—not just military power, but all the different kinds of power at our disposal.

History tells us that time and again nations that were stronger militarily, stronger economically, even nations that had the edge in will and courage, were defeated because their enemies used power more effectively. In World War III the Soviets have both a goal and a strategy for victory. Their goal is total, unconditional victory, and unconditional surrender for the West, and their strategy involves the use and orchestration of all means as prudently as possible toward that end.

The nations of the world want to be on the winning side. Most of them have lost wars. Most—and this especially includes Japan and Germany—do not want to be on the losing side again. The American people want to win. This is why MacArthur struck such a responsive chord, why he drew such a gut-level response. One of the most devastating results of the outcome in Vietnam was that America felt that for the first time it had lost a war.

In World War III, in the long run the alternative to victory is not an uneasy truce, but defeat in war or surrender without war. This is not acceptable.

Americans are unaccustomed to thinking in global terms, and uncomfortable with the exercise of power unless directly provoked, as we were at Pearl Harbor. It should be clear by now, however, that the Soviet challenge is such a provocation on a global scale.

A somewhat oversimplified but useful way of looking at the evolution of America's response to that challenge during the thirty-five years from the end of World War II through the 1970s is to view it as a progress from confusion to containment to détente. In the wake of the Soviet move into Afghanistan, the 1980s began with a rash of hasty obituaries for détente. Most missed the point of détente, of how and why it worked when it did. Afghanistan interrupted détente. But looking to the future, we need a steady policy that will again make it in the Soviet Union's interest to negotiate with the United States on a realistic quid pro quo basis. A successful détente can help make victory for the West possible—without war. But first we must recognize that containment is an essential element of détente. It is, in fact, what makes a successful détente possible.

Containment

In the immediate aftermath of World War II the West, weary of war, disarmed and turned its attention to rebuilding from the ashes of conflict. Europe lay devastated and powerless. The Soviets moved into the vacuum, cementing their hold on Eastern Europe. With Soviet support, the communists swept to power in China and fastened their hold on North Korea.

In responding to the Soviet moves after World War II the United States evolved what came to be known as the policy of containment. On the European front the Truman Doctrine in 1947 and the establishment of NATO in 1949 checked further Soviet advance. Then, in 1950, with both Soviet and Chinese support, North Korea invaded South Korea. A swift military response by the United Nations, with the United States taking the lead, checked communist aggression there, and the American policy of containment was visibly in place.

George F. Kennan, then the director of the Policy Planning Staff at the State Department, set forth the principles of the policy in an article he wrote anonymously—under the pseudonym "Mr. X"—for the magazine *Foreign Affairs* in 1947. In it he urged "a policy of firm containment, designed to confront the Russians with unalterable counterforce at every point where they show signs of encroaching upon the interests of a peaceful and stable world."

Kennan argued that by keeping the contradictions within communism confined to the communist bloc and preventing their escape via expansion, this policy would "promote tendencies which must eventually find their outlet in either the break-up or the gradual mellowing of Soviet power." In effect, he reflected the insights of that adviser to Catherine the Great two centuries earlier, who had counseled that what ceased to grow would begin to rot.

Kennan was wise enough to know that military prowess alone would not carry the day for a democracy. He said the United States would have to create "among the peoples of the world generally the impression of a country which knows what it wants, which is coping successfully with the problems of its internal life and with the responsibilities of a World Power, and which has a spiritual vitality capable of holding its own among the major ideological currents of the time."

He warned that if instead of firm containment and an attitude of self-confidence and strength, the United States were to exhibit "indecision, disunity, and internal disintegration," this would have an "exhilarating effect on the whole Communist movement." These tendencies would cause "a new jauntiness . . . in the Moscow tread"; new groups of foreign supporters would climb onto what they would see as the "band wagon of international politics"; and, instead of a "break-up or the gradual mellowing of Soviet power," "Russian pressure" would increase "all along the line in international affairs."

Looking back over the thirty years since Kennan's words were written, it is clear that his analyses were prophetic. Eight countries in Europe and two in Asia became communist between 1945 and 1949. But in the twenty-five years from 1949 to 1974, with the policies of containment fully in place, only two—North Vietnam and Cuba—turned communist. Few foreign policies have been followed so effectively.

During this period the only action the Red Army saw was against the Soviet Union's own allies in Eastern Europe. In East Germany in 1953, in Hungary in 1956, and in Czechoslovakia in 1968 rebellions were put down and liberalization strangled. The Sino–Soviet bloc became the Sino–Soviet split, the fissure growing so wide that the two former allies came to the brink of war in 1969.

Containment was well suited to the realities it was designed to address. It utilized our great economic and military strengths, and it took advantage of the internal weaknesses of the enemy. But by the time my administration took office in 1969 containment alone was not enough. Conditions had changed, partly as a result of the success of containment. There were new opportunities. There were also new dangers. The Soviets had grown much stronger militarily, but they had serious economic difficulties. They were worried about nationalistic and democratic ferment in their Eastern European satellites, and they faced an angry and bitterly resentful potential superpower on their eastern flank.

We saw that the nations of Eastern Europe were quietly and steadily pushing to expand their freedom of action. China was beginning to perceive the U.S.S.R. rather than the United States as its principal enemy. The policy of containment had been designed to deal with a monolithic communist world. Now there were deep divisions within that world that we could exploit to our benefit. Our policies needed an added dimension.

Militarily, as we had gone from nuclear monopoly to superiority to parity, the deterrent effect of our nuclear advantage was no longer decisive. At the same time the dangers of miscalculation were increasing to a very high level. The tremendous destructive force of the new weapons presented new and chillingly clear dangers to both superpowers. The constant jockeying for position, the unending moves and countermoves of the cold war, had become ominous. There was a real and ever-increasing danger that nuclear war could be set off by an unintended and unwanted escalation.

Around the world the bipolar system of the postwar world had given way to a more amorphous and complex international structure. Fifty-one nations joined the United Nations at its founding in 1945; twenty-five years later there were 127 members and their numbers have kept increasing. A bloc of "nonaligned" nations emerged, and most nations now categorize themselves as belonging to this group.

Finally, the burdens that America had been carrying for the rest of the world for twenty-five years had begun to take their toll. Long before 1950 we had the great-power responsibility for keeping the peace in Central and South America, assumed under the Monroe Doctrine. When Japan attacked China and the balance of power in Northeast Asia collapsed in the 1930s, it was eventually the United States that restored it in the 1940s and pledged to maintain it, especially after the Korean invasion in 1950. In 1947 we took over the job that the British had been doing in Greece and Turkey, and in 1948 we committed ourselves both to the defense and to the rebuilding of Europe. After the Suez crisis in 1956 the credibility of Britain and France as peacekeepers in the Middle East evaporated. We assumed that responsibility as well, codified in the Eisenhower Doctrine in 1957. As the power and peacekeeping abilities of the former colonial powers shrank, the United States stepped forward to fill the gap, replacing the power of Britain, France, Japan, Germany, and others in Europe, Northeast Asia, Southeast Asia, and the Middle East. Even for us, this was becoming too much.

Just as the military balance of power began to shift to our disadvantage, we committed ourselves to the most extensive and most expensive military undertaking in the era of containment—the war in Vietnam. At the very same time the Johnson administration launched a massive "war on poverty" at home. This enormous double burden on the social and economic structure of our society came at a time of supreme self-confidence, but also at a time when the power advantage that underlay that self-confidence was being eroded. The double maximum commitment overloaded our systems, and we short-circuited.

When I took office it was a time for consolidation, for retrenchment, both at home and abroad. New conditions called for a new strategy to deal not only with the old problems but also with the new challenges and opportunities that had emerged. That new strategy included the Nixon Doctrine, under which we undertook to provide arms and money to nations in the path of direct or indirect aggression, if they would provide the men. It included our opening to China. It included new openings to nations of Eastern Europe that wanted to reach out to the West. It also included a calculated move from confrontation toward negotiation with the Soviet Union, in an effort to channel as much of our competition as possible into peaceful paths, to limit nuclear arms, to create a web of interdependencies that would raise the cost to the Soviets of future aggressiveness and would reduce the danger of nuclear war.

Détente—The Myth and the Reality

Much of the opposition to détente arises from a misunderstanding of what détente is and what it is not. Détente is not entente. An entente is an alliance between nations with a common interest. Détente is an understanding between states with different interests. This is the situation that exists between the United States and Russia. We differ in very basic ways from the Soviet Union. Our interests are, for the most part, fundamentally opposed to theirs and will continue to be so.

Theodore Draper writes that détente has become "a profoundly ambiguous means to an evasively contradictory end." And so it has. The meaning of détente, as originally envisaged by my administration, has become so distorted, both by Soviet behavior and by misunderstanding in the United States, that the term has lost its usefulness as a description of Soviet-American relations. When détente is said to be the "alternative to the cold war" it even becomes an obstacle to clear thought.

What I meant by détente was not an "alternative to the cold war." Both détente and cold war are alternatives to hot war, specifically to nuclear war, between the two powers. The major object of détente is the avoidance of nuclear war. But détente alone will not avoid nuclear war. Sufficient U.S. strength to maintain the nuclear balance, and the demonstrated capacity and determination of the United States to deter Soviet aggression, are indispensable to that purpose.

Competition is an inevitable element in Soviet-American relations, but even so, some cooperation is possible and, in fact, essential. Détente was an attempt to expand the cooperative element and to place certain limits on the competitive. It did not call for a relaxed vigilance on the part of the United States or reduced opposition to Soviet attempts to advance their interests at the cost of our own. Détente allowed hope, it did not provide a basis for euphoria.

We did not expect that the Soviet leaders would abandon their fundamental objectives, but rather that they might be more cooperative in arrangements to promote our mutual interests. We knew that they had no intention of ceasing their struggle against the West. Brezhnev, during his talks with me at three U.S.-Soviet summits, even in his most conciliatory moments, never backed away from the premise that the Soviet Union would continue to support "wars of liberation." The same was true of the Chinese leaders in my talks with them. And I was just as firm in indicating that the United States would continue to resist such efforts, as we had in Vietnam. The Soviet leaders called for intensification of the "ideological struggle." To them, as Walter Laqueur has pointed out, that does not "refer to philosophical debates over the merits of the respective social systems but to real political struggle which may well involve limited military operations. It means, for all practical purposes, the extension of the Soviet sphere of influence." Détente did not require that we ignore that reality, and it did not mean that we would fail to oppose Soviet attempts to expand their domination. In fact, to gain cooperation we had to show the Soviet leaders that we were capable of effective opposition if forced to it. That is why my decision to mine Haiphong and increase bombing of North Vietnam in reaction to the Soviet-supported offensive against South Vietnam before the 1972 summit meeting in Moscow was essential. There can be no détente without containment, for we must expect the Soviets to take advantage of any opening we give them. And that is what many people have tended to forget, which is why the term *détente* has become so distorted.

• • •

In considering strategies for dealing with the Soviets in the future we should think of détente as a complement to containment rather than as a substitute for it. Containment, the task of resisting Russian expansionism, must remain the *sine qua non* of U.S. foreign policy, for if we do not present the Soviets with penalties for aggressive behavior, they will have no reason to be deterred from it. And détente, an attempt to avoid possible fatal miscalculations, to reduce differences where possible through negotiation, and to provide positive incentives for the Russians and the Chinese to cooperate with us in maintaining a stable world order, is only good sense in the nuclear age.

Containment without détente is both dangerous, because of the awesome nuclear arsenals of the superpowers, and foolish, because it prevents us from taking advantage of the differences between the U.S.S.R. and China. But détente without containment is a hollow illusion. The Russians will have no incentive to moderate their aggressive behavior if they find that aggression pays. If the positive inducements of détente are offered without the threat of the negative sanctions of containment, then in practice détente will amount to self-delusion and appeasement.

If the Russians think they can get away with using détente as a cover for aggression, either direct or indirect, they will try. In recent years they have not only tried but succeeded, just as they have succeeded in using aggression as a cover for shifting the military balance in their favor. But this is not an indictment of détente itself. Rather, it reflects the fact that the United States has not demonstrated the resolve needed to make détente work in our interests, while the Soviets have shown that they can make it work in their interests. Détente can still provide a basis for a successful U.S. approach, but only in conjunction with those policies of strength, courage, and will that are necessary to it.

Both containment and détente are appropriate policies for dealing with a dictatorship. The British strategist B.-H. Liddell Hart succinctly explained why the Russians will understand us when we speak the language of force: "The less that a nation has regard for moral obligations the more it tends to respect physical strength." He cautions:

> It is folly to imagine that the aggressive types, whether individuals or nations, can be bought off—or, in the modern language, "appeased"—since the payment of danegeld stimulates a demand for more danegeld. But they can be curbed. Their very belief in force makes them more susceptible to the deterrent effect of a formidable opposing force. . . .
>
> While it is hard to make a real peace with the predatory types, it is easier to induce them to accept a state of truce—and far less exhausting than an attempt to crush them, whereby they are, like all types of mankind, infused with the courage of desperation.

The Russians understand power and they respond to it far more readily than they do to high-sounding calls to cooperate for the good of all mankind. They actually trust us more when we talk the language of power than when we preach to them about our ideals.

Winston Churchill once said, "I cannot forecast to you the action of Russia. It is a riddle wrapped in a mystery inside an enigma; but perhaps there is a key. That key is Russian national interest." Now, as then, the Russians will not cooperate with us unless it is in their interest to do so.

Détente does not magically eliminate differences in attitudes, values, and interests that are grounded in the outlooks nations inherit, the ideologies they embrace, and the economic and military realities they face. Instead it is a process whereby nations seek to live with their differences rather than die for them. The differences cannot be obliterated. The options are limited to trying to come to grips with these tensions and managing them, or letting them totally determine the nature of international relations. One of the best rationales I have heard for détente was expressed by the British Governor-General of Australia, William Slim, when I saw him in 1953. He felt strongly that "we must break the ice. If we don't break it, we will all get frozen into it so tight that it will take an atom bomb to break it."

This is what détente is about, from the American standpoint—breaking the ice, where that is possible, and trying to approach our differences rationally.

The negotiated Berlin agreement of 1971 is an example of what détente can accomplish. In 1948, and again in 1958, tensions over Berlin threatened to involve the United States and the U.S.S.R. in an escalation that neither wanted. Afterward, Berlin—divided between East and West, and located deep within East Germany—remained a sore spot for both sides and a constant source of possible confrontation. In 1971, after sixteen months of intense negotiation, we reached agreement with the Soviet Union on access to Berlin and on other related and potentially dangerous problems. These Berlin agreements covered matters that might in themselves have seemed relatively minor, but that were extremely touchy for both sides, and the dangers they eliminated were very great. In reaching the agreements we had successfully replaced confrontation with negotiation. It was the Berlin Agreement that paved the way for the first U.S.-Soviet summit of my administration in 1972. We felt that if we could resolve our differences on such a thorny, long-lived controversy, we might be able to reach agreement on other issues.

What détente *can* do is to reduce the possibilities of a miscalculation leading to nuclear war, and eliminate some of the trouble spots by replacing confrontation with negotiation.

There are many things détente *cannot* do. It cannot suddenly turn the Russians into "good guys." And it cannot eliminate the fact that we are in competition with them all over the world and that some of these tensions are inevitably going to lead to confrontations. What we can hope is that détente will minimize the dangers in the minor areas by replacing confrontation with negotiation, and provide ways to resolve peacefully the confrontations in the major areas. As superpowers with the ability to destroy each other, we both have a stake in seeing that confrontations are not allowed to get out of hand.

Some apparently think that if we really tried to get to

know the Russians we could resolve all our differences and come to an understanding. To believe this is to ignore centuries of totally different national experiences, to disregard the effects of diametrically opposed ideologies, to lose sight of the tense geopolitical and military rivalry that pervades our relationship with the Soviet Union. "Getting to know you" does not necessarily mean getting to like you. In fact, in this case, it may mean finding out that we like each other even less than we thought.

Liking each other is one thing. Learning to live with each other is another. If we can talk to each other, at least we stand a chance of finding and cultivating some areas of common interest and avoiding the miscalculation and suspicion that occur when two sides are isolated from each other. If we do not talk, we will not find anything on which to cooperate and our differences will only grow and our hatreds harden. Then it may really taken an atom bomb to break us out of the ice.

Churchill remarked many years ago that "Russia fears our friendship more than our enmity. The Soviet dictatorship could not stand free intercourse with the West." His solution: "We must make Moscow fear our enmity more than our friendship." This concept is central to a successful détente. We can make the Soviets fear our enmity more than our friendship by showing them we are a dangerous enemy, but it also will help if we can demonstrate that we are a worthwhile friend. Economically they desperately need our cooperation. This is something we can offer them—if they moderate their aggressive behavior.

Détente is not a matter of changing the Russians' intentions. It is a matter of changing their cost-benefit calculations. It is a matter of making their aggressive actions more costly, and therefore less worthwhile, and their peaceful initiatives more beneficial from the viewpoint of their own national interest. The usual academic search for clues to Russian behavior is not only futile, it misses the fundamental point, which is that what they do depends on what we do. If we demonstrate a willingness to stand up to them when they try to push us around and to sit down with them when they behave more reasonably, they will be more accommodating. The key to the behavior of the Russians lies as much with us as it does with them. In order to be able to sit down with the Russians you must first be able to stand up to them.

The optimists have naïvely believed that détente can erase all the problems and conflicts of national interest between us and the two great communist powers. The critics of détente are equally in error in concluding that because détente cannot do everything, it can do nothing. The fact is that the Soviets are committed to the expansion of their power *to as great an extent as they can safely and profitably achieve*. They will not stop pressing us, testing for weak points, probing for areas of expansion. If we demonstrate that the economic and diplomatic payoff to them will be greater if they cooperate with us rather than confront us, they will draw the obvious conclusion. But if we are pushovers in opposition and niggardly in friendship, they will again draw the obvious conclusion. The choice, in many ways, is ours.

Détente—The Personal Equation

Stating general principles for a realistic détente is one thing. Applying those principles is another. No area of foreign policy is covered with more mine fields for an American President than this. A misstep—whether by being too soft or by being too tough—can lead to disaster. It is vitally important to avoid violent swings between euphoria and total disillusion.

One major problem a President has in carrying out a policy of détente is to justify following what appear to many to be two completely contradictory concepts. Throughout my public career I had earned a reputation for adamantly opposing communism and all it stands for. My visits to China and the Soviet Union in 1972 puzzled, disappointed, and even outraged many of my strongest supporters. How, they asked, could I possibly tip tea cups with Mao, drink maotai with Zhou Enlai and vodka with Brezhnev? How could I justify proposing toasts, exchanging gifts, smiling, and shaking hands with these ruthless, atheistic leaders of oppressive, aggressive regimes who opposed everything we stood for? Did this mean that I had changed my views with regard to the threat that totalitarian communism posed to the West? If not, what good purpose could possibly be served by "fraternizing" with those whose avowed goal is to impose their system on us and all free nations?

When I went to Moscow in 1972 I had no illusion whatever about the aggressive nature of Soviet intentions. During my first three years in office the Soviets had tested us in Cuba, in the Mideast, and in South Asia; they tested us again in Vietnam just two weeks before the summit. The fact that we had stood firm in each case, and had even met with the Soviets' deadly enemies in Peking before going to Moscow, did not "torpedo" the summit, as some had predicted it would. On the contrary, I am certain that our firmness helped to convince the Soviets that they had no choice but to negotiate with us.

I did not expect that personal meetings with the Soviet leaders would change their views. I knew that Brezhnev and his colleagues were all dedicated communists. However, I believed then, and I believe now, that while such meetings will not erase major differences in basic philosophy, they can be useful for narrowing the areas of potential conflict and exploring the possibilities of cooperation for mutual benefit. In a broader sense, the Soviet Union and the United States are the only two world nuclear superpowers; we therefore have an obligation to ourselves, to each other, and to the rest of the world to explore every possible avenue to see that our awesome power is not used in a way that could bring massive devastation to ourselves and to civilization as we know it.

It is essential to keep in mind the limits of what détente can achieve. It is equally important to know our adversaries and how to deal with them if we are to achieve even these limited goals. The Soviet leaders I have met, going back to 1959 when I first visited Moscow as Vice President, are very different from the old stereotypes of the bomb-throwing Bolsheviks of the twenties or the sleazy subversives of the thirties and forties. As individuals, Russians, and communists, they are far more complex—less forbidding but potentially more dangerous.

As Russians, they are very hospitable hosts; they are generous, strong, and courageous; above all, they are proud of their Russian background and extraordinarily sensitive to personal put-downs or affronts.

As Soviet communists, they lie, cheat, take advantage, bluff, and constantly maneuver—trying always to win by any means necessary to achieve their goal.

As individuals, they differ widely in background and personal characteristics. Khrushchev was crude and boorish, with a quick intelligence and a devastatingly effective sense of humor. Brezhnev gave the appearance of being warmhearted, earthy, and very physical—in the way he would often grab my arm to make a point he reminded me of Lyndon Johnson. While not as quick in intelligence, he was more steady and less impulsive than Khrushchev. Kosygin was cold, aristocratic, a smooth technocrat; if he had been born in Chicago instead of Leningrad, he might well have ended up as the chief executive officer of a U.S. multinational corporation. Gromyko was dour, tough, maddeningly persistent, and inflexible in pushing his government's foreign policy line. Dobrynin was enormously able, smooth, gregarious, and sophisticated; considering the responsibilities he had, he was without doubt the best ambassador in Washington in my memory. Suslov, the hard-line Marxist theoretician, talked and acted with the dignified self-assurance of an American college profesor on tenure. All of them appeared to be genuinely devoted family men and, with the exception of Khrushchev, had good manners and dressed impeccably.

Considering these traits, several rules for conduct in negotiating with the Soviet leaders emerge. As individuals, they of course should be treated courteously. As Russians, they are extremely sensitive to being treated as inferiors. As Prime Minister Harold Macmillan once told me, the Soviet leaders desperately want to be welcomed as equal members of the international club of top world statesmen. In nations as well as individuals insecurity often breeds belligerent aggressiveness, especially if the sensitive party thinks he is being insulted or ridiculed. Overt put-downs infuriate the Russians and cause them to become more belligerent. We must be sensitive to these concerns.

I am not suggesting that good or bad personal relations will have a major effect on state relations. However, the two cannot be separated; one affects the other. We should not assume that better personal relations will automatically improve bad state relations. Still, poor personal relations will make it more difficult to improve bad state relations, and could even aggravate them.

I would suggest these rules for those who negotiate with the Soviet leaders:

1. Any President who believes he can get the men in the Kremlin to change their policies by "charming them" or simply through personal persuasiveness is due for a rude awakening. Franklin D. Roosevelt tried at Tehran and Yalta and failed. The disillusionment that quickly dissipated the euphoric spirits of Geneva in 1955, Camp David in 1959, Vienna in 1961, and Glassboro in 1967 is stark testimony that charm and conciliatory rhetoric have no lasting effect on the tough, pragmatic Soviet leaders.

2. Conduct on the part of the President that conveys any sense of weakness or indecision can lead to miscalculation by Soviet leaders and to a testing of American will, as was the case when Khrushchev followed the Vienna summit of 1961 by putting missiles into Cuba in 1962.

3. While mushy sentimentality should be avoided, a President achieves nothing by bluster and belligerency. The Russians are masters of the bluff and can usually detect that tactic when it is used against them. Bluster and bad manners may intimidate the weak but never the strong. Talking softly but firmly, while carrying a big stick is the most effective way to deal with the Soviets.

4. The Soviet leaders are taught to be conspirators vir-

tually from birth. Therefore, it is important not to lay all your cards on the table. Above all, never tell them what you will *not* do; they may think you might do more than you can or will.

5. We must not make the common mistake of attributing our values to the Soviets. For example:

(a) The West is affected by world public opinion; the Soviets are affected only by their interests. UN resolutions condemning their actions not only fail to constrain the Soviets; the Soviets greet such resolutions with contempt.

(b) Ruling out force is considered an act of virtue in the West; the Soviets and other potential aggressors consider it a sign of weakness. Ruling out American use of force provokes the use of force against us.

(c) "Sincerity" is an idealistic Western concept that means nothing to the Soviet leaders. Our former ambassador to Russia, Charles E. Bohlen, once told me, "Trying to determine whether the Soviet leaders are sincere about anything is a useless exercise." Pointing to a coffee table, he added, "They are pure materialists. You can no more describe them as being sincere than you could describe that table as being sincere."

(d) Western and communist attitudes toward peace also are poles apart. Before I went to Moscow in 1959 I asked John Foster Dulles what he thought of the view of some foreign policy experts that my major purpose should be to convince Khrushchev that the United States was for peace. He replied, "I totally disagree. He knows we are for peace. You must try to convince him that he cannot win a war."

6. We should never negotiate from weakness. No further arms control talks, for example, should be held until the United States has firmly in place a credible program for restoring the military balance, vis-à-vis the Soviets, across the board. Otherwise, the Soviet leaders will be looking down our throats. At the conference table we can only negotiate on the basis of what we and they are definitely going to have in the arsenal.

7. Consistency coupled with firmness is absolutely indispensable. As UPI's veteran Moscow correspondent Joseph Galloway recently pointed out:

> In my dealings with the Russians like many before me I found it best to state your purpose, your aims, and your course clearly and firmly at the outset, and then hew to that line with every ounce of determination and doggedness you can muster.
>
> If you bend even the smallest of your principles you convince the other side that there is at least a chance you will bend the larger ones, and that possibility is enough to keep the Russians working on you forever.
>
> The conduct of American diplomacy with the Soviet Union over the past two and a half years has broken those simple rules of conduct time and again.
>
> Unilateral decisions have been made without seeking any Soviet concession in return. An amateurish eagerness to reach agreement has been displayed at the outset of difficult negotiations. Extraneous issues have been raised and the American prestige committed in their support, only to be allowed to fade and die. Rather than a single determined voice, the Russians hear a babble of diametrically opposed hard and soft lines from official Washington.

Many U.S. opinion makers regard the Soviet leaders as less formidable than I have found them to be. Arthur Schlesinger, for example, argues that: "Our hard-liners like to think that the Soviet Union is a dynamic and purposeful state following a policy laid down with consistency, foresight and coherence. But it may as well be that the Soviet Union is a weary, drab country, led by sick old men, beset by insuperable problems at home and abroad and living from crisis to crisis. . . ."

I would like to think that he is right. But looking at the Soviets' virtually unbroken record of successful conquests over the past five years, I fear he is wrong. And what we must constantly bear in mind is that the new generation of Soviet leaders will be at least as tough as the old; possibly tougher since, unlike Brezhnev, Gromyko, Kosygin, and most of the other present members of the Politburo, they will not be inhibited by vivid personal memories of the horrors of World War II. Of one thing we can be sure: like those they succeed, they will have a strategy of victory. Only a firm strategy of victory on our side will avoid defeat. The West must match them with leaders just as strong, just as intelligent, and if anything, more determined to defend what is right than they are to pursue what is wrong.

Victory

We can lose World War III, or we can win it.

We can lose it by defeatism: by imagining that the contest is unwinnable or unworthy. We can lose by waking up too late to the importance of the conflict, and thus acquiescing too long in those incremental gains by the Soviet side that cumulatively can amount to a major, even a decisive, Soviet victory. We can lose by disdaining allies that are imperfect, or contests that affront our sensibilities. We can lose by self-indulgence, by telling ourselves that the sacrifice can wait until tomorrow, by postponing hard decisions until the need becomes so obvious that the decision comes too late. We can lose through a sort of "paralysis by analysis," concocting overly intellectualized rationales for each new Soviet advance, and using these as an excuse for inaction.

Or we can win—if we decide to.

The first necessity is to recognize that we can win, and that we should win.

The next is to insist that we must win, and to make and stick to the basic political decision that we will do whatever is necessary to ensure victory. This sounds simple. It is not. It requires a conscious return to the concept of peace through strength. It requires discarding a lot of well-worn intellectual baggage and abandoning a lot of popular slogans. It requires overriding the clamorous voices of a lot of separate interests, all insisting that someone else sacrifice instead of themselves. It requires accepting risks.

America and the West need to be jolted into a sense of urgency. We no longer have the margin for error that we had even a few short years ago. That margin vanished with our advantage in strategic weapons.

When the United States had a decisive advantage in strategic nuclear power, relatively minor shifts in the geopolitical balance were of relatively minor consequence. But with the loss of that advantage, these shifts, when they go against us, are far more ominous, just as a misplaced step matters more to the tightrope walker than to the sidewalk stroller. With the West's oil jugular—the Persian Gulf—now directly imperiled, we are losing our margin of safety along with the margin of error.

More than two decades ago the late Dean Acheson wrote of

> the myriad decisions which will cumulatively determine whether or not our country becomes what it must be, and does what it must do, if the non-Communist world is to be pulled together, held together, and led, still strong and free, through "peaceful competition," or "cold war," warm war, or hot war, or, perhaps, all of them separately or together. These decisions will be put to us not with the dramatic simplicity with which the thunder of bombs posed the issue at Pearl Harbor. A democracy can seal its fate with a gradualism and apparent inevitability which seems to blind its leaders to the nature of the road ahead, as they were blinded in the years before the Civil War.

Acheson's observation is even more true today.

We can drift down that path of gradualism. Or we can pull ourselves up short and decide to change course.

We can afford a vastly increased defense effort—if we *decide* to. We can postpone desirable social goals in order to ensure survival—if we *decide* to. We can carry the twilight war to the enemy—if we *decide* to. But we have to make the decision.

Having made the decision that we are going to do what is necessary, we then have to pursue it through a carefully coordinated strategy that embraces the short term and the long term simultaneously.

Containment and détente have both been essentially defensive strategies, designed to keep the Soviets from advancing and to keep World War III from escalating. Now, with the West having let down its guard, the walls of containment have been ruptured and the Soviets have made ominous moves toward escalation. We need a defensive strategy in the short term to counter these Soviet thrusts. We also need a forward strategy for the longer term. Soviet strategy is not defensive; it is designed to secure victory. The only answer to a strategy of victory on the Soviet side is a strategy of victory for the West.

The Soviet goal remains what it has been: to win without war if possible, with war if necessary. Victory for the West does not necessarily mean victory in war. But victory without war requires us to be strong enough to prevent the Soviets from winning either with war or without it.

We must restore our military strength, so that once again we will unquestionably have both the power to defend our interests and the capacity to project that power to trouble spots around the globe. This will take time, and time is running out. If we begin quickly and vigorously, we can lessen that period of acute peril during which the Soviets will have military superiority over us. A 5 percent increase in the military budget is wholly inadequate to turn the tide. This would still leave the Soviets outspending us by a wide margin, and therefore widening their military lead over us in the dangerous years of the early and mid-1980s. All a 5 percent increase will do is reduce the rate of increase of Soviet strength relative to that of the United States. This is not a mark of resolve. It is a mark of temporization.

Our friends and adversaries alike are well aware that either a guarantee or a warning by the United States is only as strong as the forces backing it up. Further, it is only as strong as the demonstrated will of the President to use those forces if necessary. When a President repeatedly makes a political issue out of the claim that no American has been killed in combat during his administration, he wins points at home but loses clout abroad; other leaders must wonder how far he would let himself be pushed before he would risk that record.

A strategy of victory requires that we move urgently to

restore both the intelligence and the covert arms of the CIA, so that we can have better information and more means of dealing with threats to ourselves and others—and so that we too can fight the twilight war on those many hidden fronts on which our adversary is engaged, now too often without effective opposition.

We should restore honor to those who fight the nation's wars, whether in the uniform of the armed forces or in the often more hazardous mufti of the CIA.

The nations most directly in the path of Soviet ambition are often weak and unstable. Aggression in World War III comes more often under borders than over them, in the form of Soviet-supported coups or insurgencies. The United States has been taking a beating all over the world because the deck has been stacked: neutral or Western-oriented nations have been open hunting grounds for the Soviets and their proxies, while Communist-oriented countries have been privileged sanctuaries; and the Russians have been giving their clients guns, while we have been giving ours lectures on human rights.

On both these counts the United States should serve clear public notice that its policies are going to change. The Third World is the battleground on which much of the present phase of World War III is being fought. It is in the interests of Third World peoples and nations, as well as our own, that our side prevail. If we win World War III, all peoples can survive and go their own way, with the chance to advance toward freedom and prosperity. If the Soviets win, all will become slaves and satellites.

Nations confronting Soviet-supported threats need arms to defend themselves, and this includes the majority of such regimes that are nondemocratic as well as the minority that might be called democratic. We should not collapse in a flutter when accused of being "arms merchants." In World War II we proudly declared ourselves "the arsenal of democracy." In World War III it is just as vital that our friends have the arms to defend themselves. We should be less fastidious and more forthcoming in supplying arms where they are needed to stem the Soviet advance. We should stop condemning a friendly government and refusing it aid when its existence is threatened, merely because its elections are no more honest than our own have sometimes been in places like Boston or Chicago. Even if the regime is repressive or authoritarian, the communist alternative is likely to be not only worse for the West, but worse for the people of the country itself.

A more fundamental step we should take is to knock down the "no trespassing" signs that surround the Soviet empire and that have limited the war to our side of the border. We should declare that henceforth we will consider ourselves as free to forage on the Soviet side as they have been to forage on ours.

This does not mean automatically supporting any and all liberation movements within the Soviet sphere. The same sort of practical constraints that kept the West from intervening to help the Hungarians in 1956 and the Czechs in 1968, for example, still operate, and it would be a cruel disservice to hold out false hopes of assistance to those who would not receive it. But we should consider ourselves free to support those we perceive it is in our interest to support, either overtly or covertly, and we should do so without apology. A popular, pro-Western rebel leader such as Jonas Savimbi in communist-ruled Angola should not be turned away when he comes to the United States seeking support.

A strategy for victory requires, over the long term, that we check Soviet strengths and exploit Soviet weaknesses. The principal Soviet strength is military, and Soviet strategy is based on force. Economically, we outproduce them. In terms of providing what people want, of satisfying the strivings of the human spirit, there simply is no contest between the two systems; the West wins hands down. The Soviets can conquer, but they can never persuade. Moscow has been very successful in extending its domination over other nations, but totally unsuccessful in winning the support of the people of those nations.

More than 2,000 years ago the ancient Chinese strategist Sun Tzu set forth this principle: Engage with the ch'eng—the ordinary, direct force—but win with the ch'i—the extraordinary, indirect force. In his wisdom he saw that the two are mutually reinforcing and that the way to victory is by the simultaneous use of both.

In our own time we have no choice but to engage with the ch'eng—to counterpose our military strength to that of the Soviet Union, to hold our alliances together and increase the combined strength of the West. This is the way to avoid defeat; this is the way to contain Soviet advance. It is an essential first step, just as the tide has to stop coming in before it goes out. The next step—to go on toward victory, to win with the ch'i—is at once more complex, more subtle, and more demanding. Yet here again the West has the greatest advantages, if only we can marshal and use them.

This requires patience. It requires perseverance. The pattern of Soviet advance has been two steps forward and, occasionally, one step backward; the pattern of a successful reversal of that advance will be one step backward and two steps forward.

Defeat, if it comes, is likely to be incremental, coming upon us with that "gradualism and apparent inevitability" that Acheson warned of. By the same token, victory, if it comes, will come step by careful step, and it will be achieved by avoiding missteps. We have to learn to recognize incremental gains as real gains. The *direction* of change, the momentum of history, as it is perceived by the leaders of other nations, will be a vital element in our success or failure. We will have to work at the small victories that, cumulatively, will reverse the backward momentum and signal those leaders looking for a bandwagon that the West is moving forward. When a river floods, those who live along its unprotected banks gather up their belongings and flee to safety. But those who live on protected banks are secure against the flood. The combination of the West's military strength and its demonstrated will to use it is, in effect, a levee that will contain the rising river of Soviet expansionism. As long as that levee remains high enough and sound enough, the nations that live along its banks will have the

courage to stand rather than flee. As more stand successfully, more will be emboldened to join them in making a stand.

The Soviets' goal is total victory and everything they do
is designed to achieve that goal. Their favorite tactic is to
identify a potential Western or Third World weak point,
and then concentrate overwhelming force on that particular
point. At various times that weak point has been an unstable
government, as in Italy; an unpopular government, as in
Nicaragua; a nation's will, as in their attempts to win the
Vietnam War on the American home front; or guilt, as in
their efforts to make the West defensive about anything to
which the communists attach the label "imperialism." They
have had some very significant successes with these tactics,
but they too have weak points, on which they are extremely
vulnerable.

One weak point is that they consistently act in ways
that make them intensely unpopular. Their aggressive bullying breeds an angry response in others. To the Soviets, alliances are only a pit stop on the road to satellization; other
nations are targets of aggression, potential Soviet Socialist
Republics. When Lenin commented that "we will support
Kerensky as the rope does the hanged man," he neatly defined the nature of Soviet friendship. This has not been lost
on those whose friendship the Soviets seek to cultivate.

When they do get a foot in the door, the Soviets often
behave so boorishly and heavy-handedly that their hosts
throw them out. Soviet advisers were thrown out of Egypt
in 1972 and Somalia in 1977. Pro-Soviet governments were
ousted in Chile in 1973, in Peru in 1976, and in Ghana in
1966. Nor do they always manage to establish a foothold
when they try. Communist or communist-backed rebellions
have been put down in many countries, including Greece in
1949, the Philippines in 1953, Malaya in 1960, the Congo in
1962, and Oman in 1975. Communist coup attempts have
been successfully foiled in the Dominican Republic and Indonesia in 1965, in the Sudan in 1971, in Portugal in 1975,
and in many other places as well.

• • • •

The Chinese formerly referred to the Soviets as their "elder brother"; now China has become the Soviet Union's bitterest enemy, a giant that shares 4,000 miles of border with the U.S.S.R. and claims parts of its territory.

There has been a great deal of talk about "playing the China card." This talk is insulting to the Chinese, who do not like to be considered a "card" to be "played." Some say we sought closer relations with Peking during my administration so we could use the Chinese against Moscow, and that Moscow was then forced to seek better relations with us. This is a valid assessment, but it is only a half-truth. Even if there had been no differences between Russia and China, it would still have been in our interest to improve relations with China. Further, as Henry Kissinger has pointed out, the notion "that we use China to annoy the Soviets as a penalty for Soviet conduct" is dangerous for two reasons: because "China is an extremely neuralgic point for the Soviet Union and they may not react rationally," and also because "it may even have a bad effect in Peking. If we improve our ties with Peking in order to punish the Soviet Union, this may leave the implication that if we want to improve our relations with the Soviet Union or if the Soviet Union makes some concessions to us, we may lower the level of our activities with Peking. So we ought to have a settled, long-range policy."

It is in our interest to have a strong China, because a weak China invites aggression and increases the danger of war. We and our European allies should do what is necessary to see that China acquires the military strength necessary to provide for its defense. For their part, the Chinese want to see a strong and resolute United States. If they see us backing down before the Soviets, they may decide that their interests lie in a rapprochement with the Soviet Union—not because they will suddenly agree with the Soviets or stop hating and fearing them, but because the combination of Soviet strength and U.S. weakness will cause them to reassess where their interests lie.

Promoting Sino-Soviet rivalry cannot, in and of itself, be a U.S. policy. But the rivalry is there, and it provides an opportunity, an environment, in which to design a policy. Triangular diplomacy can work to our advantage or our disadvantage. As long as that rivalry persists, however, it not only ties down a large portion of the Soviet forces militarily and affects the overall balance of power; it also seriously undermines the Soviet position in the Third World. In speaking to many Third World leaders China has credentials the United States cannot match. They will listen to Chinese warnings when they might discount our own.

The Soviets have reason to feel insecure. Theirs is a system that can only be kept in power by force. Wherever their capacity to exercise force weakens, their rule is threatened.

The peoples of Eastern Europe hate their Russian overlords. In the short term the chance that any of these nations will detach itself from the Soviet embrace is slim. The Soviets have shown that they have the will to use whatever force it takes to crush an East European rebellion. They know how shaky their hold is on Eastern Europe and how vulnerable the whole area would be to the "domino effect" if one nation should successfully break free. But Eastern Europe will remain a perpetual problem for the Soviet Union. The peoples of Eastern Europe have tasted freedom, something the Russian people have never tasted, except for a few brief months in 1917. Eventually, unless the Soviet Union first succeeds in its goal of world domination, the nations of Eastern Europe will become free.

Until they do, suppressing their urge to freedom will be a constant drain on Soviet resources. When they do, the Soviets may find that they cannot post a "quarantine" sign on their own borders to keep out the contagion of freedom.

Among the strongest potential allies we have in the struggle against the Kremlin leadership are the people of the Soviet Union. As one of the most powerful voices of the Russian people, Alexander Solzhenitsyn has pointed out: "All oppressed peoples are on the side of the West: the Russians, the various nationalities of the U.S.S.R., the Chinese, and the Cubans. Only by relying on *this* alliance can the West's strategy succeed. Only together with the oppressed will the West constitute the decisive force on earth. These people are communism's Achilles' heel. They can be freedom's secret weapon if we recognize their immense strategic importance."

History shows that among nations, alignments change. In World War II we and the Soviet Union fought together against Germany and Japan; now Japan and West Germany are our allies against the Soviet Union. China was our ally in World War II, then our enemy in Korea and Vietnam; now China is, not our ally, but our friend, and the enemy of the Soviet Union.

As we look at the potential strengths of the Western side, we can count among them not only our allies but also those other nations that stand in an uneasy relation to the Soviet Union, half in and half out of the Soviet embrace. Even if they do not come over to our side, we gain when they move away from the Soviet side.

The freely associated nations of the West can use all their forces to ward off aggression. The Soviet Union has to use part of its forces to keep its "allies" under control. The Western alliance is strengthened by the innate desire of man to be free. The Soviet Union is vulnerable to the innate resistance of man to tyranny.

In this struggle, the strength of the Soviets is military. They seek victory through aggression and intimidation; in order to achieve this, they seek military superiority. They rule by force, and they seek to extend their rule by force.

We must check this ambition. We must have the strength and the will to prevent their winning by force. But then we must carry the struggle into those areas where they are weak and we are strong. Despite their strength militarily, they fail utterly at providing what people want.

People want peace. They want material progress. They want to be free from foreign domination. They want the "higher values"—freedom of speech, travel, worship, choice; liberty in all its aspects.

The Soviets promise peace, and bring war; they promise

economic progress, and bring poverty; they promise "liberation," and bring a new imperialism; they promise freedom, and bring slavery. In all these areas, their own record is the best answer to their rhetoric. Wherever the Soviets and the West are matched in competition, there simply is no contest.

We must hold the line against aggression, both direct and indirect, so that those who opt for the West need not fear that they will be on the losing side. We must stand by our friends, so that those who want to be our friends will not fear to be our friends. We should use our enormous economic power to further the progress of our friends, and to squeeze our potential enemies.

In the short term—if we restore the strength of our defenses—we can halt, and then turn back, the tide of Soviet advance by concentrating our efforts in the immediate target areas and showing a steadfast determination to do what is necessary to keep aggression from succeeding. As the nations of the West grow stronger, as they visibly muster their will, as they demonstrate that they will not repeat the mistakes of Munich, two things will happen. Third World leaders who want to ride with a winner will look more respectfully on the West, calculating the advantages that friendly relations with us can bring. And the Soviet leaders will reevaluate the costs of adventurism, recognizing that as the strength, cohesion, and will of the West increase arithmetically, the costs of aggression will go up geometrically.

Over the longer term we can encourage peaceful evolution within the Soviet Union itself. However, this is a task not of decades but of generations. Pressed too rapidly, it would bring a brutal repression; developed gradually, so that it less directly threatens those in power at any given time, it can gradually show results, just as it did under the Tsars in the nineteenth century.

The task that confronts us is not one for the United States alone. As the present threat to the Persian Gulf makes starkly clear, the entire West has an immediate stake in the struggle. So do the threatened nations themselves. It makes no sense for the United States to provide the arms, the money, and the men to meet every crisis. There are more than 3 billion people outside the Soviet bloc, of which only 200 million are Americans. As the French have shown in Africa, sometimes our allies can respond more effectively than we can, especially in areas with which they have a long familiarity. The oil-rich Moslem nations of the Persian Gulf share a common interest in defending their own independence, and Islam, against any expansion of the Soviet thrust into Afghanistan. But the West does look to the United States for leadership. And the Soviets do look at the United States in calculating what they can get away with.

If the Soviet leaders look westward and see an American leadership that eyes their moves in a measured way, that clearly refuses to bow, that walks without faltering, that knows what it is doing, that is determined to do whatever has to be done in order to ensure the survival and security of the West, then those Soviet leaders will not be tempted to gamble all in a high-stakes throw of the dice. They will make their cost-benefit analyses, and postpone or abandon ambitions that no longer seem worth the candle. Then we will see how preparation for war can help avert war; how having strength can free us from the necessity of using it.

I have often cited Sir Robert Thompson's equation: national power equals applied resources plus manpower times will. The will to use power multiplies its effectiveness; when that will is clearly perceived by the adversary, the actual application of power may be unnecessary.

Power by itself is neutral; it can be used for good or for evil. Its results are not measured by intentions. Power used with good intentions, but ineptly, can be as destructive as power used with bad intentions. The greatest tragedy of all, however, occurs when those who have power fail to use it, and because of that failure lives and even freedom itself are lost.

The human spirit has time and again transcended the most terrible assaults on it; civilizations fall to barbarians, but eventually barbarism succumbs to civilization. But this victory of the spirit takes place over a very long term. Our challenge now is to show that a particular civilization—ours—can triumph over a particular barbarism—Soviet communism—so that freedom will be preserved for our children and grandchildren.

12
The Sword and the Spirit

> There are only two powers in the world, the sword and the spirit. In the long run the sword will always be conquered by the spirit.

> —*Napoleon*

Britain's former Prime Minister Harold Macmillan, still crisply lucid at eighty-five, recently compared the present situation in the world with that in Europe before World War II. "Speaking honestly," he declared, "I would say that we are now at 1935 or 1936." He went on to warn: "We can save ourselves only by looking at the realities, and by organizing the resistance which we must create if what we have won in two world wars we shall not lose in the third."

In the late 1930s the nations in Hitler's path had time to stop World War II before it started, but they ignored the warnings and frittered away that time.

In his "Iron Curtain" speech at Fulton, Missouri, in 1946 Winston Churchill recalled:

> Last time I saw it all coming, and cried aloud to my own fellow-countrymen and to the world, but no one paid any attention. Up till the year 1933 or even 1935, Germany might have been saved from the awful fate which has overtaken her and we might all have been spared the miseries Hitler let loose upon mankind.

> There never was a war in all history easier to prevent

by timely action than the one which has just desolated such great areas of the globe. It could have been prevented, in my belief, without the firing of a single shot, and Germany might be powerful, prosperous and honored today; but no one would listen and one by one we were all sucked into the awful whirlpool.

The nations in Moscow's path today have time to avoid the fate of those in Hitler's path in the 1930s; but only barely.

The outcome of the "protracted conflict" between East and West will depend on our military arsenals, our strategic vision, and our control of those material resources that are needed to build the weapons of war and the sinews of peace. But it will also turn on how we use another resource, the most precious of all, and the one that for each and every one of us is finite: time. If the West loses this conflict, MacArthur's warning will be its epitaph: "The history of failure in war can be summed up in two words: Too Late."

The whole history of freedom is a narrative of the struggle to become free and remain free. Freedom is not cheap and maintaining it is not easy. Fate, history, God, chance—to whatever we may ascribe it, we hold a responsibility to the future unique to our time and place. Nothing that today's generation can leave for tomorrow's will mean more than the heritage of liberty. That heritage is under more severe threat now than ever before.

Today's "new frontiers," unfortunately, are the frontiers of Soviet expansionism: the frontiers of Soviet advance in Africa, in the Middle East, in central Asia; the frontiers of more and more commanding Soviet influence through indigenous Communist parties in Western Europe, through "liberation" movements, through the calculated rewriting of history, through agitation and propaganda and attacks on those institutions and those governments that stand in the way of Soviet ambitions.

The plain, harsh fact is that on all of these fronts the West is in retreat and the Soviet Union is advancing; freedom is in retreat, and totalitarianism is on the march.

The Soviet Union has 6 percent of the world's population and 10 percent of its production; yet it successfully bullies its neighbors and threatens the world. The other 94 percent of the world's people, with the other 90 percent of its production, seem increasingly helpless in the face of Soviet ambitions.

Why should this be?

The answer is that it shouldn't be and it needn't be.

Unless a great power acts like one, it will leave a power vacuum that another great power will fill. The United States has been floundering, uncertain and irresolute, and the Soviet Union has rushed to fill the vacuum created by our inaction. The United States and the U.S.S.R. form the two sides of the basic power equation that will dominate the final decades of the twentieth century. The direction of future world history will be set by the direction in which the balance between our two nations appears to be shifting.

The Soviet leaders may be crude philosophers but they are sophisticated wielders of power. Lacking those qualms of conscience that inhibit the West, they can be utterly ruthless and totally opportunistic in their uses of power. In a time of power equivalence this makes them a formidable adversary. Only if the West develops a sense of purpose equal to theirs—though different from theirs—can we hope to shift the balance in our favor.

There was a famous Frenchman, Emmanuel Joseph Sieyés, who somehow managed to get through the ten grim and tumultuous years between 1789 and 1799, between the time when the Third Estate met in the tennis court at Versailles and the time when the Consulate was established. When he was asked much later, "What did you do in all those years of revolution?" he replied, "I survived."

This is the immediate task the defenders of liberty face in the grim years just ahead: to survive, and by surviving to keep liberty itself alive. Unless the West survives these decades Western civilization as we know it, with all its ideals, its culture, its high aspirations, will crumble into the dust of history.

With this priority clearly in mind, the West can survive. Without it, the dawn of the twenty-first century may be the opening chapter in a new age of barbarism on a global scale. For survival is no longer automatic. We are entering a period in which we have to work to ensure it, in which we have to sacrifice other priorities in the name of that supreme priority. We will have to compromise some of our cherished ideals, as well as spend more of our wealth than we would wish on weapons and other forms of defense.

To say that we must oppose the march of the new despotism with every effort required does not mean launching a holy war; it does not mean launching a war at all. It does, however, mean arming sufficiently to dissuade the other side from launching a war; and it does mean active intervention where necessary to thwart Soviet expansion at those points at which Moscow is testing the limits of its new frontiers.

It would be comforting to rely on Napoleon's comment that "There are only two powers in the world, the sword and the spirit. In the long run the sword will always be conquered by the spirit." But the comment says more for Napoleon's modesty as a soldier than it does for his accuracy as a historian.

The spirit may prevail in the long run, if we measure the long run in millennia. But in the shorter run of decades, generations, and even centuries, time and again the spirit has been extinguished by the sword. For the generation whose cities are sacked, whose sons are killed, and whose liberties are crushed by a conquering army, the prospect that a millennium hence the spirit might rise again is cold comfort. In that short run in which we all live, the sword is the essential shield for the spirit.

One of our strengths in this struggle, however, is that the spirit itself can be a weapon—and while the Soviets have the sword, ours is the side that has both the sword and the spirit.

In 1839 the Marquis de Custine visited Russia and noted: "One word of truth hurled into Russia is like a spark landing in a keg of powder." Today, the fact that the Soviet system lives on lies makes it extremely vulnerable to the truth. Truth can penetrate borders. Truth can travel on its own power, wherever people and ideas of East and West meet. Russia has heavy censorship, but its people are starved for the truth. Sending the West's message through every totalitarian barrier—whether by exchange of visitors, or books, or broadcasts—will give hope to millions behind those barriers, and will gradually eat away at the foundations of the Soviet system just as seeping water can erode the foundation of a prison.

We should not shrink from the propaganda war, either within the Soviet empire or in the rest of the world. We should revitalize Radio Free Europe and Radio Liberty, and set up counterparts of them that can compete directly with Soviet propaganda in those areas of the Third World the Soviets have targeted for aggression.

Khrushchev often challenged the West to competition with communism. In 1958, in an address I made to the English-Speaking Union of the Commonwealth at Guildhall in London, I urged that the West both accept the challenge and broaden it. I said then:

> We say—broaden this competition and include the spiritual and cultural values that have distinguished our civilization. . . .
>
> Man needs the higher freedoms, freedom to know, to debate freely, to write and express his views.
>
> He needs the freedom that law and justice guarantee to every individual. . . .
>
> He wants the freedom to travel and learn from other peoples and cultures.
>
> He wants freedom of worship.
>
> To us, these are the most precious aspects of our civilization. We would be happy if others were to compete in this sphere and try to surpass our achievements.

Whether or not the Soviets choose to compete in these areas, we should compete with all the vigor at our command. Let the idea of liberty hammer at the barricades, reach through the bars of the prisons, take tyranny by the throat and shake it. The Soviets need contact with the West. They need our technology and our trade. They cannot keep out our radio broadcasts. They cannot seal themselves off totally from the world. When they crack open the door to reach out for what they want, we should push through it as much truth as we can. And in those parts of the world where their police power does not reach—in the target areas, where the immediate battles of World War III are being waged—we can wield truth as a sword.

Marx dismissed religion as the opiate of the masses. Today's Kremlin leaders are finding it an unbreakable rock. Pope John Paul II's triumphal return to Poland forced the Soviets to chew hard on Stalin's words in the 1930s, when he contemptuously asked, How many divisions has the Pope? The Pope does not have armored divisions, but the forces he has cannot be crushed by Soviet tanks. The emotions he has unleashed reach to the core of the human spirit; religious faith is a force often underestimated by those who do not understand it.

In the final analysis victory will go to the side that most effectively builds, maintains, concerts, and uses its power—not just its military power, but all of its strengths combined.

The road to victory is circuitous. Like a mountain trail, it sometimes doubles back before going on. Like a mountain trail, it requires patience and perseverance to traverse. The one who tires and drops by the wayside does not attain victory.

Power is the ability to make things happen, to influence events, to set the course of history. Some kinds of power operate effectively in the short term; some only over the course of many generations.

Traditionally, the Chinese think in terms of millennia, the Russians in terms of centuries, the Europeans in terms of generations, and we Americans in terms of decades. We must learn to take a longer view. Then we will be more likely to take the actions in the short term that are necessary to achieve the results we want in the long term. Then we will recognize that victory, if it comes, will come incrementally, and therefore that each front in World War III is important, that each battle is important, that all of them will combine to bring us either defeat or victory.

Woodrow Wilson spoke of making the world safe for democracy. Our task today is to make the world safe for liberty.

Democracy is political, a system devised by human reason. Liberty is personal, a striving of the human spirit. Democracy is a particular form of government, which evolved out of the parliamentary traditions of Western Europe, which was brought here to North America by the European settlers and then developed as our country grew. Liberty is a human condition.

Liberty can survive and even flourish in other systems besides democracies. In this country, thanks to centuries of political evolution, we are fortunate enough to have liberty and democracy. We should not make the mistake of attempting to impose instant democracy on nations not ready for it, and in the process pave the way for the destruction of such liberties as they have.

Making the world safe for liberty, then, does not mean establishing democracy everywhere on earth. It does mean making liberty secure where it exists: secure against overt aggression, and also against externally supported subversion. If we make liberty secure where it exists, then by the force of its example liberty will become the wave of the future.

To the extent that the United States prevails, the world will be safe for free nations. To the extent that the Soviet Union prevails, the world will be unsafe for free nations. Soviet-style tyranny survives by expanding. Liberty will expand by surviving. But to expand, it must first survive.

De Gaulle once said of France, a great nation is never its true self unless engaged in a great enterprise. Ensuring the survival and ultimate triumph of human liberty is the greatest enterprise to which a nation can be summoned.

Victory without war requires that we resolve to use our strength in ways short of war. There is today a vast gray area between peace and war, and the struggle will be largely decided in that area. If we expect to win without war, or even not to lose without war, then we must engage the adversary within that area. We need not duplicate his methods, but we must counter them—even if that means behaving in ways other than we would choose to in an ideal world.

The uses of power cannot be divorced from the purposes of power. The old argument over whether "the end justifies the means" is meaningless in the abstract; it has meaning only in concrete terms of whether a particular end justifies a particular means. The true test of idealism comes in its results. Some ends of transcendent moral value do justify some means that would not be justified in other circumstances.

Preserving liberty is a moral goal, defeating aggression is a moral goal, avoiding war is a moral goal, establishing conditions that can maintain peace with freedom through our children's generation is a moral goal. Failure to take whatever means are needed to keep liberty alive would be an act of moral abdication.

Victory does not mean being "the world's policeman." It does mean establishing, very explicitly, that we regard the frontiers of Soviet advance as the frontiers of our own defense, and that we will respond accordingly. And it does require a firm, unflagging faith, as Lincoln would put it, that we are on God's side, that our cause is right, that we act for all mankind.

It may seem melodramatic to treat the twin poles of human experience represented by the United States and the Soviet Union as the equivalent of Good and Evil, Light and Darkness, God and the Devil; yet if we allow ourselves to think of them that way, even hypothetically, it can help clarify our perspective on the world struggle. As the British writer Malcolm Muggeridge has pointed out, "Good and evil . . . provide the theme of the drama of our mortal existence. In this sense, they may be compared with the positive and negative points which generate an electric current; transpose the points and the current fails, the lights go out, darkness falls and all is confusion."

The United States represents hope, freedom, security, and peace. The Soviet Union stands for fear, tyranny, aggression, and war. If these are not poles of good and evil in human affairs, then the concepts of good and evil have no meaning. Those who cannot see the distinction have little claim to lecture us on conscience. It is precisely because so many have "transposed the points" that the light of reason has dimmed and a dangerous confusion has spread. Ending that confusion is the first step toward seeing the path to victory.

America recently celebrated the tenth anniversary of man's first walk on the moon. That adventure captured the human imagination as few events in history have, but the venture that now beckons is in its own way greater still. In traveling to the moon, man stepped into the heavens. In meeting this great challenge here on earth, we can make the world safe for liberty and thus achieve what for centuries philosophers have set as mankind's goal.

Space caught man's imagination less for its technical wizardry than for its mystery. And yet it was not mystery that took us there. It was the genius, vision, courage, perseverance, and the dogged hard work of thousands of human beings joined in a common enterprise.

The obstacles confronting us in our present enterprise are no less formidable—and like our venture into space, this too is achievable.

This is a struggle of titans, the like of which the world has never seen. We cannot prevail by the short-term expedient of declaring a sudden emergency, and creating the illusion that the challenge can be dealt with quickly and then put behind us. The challenge we face will not end in a year, or a decade; to meet it we have to prepare ourselves for a sustained level of will and fortitude. Victory in this struggle will come through perseverance, by never giving up, by coming back again and again when things are tough. It will come through the kind of leadership that in one crisis after another raises the sights of the American people from the mundane to the transcendent, from the immediate to the enduring.

If we determine to win, if we resolve to accept no substitute for victory, then victory becomes possible. Then the spirit gives edge to the sword, the sword preserves the spirit, and freedom will prevail.

Selected Source Notes

Chapter One

p. 1.   William Manchester, *American Caesar* (Boston: Little, Brown and Company, 1978), p. 182.

p. 7.   Walter Lippmann, *The Public Philosophy* (Boston: Little, Brown and Company, 1955), p. 4.

Chapter Two

p. 19.   "An Interview with Teng Hsiao-p'ing [Deng Xiaoping]," *Time*, February 5, 1979, p. 34.

p. 19.   Brian Crozier, *Strategy of Survival* (New Rochelle, N.Y.: Arlington House, 1978), p. 9.

p. 19.   "This war is not as in the past . . ": see Michael B. Petrovich, trans., *Conversations with Stalin* by Milovan Djilas (New York: Harcourt, Brace, and World, 1962), p. 114.

p. 23.   "the capability to control . . .": see Charles M. Kupperman, "The Soviet World View," *Policy Review*, Winter 1979, p. 45.

p. 31.   Francis X. Maier, "The Jonas Savimbi Interview," *The American Spectator*, January 1980, p. 8.

p. 43.   "Dangling from the trees . . .": see Uwe Siemon-Netto, remarks to an Accuracy in Media banquet, *The AIM Report*, November 1979, p. 2.

p. 47. B. H. Liddell Hart, *Strategy*, 2nd ed. (New York: Frederick A. Praeger, 1967), p. 164.

p. 48. Refugee quote from *Los Angeles Times*, July 11, 1979, Part 1, p. 13.

p. 49. Iving Kristol, "Foreign Policy: End of an Era," *Wall Street Journal*, January 18, 1979.

Chapter Three

p. 51. Henry Reeve, trans.; Henry Steele Commager, ed., *Democracy in America* by Alexis de Tocqueville, Book I, Chap. XIX (London: Oxford University Press).

p. 56. The nineteenth-century writer quoted is Tibor Szamuely, *The Russian Tradition* (London: Secker and Warburg, 1974), p. 25.

p. 61. The description of the Novgorod attack taken from Szamuely, *The Russian Tradition*, p. 33.

p. 64. "virtually a Soviet colony": see Harry Schwartz, *Tsars, Mandarins, and Commissars* (Philadelphia and New York: J. B. Lippincott and Company, 1964) p. 118.

p. 65. "long-mute Russia": see Bertram D. Wolfe, *Three Who Made a Revolution*, 4th ed. (New York: Dell Publishing, 1978), pp. 17, 24.

p. 67. Robert Conquest, "The Human Cost of Soviet Communism" (Washington, D.C.: United States Government Printing Office, Document 92–36, July 16, 1971), p. 23.

p. 67. The statistics on deaths in the forced-labor camps and during the famine taken from Harris L. Coulter and Nataly Martin, trans., *Warning to the West* by Aleksandr I. Solzhenitsyn, Alexis Klimoff, ed. (New York: Farrar, Straus & Giroux, 1976), p. 19; and Thomas P. Whitney, trans., *The Gulag Archipelago*, Vols. I and II, by Aleksandr I. Solzhenitsyn (New York: Harper and Row, 1973), pp. 432–435 and 438–439.

p. 67. The quote from Molotov is from Victor Kravchenko, *I Chose Freedom* (New York: Charles Scribner's Sons, 1946), p. 87.

p. 68. Winston Churchill, *The Unknown War* (New York: Charles Scribner's Sons, 1931), pp. 1–2.

pp. 68–69. "An inordinate .. ambition . . .": see Phyllis Penn Kohler, trans. and ed., *Journey for Our Time* by Marquis de Custine (Chicago: Henry Regnery Company, 1951), p. 363.

p. 69. "The Russian people will . . .": see Szamuely, *The Russian Tradition*, p. 133.

p. 69. Zbigniew Brzezinski, *Ideology and Power in Soviet Politics* (New York: Frederick A. Praeger, 1967), p. 132.

p. 74. "the United States was not merely . . .": see John Spanier, *American Foreign Policy Since World War II*, 6th ed. (New York: Frederick A. Praeger, 1973), p. 8.

p. 75. Hajo Holborn, *The Political Collapse of Europe* (New York: Alfred A. Knopf, 1960), pp. ix–x.

p. 75. Charles E. Bohlen, *The Transformation of American Foreign Policy* (New York: W. W. Norton and Company, 1969), pp. 14–15.

Chapter Four

p. 78. Wilson quoted in Dale R. Tahtinen, *National Security Challenges to Saudi Arabia* (Washington, D.C.: American Enterprise Institute, 1978), p. 1.

p. 78. Molotov quoted in Foy Kohler, *Understanding the Russians* (New York: Harper and Row, 1970), p. 398.

p. 79. Guy V. Daniels, trans., *My Country and the World* by Andrei D. Sakharov (New York: Alfred A. Knopf, 1976), p. 81.

p. 80. Harry S. Truman, "Truman Charges Inaction on Syria," *New York Times*, August 25, 1957, p. 23.

p. 82. "highly strategic and political . . .": see Anthony Sampson, *The Seven Sisters* (New York: The Viking Press, 1975), p. 128.

pp. 96–97. Edward Luttwak, "Cubans in Arabia?" *Commentary*, December 1979, p. 65.

p. 100. Chaim Herzog, "Why Was the West Unprepared?", *Wall Street Journal*, December 24, 1979.

Chapter Five

p. 105. B. H. Liddell Hart, *Strategy*, p. 17.

p. 105. Sir Robert Thompson, *Revolutionary War in World Strategy, 1945–1970* (New York: Taplinger, 1970), p. 117.

p. 105. George McGovern quoted in *The Congressional Record*, June 22, 1970, p. 20737.

p. 106. Thompson, *Revolutionary War in World Strategy*, pp. 31, 32.

p. 111. "Only the American press . . .": see Thompson, *Peace Is Not at Hand* (London: Chatto and Windus, 1974), p. 32.

p. 112. "The camera . . .": see ibid., p. 38.

p. 118. Sihanouk quoted in Henry Kissinger, *White House Years* (Boston: Little, Brown and Company, 1979), pp. 250, 251, 459.

p. 120. L. Shelton Clarke, Jr., *New York Times*, Letters to the Editor, October 4, 1979, p. A–30.

p. 121. Kissinger quoted in *The Economist*, September 8, 1979, p. 7.

p. 122. Thompson, *Peace Is Not at Hand*, p. 101.

pp. 126–27. Thompson, *Peace Is Not at Hand*, p. 137.

p. 129. Dung quoted in Guenther Lewy, *America in Vietnam* (New York: Oxford University Press, 1978), p. 208.

p. 130. Crozier, *Strategy of Survival*, p. 62.

p. 132. Quotes on Cambodian genocide taken from John Barron and Anthony Paul, *Murder of a Gentle Land* (New York: Reader's Digest Press, 1977), pp. 134–136, 206; and *A Report to the Division of Human Rights of the United Nations, the Subcommission on Prevention of Discrimination and Protection of Minorities of the Human Rights Commission, Geneva, Switzerland*, 1978 Session (Washington, D.C.: United States Department of State, July 6, 1978), refugee interviews.

p. 135. William E. Colby and Peter Forbath, *Honorable Men: My Life in the CIA* (New York: Simon and Schuster, 1978), p. 286.

Chapter Six

p. 144. O. Edmund Clubb, *Twentieth Century China* (New York: Columbia University Press, Columbia Paperback ed., 1965), p. 4.

Chapter Seven

p. 163. Robert Rhodes James, ed., *Winston S. Churchill: His Complete Speeches 1897–1963*, Vol. VII (New York and London: Chelsea House Publishers, 1974), p. 7287.

p. 163. Victor Utgoff, remarks at a National Security Conference, February 1, 1978, Monterey, California, sponsored by the American Institute of Aeronautics and Astronautics.

p. 173. Paul Nitze, "Is SALT II a Fair Deal for the United States?" (Washington, D.C.: Committee on the Present Danger) May 16, 1979, pp. 8–9.

p. 177. Richard Pipes, "Why the Soviet Union Thinks It Could Fight and Win a Nuclear War," *Commentary*, July 1977, pp. 21, 34.

p. 179. *The Economist*, December 30, 1978, p. 8.

p. 180. Thompson, *Peace Is Not at Hand*, p. 175.

p. 188. Nitze, "Is SALT II a Fair Deal?", p. 6.

p. 190. Nitze, "Is SALT II a Fair Deal?", p. 13.

p. 193. Helmut Schmidt, Remarks at the Harvard University Commencement, June 1979.

p. 196. Secretary of Defense James Schlesinger, "The Theater Nuclear Force Posture in Europe, A Report to Congress," April 1, 1975, p. 10.

p. 211. Holloway and Gorshkov quoted in *Understanding Soviet Naval Developments*, 3rd. ed. (Washington, D.C.: Department of the Navy, Office of the Chief of Naval Operations, 1978), pp. 3, 61.

Chapter Eight

p. 220. George Marshall quoted in *The Marshall Plan, 1947–1951*, The Foreign Policy Association Headline Series No. 236, June 1977.

p. 220. Michael Scammell, trans., *To Build a Castle—My Life as a Dissenter*, by Vladimir Bukovsky (New York: Viking Press, 1979), p. 141.

pp. 221–22. Soviet economic dependence on the West: see Carl Gershman, "Selling Them the Rope," *Commentary*, April 1979.

p. 223. Richard T. McCormack, "The Twilight War," *Army*, January 1979, pp. 13, 18.

p. 240. Irving Kristol, "The Worst Is Yet to Come," *Wall Street Journal*, November 26, 1979.

p. 244. William E. Simon, *A Time for Truth* (New York: Reader's Digest Press, 1978), p. 67.

pp. 245–46. Milton Friedman, *Capitalism and Freedom* (Chicago: The University of Chicago Press, 1962), p. 9.

pp. 246–47. Herman Kahn quoted in the Los Angeles *Herald Examiner*, May 29, 1979.

p. 247. Robert Nisbet, "The Rape of Progress," *Public Opinion*, June/July 1979, p. 4.

p. 248. Thompson, *Peace Is Not at Hand*, pp. 172–173.

pp. 248–49. McCormack, "The Twilight War," p. 18.

Chapter Nine

p. 250. Hugh Seton-Watson, "How Right the Old Kennan Was," in *The Decline of the West?*, ed. Martin F. Herz (Washington, D.C.: Ethics and Public Policy Center, Georgetown University, 1978), p. 48.

p. 250. Paul Johnson, "Is the American Century Ending?", an interview in *Public Opinion*, March/May 1979, pp. 6–7, 59.

p. 252. Edith Hamilton, *The Echo of Greece* (New York: W. W. Norton and Company, 1957), pp. 16, 17.

p. 252. Andrei Amalrik, *Will the Soviet Union Survive until 1984?* (Evanston and New York: Harper and Row, 1970), pp. 33–34.

p. 254. Foy Kohler, *Understanding the Russians* (New York: Harper and Row, 1970), p. 117.

p. 256. Mussolini quoted in *An Ideology in Power* by Bertram D. Wolfe (New York: Stein and Day, 1969), p. 162.

pp. 259–60. Harry R. Davis and Robert C. Good, eds., *Reinhold Niebuhr on Politics* (New York: Charles Scribner's Sons, 1960), p. 34.

p. 261. Harry M. Geduld, ed., *The Rationalization of Russia* by George Bernard Shaw (Bloomington: Indiana University Press, 1964), pp. 30, 31.

p. 261. Malcolm Muggeridge, *Wall Street Journal*, December 31, 1979.

p. 261. William Pfaff, "On the Passing of a Grand Illusion," *Los Angeles Times*, March 25, 1979.

p. 262. Eric Hoffer, *Before the Sabbath* (New York: Harper and Row, 1979), pp. 3–4.

p. 262. Hugh Seton-Watson, "How Right the Old Kennan Was," p. 43.

pp. 262–63. Norman Podhoretz from an interview with Edmund Fuller, *Wall Street Journal*, October 31, 1979.

p. 265. Nisbet, "The Rape of Progress," p. 55.

p. 265. Aleksandr I. Solzhenitsyn, "A World Split Apart," remarks at the Harvard University Commencement, June 1978.

Chapter Ten

p. 269. James MacGregor Burns, *Leadership* (New York: Harper and Row, 1978), p. 388.

p. 269. Hugh Sidey, "We Argue About Courage Again," *Time*, March 5, 1979, p. 13.

p. 273. Liddell Hart, *Strategy*, p. 371.

p. 274. Sir Harold Nicolson, *Diplomacy* (New York: Oxford University Press, Galaxy Books ed., 1964), p. 43.

pp.   Dwight D. Eisenhower, *The White House Years*, Vol. II,
276–77. *Waging Peace* (Garden City, N.Y.: Doubleday and Com-
           pany, 1965), p. 97.

p. 286. Nicolson, *Diplomacy*, p. 52.

p. 297. Hoover Institution Study: see George Lenczowski, ed.,
           Iran Under the Pahlavis (Stanford, Cal: Hoover Institution
           Press, 1978), p. xv.

Chapter Eleven

p. 303. Winston Churchill quoted in C. L. Sulzberger, *Seven Con-
           tinents and Forty Years* (New York: Quadrangle/The New
           York Times Book Company, 1977), p. 125.

p. 303. B. H. Liddell Hart, *Strategy*, pp. 366, 370.

p. 305. George F. Kennan, "The Sources of Soviet Conduct,"
           American Diplomacy 1900–1950 (Chicago: The University
           of Chicago Press, 1951), pp. 126–127.

p. 310. Walter Laqueur, "The Psychology of Appeasement,"
           Commentary, October 1978, p. 49.

pp.   B. H. Liddell Hart, *Strategy*, p. 372.
311–12.

p. 320. Joseph Galloway, Remarks to the UPI Advisory Board,
           reprinted by San Diego *Union*, December 26, 1979.

p. 320. Arthur Schlesinger, Jr., "Is This Journey Necessary?",
           Wall Street Journal, January 18, 1980.

p. 322. Dean Acheson, *Power and Diplomacy* (Cambridge, Mass.:
           Harvard University Press, 1959), pp. 26–27.

p. 328. Henry Kissinger, interviewed in *Wall Street Journal*, Jan-
           uary 21, 1980.

Chapter Twelve

pp.   Malcolm Muggeridge, "Muggeridge Sees Deliverance De-
341–42. spite West's Despair," *Los Angeles Times*, June 17, 1979.

Author's Note

This book is the final product of my time in San Clemente, California, where I bought a home and established the Western White House in 1969, and where I later lived for exactly five and a half years after resigning the Presidency—from August 9, 1974 until February 9, 1980. During those five and a half years I wrote two books, my *Memoirs* and this volume. It was a time of intensive reflection on the lessons of a third of a century in public life, and of attempting to apply those lessons to the challenges facing the West in the years ahead. Essentially, the *Memoirs* were a look back, whereas this is a look ahead.

In the process, I found that no longer being either a public official or a candidate for office has certain advantages, not least of which is that it allows greater directness and candor. Former British Prime Minister Harold Macmillan, who also served as Foreign Secretary, once said that a Foreign Secretary is "forever poised between a cliche and an indiscretion." Being out of power and thus unable to shape events directly is often frustrating, particularly after having been at the center of events, but not having to be so discreet is one of its compensations. If I have stated my views more bluntly in this volume than people were accustomed to when I was Vice President or President, the bluntness reflects that freedom.

It is much easier to pinpoint when the work on this book ended than when it began. I completed the basic manuscript in the summer of 1979, then continued editing and updating during the usual phases of a book's production; as it worked out, the final page proofs arrived from the printer just before I left San Clemente to move to New York. I corrected page proofs during a brief stay in Florida en route from San Clemente, and delivered them back to the publisher on the same day that I arrived in New York to live—February 14, 1980. Several people who read the original draft in September 1979 commented that it was a mistake to feature the Soviets' 1978 move into Afghanistan so prominently in Chapter 1; by early 1980, after the Red Army moved in, they no longer considered it a mistake.

In one sense, the work on this book began after I completed my *Memoirs* in April, 1978, when I turned to the writing of this volume as my principal activity. In another sense its roots go back thirteen years, to 1967, when I began work on a book on foreign policy prior to the 1968 presidential campaign. It soon became clear that the demands of the book conflicted too much with the demands of the campaign, so I laid the book on the shelf—though much of the work I had done on it found its way into speeches, and the ideas I was developing in it found their way into the policies of my administration.

In a more fundamental sense, however, this book's origins go back more than thirty years, to my early days as a Congressman in the period immediately following World War II. It was then that I toured war-devastated Europe as a member of the Herter Committee, as we sought to chart what America's role should be in helping its recovery. From then on, foreign policy was the chief focus of my concern in public life. In 1953, during my first year as Dwight D. Eisenhower's Vice President, I made a seventy-day trip to twenty-one countries, the most extensive that had ever been undertaken by an American President or Vice President. On that trip I visited Hanoi, when it was still French; Mrs. Nixon and I were Japan's first state visitors since World War II. The leaders I met ranged from the Shah of Iran to South Korea's Syngman Rhee; many of the insights I picked up from them and from the trip itself have stayed with me ever since. I continued extensive foreign travels throughout the eight years of my Vice Presidency and the eight years as a private citizen that followed. By the time I took office as President, I had already visited seventy-three countries.

A book speaks with its author's voice, but is the product of many hands. The views expressed on the complex and controversial issues discussed in this volume are my own and are not necessarily shared by those who assisted me in preparing the manuscript. But many did help, and any listing can only be partial.

For their help in producing and keeping track of the manuscript, I want to thank my long-time associates Rose Mary Woods and Loie Gaunt, and also Marnie Pavlick and Cathy Price.

Many friends and associates offered information, ideas and counsel; four whose help on the book was especially extensive were former ambassador to NATO Robert Ellsworth; Lt. Gen. Vernon G. Walters, formerly deputy director of the CIA; Dr. William L. Van Cleave, director of the University of Southern California's Defense and Strategic Studies Program; and John Lehman, formerly a senior member of my National Security Council staff. Two recent graduates of Harvard College and the Harvard Business School, respectively, Hugh Hewitt and Todd Leventhal, worked with me for many months on the project, and provided enormously useful research and editorial assistance. Raymond Price, formerly chief of my White House speech staff, helped me throughout the project as my principal editorial coordinator. His encouragement and wise counsel were indispensable elements in enabling me to produce the final manuscript.

—R.N.

Index